SOTERIOLOGY AND MYSTIC ASPECTS
IN THE
CULT OF CYBELE AND ATTIS

ÉTUDES PRÉLIMINAIRES
AUX RELIGIONS ORIENTALES
DANS L'EMPIRE ROMAIN

PUBLIÉES PAR

M. J. VERMASEREN

TOME CENT-TROISIÈME

GIULIA SFAMENI GASPARRO

SOTERIOLOGY AND MYSTIC ASPECTS
IN THE
CULT OF CYBELE AND ATTIS

LEIDEN
E. J. BRILL
1985

Bust of Attis. Roman terracotta lamp from Agrigento (Archaeological Museum, Inv. no. 7545). Unpublished. Courtesy of Prof. E. De Miro, Superintendent of the Museum.

GIULIA SFAMENI GASPARRO

SOTERIOLOGY AND MYSTIC ASPECTS IN THE CULT OF CYBELE AND ATTIS

WITH A FRONTISPIECE

LEIDEN
E. J. BRILL
1985

Published with the help of the Consiglio Nazionale delle Richerche
and of the Ministero della Pubblica Istruzione della Repubblica Italiana

ISBN 90 04 07283 7

FOR MY MOTHER

CONTENTS

ABBREVIATIONS

AA	Archäologischer Anzeiger.
ABSA	Annual of the British School at Athens.
ABull	The Art Bulletin. A Quarterly published by the College Art Association of America.
AC	L'Antiquité Classique.
AD	Ἀρχαιολογικὸν Δελτίον
AEph	Ἀρχαιολογικὴ Ἐφημερίς
AEspA	Archivo Español de Arqueología.
AFLPad	Annali della Facoltà di Lettere e Filosofia di Padova.
AIPhO	Annuaire de l'Institut de Philologie et d'Histoire Orientales et Slaves de l'Université libre de Bruxelles.
AJA	American Journal of Archaeology.
AJPh	American Journal of Philology.
AlmC	Almanacco Calabrese.
AM	Mitteilungen des Deutschen Archäologischen Instituts, Athenische Abteilung.
AntAfr	Antiquités Africaines.
AOF	Archiv für Orientforschung. Internationale Zeitschrift für die Wissenschaft vom Vorderen Orient.
Arctos	Arctos. Acta Philologica Fennica.
ARW	Archiv für Religionswissenschaft.
AS	Anatolian Studies. Journal of the British Institute of Archaeology at Ankara.
ASAA	Annuario della Scuola Archeologica di Atene e delle Missioni Italiane in Oriente.
AZ	Archäologische Zeitung.
BA	Bollettino d'Arte del Ministero della Pubblica Istruzione.
BAB	Bulletin de la Classe des Lettres de l'Académie Royale de Belgique.
BAGB	Bulletin de l'Association G. Budé.
BCAR	Bollettino della Commissione Archeologica Comunale di Roma.
BCH	Bulletin de Correspondance Hellénique.
BCTH	Bulletin Archéologique du Comité des Travaux Historiques.
BFC	Bollettino di Filologia Classica.
BIBR	Bulletin de l'Institut Historique Belge de Rome.
BICS	Bulletin of the Institute of Classical Studies of the University of London.
BiOr	Bibliotheca Orientalis.
BJ	Bonner Jahrbücher des Rheinischen Landesmuseums in Bonn und des Vereins von Altertumsfreunden im Rheinlande.
BSBAP	Bulletin de la Société Royale Belge d'Anthropologie et de Préhistoire.

CArch   Cahiers Archéologiques. Fin de l'Antiquité et Moyen Âge.
CBQ   The Catholic Biblical Quarterly.
CH   Cahiers d'Histoire.
CHM   Cahiers d'Histoire Mondiale.
CIG   *Corpus Inscriptionum Graecarum.*
CIL   *Corpus Inscriptionum Latinarum.*
CPh   Classical Philology.
CQ   The Classical Quarterly.
CR   The Classical Review.
CRAI   Comptes rendus de l'Académie des Inscriptions et Belles-Lettres.
EC   Les Études Classiques.
EJ   Eranos-Jahrbuch.
EphD   Ephemeris Dacoromana.
EPRO   Études preliminaires aux religions orientales dans l'Empire Romain, ed. M. J. Vermaseren, Leiden 1961ff.
FHG   F. Jacoby, *Die Fragmente der griechischen Historiker* (*F GR HIST*), Berlin-Leiden 1923ff.
GIF   Giornale Italiano di Filologia.
Hastings, *ERE* J. Hastings, *Encyclopaedia of Religion and Ethics*, vols. I-XIII, Edinburgh 1908-1926.
HSPh   Harvard Studies in Classical Philology.
HThR   Harvard Theological Review.
IG   *Inscriptiones Graecae.*
IGRR   R. Cagnat, *Inscriptiones graecae ad res romanas pertinentes*, vols. I-IV, Paris 1901-1927.
ILS   H. Dessau, *Inscriptiones Latinae Selectae*, vols. I-III, Berlin 1892-1916.
JDAI   Jahrbuch des Deutschen Archäologischen Instituts.
JHS   The Journal of Hellenic Studies.
JNES   Journal of Near Eastern Studies.
JÖAI   Jahreshefte des Oesterreichischen Archäologischen Instituts.
JRS   The Journal of Roman Studies.
JS   Journal des Savants.
JSS   Journal of Semitic Studies.
JThS   The Journal of Theological Studies.
JWI   Journal of the Warburg and Courtauld Institute.
Kaibel, *Epigr.graec.* G. Kaibel, *Epigrammata graeca ex lapidibus conlecta*, Berlin 1878.
KJB   Kölner Jahrbuch für Vor-und Frühgeschichte.
MAMA   W. M. Calder, *Monumenta Asiae Minoris Antiquae*, vols. I-VIII, Manchester 1928-1962.
MDOI   Mitteilungen des Deutschen Orientalischen Instituts.
MEFR   Mélanges d'Archéologie et d'Histoire de l'École Française de Rome.
MemAccLinc   Atti dell'Accademia Nazionale dei Lincei. Memorie della Classe di Scienze morali, storiche e filologiche.
MemPontAcc   Atti della Pontificia Accademia Romana di Archeologia. Memorie.

MonAL	Monumenti Antichi pubblicati dalla Accademia dei Lincei.
Nauck[2]	A. Nauck, *Tragicorum graecorum fragmenta*, Suppl. B. Snell, Hildesheim 1964.
NAWG	Nachrichten der Akademie der Wissenschaften in Göttingen, Philol.-hist.Klasse.
NC	La Nouvelle Clio.
ND	Nuovo Didaskaleion. Studi di letteratura e storia cristiana antica.
NSc	Notizie degli Scavi di Antichità.
OGIS	W. Dittenberger, *Orientis graeci inscriptiones selectae*, vols. I-II, Leipzig 1903-1905.
PhW	Philologische Wochenschrift.
PP	La Parola del Passato. Rivista di studi antichi.
PSAM	Publications du Service des Antiquités du Maroc.
PWRE	H. Pauly-G. Wissowa, *Real-Encyclopädie der classischen Altertumswissenschaft*, vols. Iff., Stuttgart 1893ff.
QUCC	Quaderni Urbinati di Cultura Classica.
RA	Revue Archéologique.
RAAN	Rendiconti dell'Accademia di Archeologia, Lettere e Belle Arti di Napoli.
RAC	Reallexikon für Antike und Christentum, vols. Iff., Stuttgart 1950ff.
RACentre	Revue Archéologique du Centre.
RAE	Revue Archéologique de l'Est et du Centre-Est.
RBi	Revue Biblique.
REA	Revue des Études Anciennes.
RechSR	Recherches de Science Religieuse.
REG	Revue des Études Grecques.
REL	Revue des Études Latines.
RendAccLinc	Atti dell' Accademia Nazionale dei Lincei-Rendiconti della classe di Scienze morali, storiche e filologiche.
RendPontAcc	Atti della Pontificia Accademia Romana di Archeologia. Rendiconti.
RevEp	Revue épigraphique.
RFIC	Rivista di Filologia e di Istruzione Classica.
RGVV	Religionsgeschichtliche Versuche und Vorarbeiten.
RH	Revue Historique.
RHLR	Revue d'Histoire et de Littérature Religieuses.
RhMus	Rheinisches Museum für Philologie.
RHR	Revue de l'Histoire des Religions.
RILomb	Istituto Lombardo di Scienze e Lettere, Classe Lettere, Rendiconti.
RivArchCr	Rivista di Archeologia Cristiana.
RM	Mitteilungen des Deutschen Archaeologischen Instituts. Römische Abteilung.
Roscher, *Myth.Lex.*	W. H. Roscher, *Ausführliches Lexikon der griechischen und römischen Mythologie*, vols. I-VI, Leipzig 1884-1937.
RPhLH	Revue de Philologie, de Littérature et d'Histoire anciennes.
RSPh	Revue des Sciences Philosophiques et Théologiques.
RSR	Revue des Sciences Religieuses.

RUM	Revista de la Universidad de Madrid.
SBHAW	Sitzungsberichte der Heidelberger Akademie der Wissenschaften, Philos.-hist.Klasse.
SEG	*Supplementum Epigraphicum Graecum.*
SIG³	W. Dittenberger, *Sylloge Inscriptionum Graecarum*, vols. I-IV, Leipzig 1921-1924³.
SMSR	Studi e Materiali di Storia delle Religioni.
TAPhA	Transactions and Proceedings of the American Philological Association.
ThRev	Theologische Revue.
Turchi, *Fontes*	N. Turchi, *Fontes Historiae Mysteriorum Aevi Hellenistici*, Roma 1930.
UCPCPh	University of California.Publications in Classical Philology.
Vermaseren, *CCCA* II	M. J. Vermaseren, *Corpus Cultus Cybelae Attidisque (CCCA)* II. *Graecia atque Insulae* (EPRO 50), Leiden 1982.
Vermaseren, *CCCA* III	Id., III. *Italia-Latium* (EPRO 50), Leiden 1977.
Vermaseren, *CCCA* IV	Id., IV. *Italia-Aliae Provinciae* (EPRO 50), Leiden 1978.
Vermaseren, *CCCA* VII	Id., VII. *Musea et Collectiones privatae* (EPRO 50), Leiden 1977.
WS	Wiener Studien. Zeitschrift für klassische Philologie und Patristik.
ZA	Zeitschrift für Assyriologie.
ZKTh	Zeitschrift für katholische Theologie.
ZNTW	Zeitschrift für die Neutestamentliche Wissenschaft und die Kunde der älteren Kirche.
ZPE	Zeitschrift für Papyrologie und Epigraphik.

PREFACE

Of all the subjects in the religious history of the ancient world not one, surely, has given rise to a more extensive literature than that of the mysteries, both Greek and Oriental. It is above all the latter which have attracted the attention of scholars as phenomena particularly representative of the spiritual climate in the Mediterranean area at the end of the pre-Christian and the beginning of the Christian era. They were, after all, cosmopolitical in character and they displayed a capacity of spreading and taking root in a variety of places. Unlike most of the Greek mysteries, such as those of Eleusis, Andania, Thebes and Samothrace, which were limited to certain sanctuaries, in fact, the Oriental mysteries were not bound to a single cultic centre.

Ever since Ch. A. Lobeck's *Aglaophamus* (Königsberg 1829), a monumental collection of sources on the Greek mystery cults, research on the subject has flourished. Towards the end of the last century and the first decades of the present century, as we know,[1] investigation found a particularly favourable terrain in the Religionsgeschichtliche Schule whose comparative method and interest in the various religious traditions of the Near East appeared to provide the ideal context for an analysis of such problems.

Yet we need hardly recall that, however much the mysteries have been examined in themselves, the study of these phenomena, even in the broader framework of the religious history of the period, has been mainly related to the research on the origins and the nature of Christianity. We see this both when the question was confronted directly and explicitly, with the object of situating the Christian episode in its historical setting, and when it was used, rather, as the background for an analysis of the mystery cults undertaken all too frequently with an implicit comparison with the themes and doctrinal contents of Christianity in mind.

This is no place to trace the history of a type of research which still gives rise to the most varied investigations and discussions. All we need note is the priority assumed by the question of the mysteries. It ended up by being affected to a greater or lesser extent by the different positions on the one hand of those who stressed the massive contribution of pagan language and concepts to the formation of Christianity, and on the other of those who denied such influences and preferred to emphasise the characteristics peculiar to the new religious message and its direct connection with the Judaic traditions.

---

[1] For a brief history of the studies and apposite bibliography see R. Pettazzoni, "Les mystères grecs et les religions à mystères de l'antiquité. Recherches récentes et problèmes nouveaux", *CHM* II, 2 (1954), 303-312, 661-667. Cf. also B. M. Metzger, "Considerations of Methodology in the Study of the Mystery Religions and Early Christianity", *HThR* XLVIII (1955), 1-20.

Indeed, this debate led all too often to a simplification of the complex and multiple phenomena gathered in the category of the "mysteries", while at the same time precedence was given, within these mysteries, to those aspects or elements which would appear to lend themselves better, by analogy or by contrast, to a comparison with Christianity, especially in its Pauline formulation.

This is how the celebrated definition of "mystery religions" was reached. Suggested by Reitzenstein and accepted more or less explicitly by numerous scholars, it seemed to confer on those cults of an esoteric and initiatory character to which it was applied an organic and autonomous religious physiognomy hardly corresponding to the historical reality of the phenomena in question. Now not only does each of these phenomena fit into a flexible religious context of a polytheistic type, but they usually represent a specific aspect of the cult attributed to a particular deity in that same context.

Thus, for example, the Eleusinian mysteries in Greece are a completely individual and historically identifiable form of the cult of Demeter, while the mysteries of Dionysus only constitute a single aspect of the varied and multiform phenomenon of the Dionysiac religion whose origins, procedure and historical development still have to be studied.

As for the mysteries of Isis, they are one of the components—and probably a late one, formed under Greek influence—of the vast panorama of Egyptian religion and of the cult of Isis itself, with a complex history stretching back over the centuries. We have a similar situation in the case of the "mysteries" of the cult of the Great Mother Cybele, of Anatolian origin but naturalised in Greece at least as early as the 6th century B.C. and officially introduced into Rome in the 3rd century B.C.

In all the cases mentioned the initiatory-esoteric rites which constitute the "mysteries" of the deities only represent one aspect of the various forms of the cult attributed to them in their areas of origin and in the centres of dissemination of that cult in the Hellenistic and Roman *oikoumene*.

The situation of Roman Mithraism is quite unique from this point of view. Although it has a certain relationship of continuity (to an extent and in forms which are still subject to definition) with the ancient Iranian cult of Mithras, it constitutes an organic and autonomous religious context which had so entirely assumed a mystery "shape" that, of all the cults with an initiatory-esoteric structure in Antiquity, this alone deserves to be defined as a "mystery religion".

The tendency to regard the mystery cults as religious forms substantially akin to one another despite the variety of the deities and the ethnic traditions from which each one originated, was due to a series of elements believed to be common to them all and to constitute their specificity from a religious historical point of view. Even if it is a slight oversimplification, we can say that in all the attempts to classify the mysteries scholars have concentrated essentially on the type of the deity who is the object of the cult, the specific ritual procedure of the cult and the apparent purposes of its celebration.

To have identified and circumscribed these three aspects of the phenomena in question was no doubt a laudable result of research into the peculiar nature of the mysteries. All too frequently, however, owing to the German School of religious history and those scholars who, to a varied degree, accepted its conclusions on this particular subject, the definition of these aspects suffered from the theoretical premises of the School itself and from the attitude described above.

In other words, the necessity of the comparative method in examining religious facts in order to detect kindred, or even common, aspects and elements was stressed; research into the mysteries was put in relation to Christianity and was thus largely dominated by the objective of "situating" the phenomena comparatively. Since the peculiarity of the Christian message seemed to reside in its being a message of salvation based on the person of Christ, a figure both human and divine who was subject to an earthly vicissitude with death and resurrection, and at the same time connected with a sacramental practice which fulfilled that salvific promise establishing a direct relationship between the worshipper and Christ, scholars sought in the contemporary pagan sphere for religious phenomena which might present some affinity to these elements peculiar to Christianity. This, as we know, often took place in the perspective of the Erklärung, where it was readily admitted that an analogy between the facts being compared automatically amounted to an "explanation" in the sense of a genetic derivation of one fact from another which was believed to be—or actually was—prior to it.

The mystery cults, then, were examined from this specific angle, which seemed the one most likely to offer solutions to the problem posed. The object was to discover whether these cults, which appeared so successful in late Hellenism and round which the most vital forces of the pagan resistance in the last years of the Empire assembled, contained soteriological elements centred on the divinity whose destiny, celebrated in a liturgical and sacramental context, was believed to have an effect on the destiny of man.

As we know, the answer to these questions was affirmative. Once Frazer's formula of the "dying and rising god" had come into its own as a definition of the nature of the mystery gods, the notion of the soteriological efficacy of the god's vicissitude on the initiate who was ritually assimilated in the destiny of the deity through a "mystic" experience of death and rebirth was fully accepted.

The soteriology of the mysteries was thus regarded as clearly, if not exclusively, orientated towards eschatology. The participant in one of the many esoteric-initiatory cults of the ancient world appeared as a man preoccupied

with his own existence after death, determined to guarantee for himself a life
of bliss in the hereafter but already capable of anticipating this happy destiny
in the ritual experience, through a process of mystically obtained inner
"regeneration", which made of him a "new" man with an intimate spiritual
relationship with his god.

Criticisms of the definition of the mystery gods as "dying and rising gods"
were advanced from various sides and present-day religious-historical
research has, in the words of Brelich, "virtually dismantled this assumed type
of divinity".[2]

This does not mean however, that we should go to the opposite extreme and
deny a certain typological affinity between the divinities at the centre of the
ancient mystery cults. Indeed, like the protagonists of the mythical-ritual
complexes usually defined as "fertility cults" (another formula which awaits
further historical and phenomenological investigation), the gods of the
mysteries are subject to vicissitudes which include crisis, disappearance,
sometimes even death, but also a positive outcome.

In some cases this outcome entails a typical alternating rhythm of presence
and absence, asserted in the myth and celebrated in the cult, as in the case of
the Eleusinian Koré-Persephone, of Adonis (whose ritual does not, however,
seem to have assumed a mystery form) and of certain Dionysiac cults whose
ritual structure and mythical background cannot, unfortunately, be
reconstructed with any certainy—suffice it to think of the ritual of the Delphic
Thyiades and the contemporary one of the Hosioi, of the cult of Lerna and
other all too little known ritual complexes. Sometimes the outcome of the
divine vicissitude includes the acquisition of a new status beyond death (as in
the case of Osiris, restored to psycho-physical integrity by the funeral
ceremonies performed by Isis with the help of Nephthys and Anubis in whose
infernal world he then becomes sovereign and judge) or of a "survival" in
death, as in the case of Attis who does not die completely and whose presence
is celebrated ritually with annual ceremonies.

A particular position is occupied in this perspective by the invincible
Mithras of Roman Mithraism. Although he experiences neither defeat nor
death he would seem to be subject to a vicissitude demanding exhausting
efforts and the most strenuous undertakings and risks when it comes to

---

[2] "Politeismo e soteriologia", S. G. F. Brandon (ed.), *The Saviour God. Comparative Studies
in the Concept of Salvation presented to Edwin Oliver James*, Manchester 1963, 44. H.
Frankfort, while retaining the definition of "dying god" to characterise figures such as Tammuz,
Osiris and Dionysus, has clearly demonstrated the difference of meaning and "function" of each
of these in their respective cultural and religious contexts ("The Dying God". Inaugural Lecture
as Director of the Warburg Institute and Professor of the History of Pre-Classical Antiquity in
the University of London, 10 November 1949, *JWI* XXI, 1958, 141-151). See also *Kingship and
the Gods. A Study of Ancient Near Eastern Religion as the Integration of Society and Nature*,
Chicago-London, 1948 (6th ed. 1969), 286-294.

accomplishing those *maxima divum* mentioned in the inscriptions of Santa Prisca and which seem to consist essentially in that enterprise of cosmic significance, the tauroctony.

A further element which the deities in question have in common is their connection, variously defined, with the sphere of nature. A certain parallelism develops between their own vicissitude and the seasonal cycle, agrarian rhythms or anyhow chthonic fertility, and the realm of animal and human fertility.

We are thus probably entitled to refer to a "category", varied and flexible but sufficiently homogeneous from a typological point of view, which covers the theme of the vicissitude that distinguishes the personality and the destiny of the "mystic" god from the type of the "Olympic" god within a polytheistic structure. The latter, of course, is characterised by stability and, despite the multiple adventures of an anthropomorphic nature of which he is the protagonist, he is extraneous to a direct contact with the sphere of suffering and death. Suffice it to recall the Homeric definition of the gods as blessed immortals, the ῥεῖα ζῶντες.

Present-day religious historical research has rejected the classificatory scheme of the "dying and rising god", which has turned out to be inadequate for the definition of the varied and multiple historical reality of the facts examined. Scholars persist, however, in attempting to detect a specific typology, suitable for including the various deities of the mystery contexts, without repressing the characteristics peculiar to each one. They are still concerned with the problem of the possible soteriological content of the cult pertaining to those deities considered essentially as "saviours".

The problem is complicated by the preliminary difficulty of defining the very notion of "salvation", both in a general sense, universally valid from a religious historical point of view, and in specific relation to the paganism of late Antiquity in which we can situate the mystery cults themselves.

Now, we can probably only talk of salvation in relation to what we want to be saved from. The concept in question thus assumes a significance in the broader framework of the particular "world picture" which every religious context expresses in so far as it is a specific component of a definite cultural tradition.

Emphasis has been rightly laid on the risk implicit in giving too broad a meaning to the notion of "salvation", understood as a guarantee of human existence provided by the superhuman beings to whom the cult is directed. In this sense all religions and nearly all superhuman entities, with the exception of those who are the object of an apotropaic cult or who are considered evil and whose intervention in human life is feared and shunned, could be regarded as "saviours", if, that is, a religious relationship has been established in

order to obtain the benevolence of these superhuman beings and the benefits
which they can bestow.

The notion of salvation was then restricted, being confined to those
religious contexts in which it appeared as the liberation from reality and from
the normal conditions of existence regarded as the result of a decline, an ac-
cident or an original sin.

In his contribution to the volume offered to E. O. James on the subject of
the "saviour god", A. Brelich accepts this meaning of the religious historical
concept of salvation and stresses the basic incompatibility between this concept and all religious structures of a polytheistic type which assume the total
acceptance of present reality, with its divine balances and its natural rhythms
in so far as it is the result of a cosmogonic activity intended to establish order
after overcoming initial chaos. In so far as they are agents of cosmogonic
enterprises or guarantors of the present functioning of the cosmos over whose
"departments" they usually preside, the gods of polytheism would thus be
intrinsically incompatible with the type of the "saviour" god. The former are
in fact almost absorbed by cosmic reality and are the custodians of the
rhythms of existence from which man in a "soteriological" context wishes to
escape.

When confronted by the problem of the mystery gods, typically polytheistic
and yet so frequently referred to as "saviours", however, Brelich admits that
"the dying (and ultimately resurrecting?) god could assume a soteriological
significance" in the Hellenistic-Roman period, when "ancient polytheism was
disintegrating" (ibid., 45). He goes on to quote the famous mystery formula
told by Firmicus Maternus (de err.prof.rel. 22) concerning the "saved god"
and the ἐκ πόνων σωτηρία in store for the initiates as the attestation of this
soteriological significance and as a possible allusion to the idea of the "resurrection" of a deity whose identity remains uncertain.

The central problem of the mysteries thus remains. Religious historical
research has to establish, beyond hypotheses and possibilities, if, and exactly
how, the divine protagonists of the initiatory-esoteric cults of the various
polytheistic contexts of the Mediterranean area have actually "adopted" that
soteriological significance.

This question is further complicated by the basic problem underlying the
definition of the concept of salvation, a problem which does not appear to
have been solved in the alternative between a broad, almost generic meaning
which would include every possible religious expression in which the
superhuman beings are regarded as beneficial to man, and the specific sense of
liberation from reality and from the conditions of present existence which
really implies a refusal of these conditions.

In fact, even if such an attitude can be said to characterise certain religious
contexts whose soteriology rests on dualistic bases of an anticosmic type (the

world and human existence considered as the products of a fall or "devolu-tion" of the divine sphere, as in Orphism and in the Gnostic systems, or as an "illusion", as in many Indian religious philosophical formulations), it still cannot be applied to the notion of salvation in other religious traditions, which are also typically orientated in a soteriological direction.

The Iranian Zoroastrian tradition, for example, with its basic dualistic in-spiration (attributing to evil an original and fundamental consistency of its own as regards certain elements of reality), elaborates a soteriology entailing a total commitment of man to his present existence in the world, in order to achieve a definitive liberation from the contamination of demoniac forces which are lethal, or in any case damaging, to the supreme value—life on all its levels.

We can turn, next, to the great religions of history, such as Judaism, Chris-tianity and Islam, where salvation appears as an individual and collective adhesion to the only creating God, architect of the whole of reality, after all obstacles have been overcome. These obstacles do not consist in reality itself or in the typically human conditions of existence, but in a complex of negative ethical conditions and forms of behaviour which remove man from God. In Christianity, in particular, salvation thus becomes salvation from sin, and certainly not from reality and the world (unless the world is only understood as a possible instrument of detachment from God). Salvation is an ever more intimate and profound communion with divine life, mediated by Christ who, after a first sinful deed at the beginning of human history and a long series of individual and collective sins, has, in his double nature of god and man, restored the harmonic relationship of the creature with his Creator.

Therefore we should delve still further into the problem in order to reach a definition (or a series of definitions) of the concept of salvation. Without lapsing into a generalisation useless to historical analysis, this concept should be sufficiently flexible to cover a whole range of religious phenomena, vast and varied, but also essentially homogeneous.[3]

This is certainly not the place to attempt such a complex undertaking. Suf-fice it to have indicated the general terms of the problem in which the more limited and specific question of the soteriology of the mystery cults can be set. This question, moreover, provides a useful starting point for the confronta-tion of the broader topic once the insufficiency of the alternative between the two meanings of the concept of salvation outlined above has been made quite clear.

On the one hand it is in connection with the mystery gods, in their own typological specificity (gods "subject to vicissitude", to dramatic adventures,

---

[3] A series of studies on the subject in A. Abel et al., *Religions de salut* (Annales du Centre d'Étude des Religions, 2) Bruxelles 1962, and, more recently, E. J. Sharpe-J. R. Hinnells (eds.), *Man and his Salvation*, Manchester 1973.

and themselves in need of "salvation"), that there emerges still more clearly the vagueness of too vast and ill-defined a use of the concept in question, and its uselessness for distinguishing the mythical-ritual complex gravitating around these deities from that pertaining to other deities. On the other hand, the meaning of salvation in the sense of liberation from the present conditions of human existence and ultimately from worldly reality, which leads us to deny any soteriological element to polytheistic systems, is somewhat limited if referred to the characters of the mystery cults. For these are typically polytheistic deities (at least as far as that part of their history accessibile to positive investigation is concerned).⁴ They are marked, however, by a particular destiny and they are the object of a cult which confers on the worshipper a specific religious connotation whose precise nature, qualities and effect on the conditions of present and future existence have yet to be analysed.

Nor can we overcome this antinomy by resorting to the idea of a transformation undergone by these deities and their respective cults in the late Hellenistic period entailing a soteriological significance which was formerly lacking.

If by "transformation" we mean the passage of some of these figures from "mystic" to "mystery" deities, in other words to deities of an initiatory-esoteric cult which celebrates their vicissitude and establishes a special relationship between the devotee and the god himself (as does indeed seem to have occurred in many cases), then the basic terms of the problem remain unchanged. On the one hand, however, they move in time, and on the other, they raise the historical and phenomenological question of the mysteries.

We must ask ourselves what religious motivations attended such a transformation, if it is an internal process of development or an influence exerted by other cults, themselves already constructed according to the mystery pattern, or an adaptation to such a pattern considered more suitable for the expression of certain religious values.

These religious values include that very same soteriological significance which the figures and the cults in question would have "adopted". So further questions arise: was this soteriology inherent in the "type" of the mystery god as such? do the deities of non-mystery origin adopt it when they adopt that particular "mystery" dimension? or is it a process of transformation which affects all the cults with an initiatory-esoteric structure, from the earliest, like

---

⁴ I refer to the interpretation proposed by A. Brelich ("Quirinus. Una divinità romana alla luce della comparazione storica", *SMSR* XXXI, 1960, 92-98), according to which "the dying or dead god", in other words the character "subject to vicissitude" in the "fertility cults" and the mysteries, is a divinity whom the polytheisms have "inherited" from earlier cultural complexes, namely from those civilisations of primitive agriculturalists in which we get the figure of the "dema" as illustrated in the studies of A. E. Jensen (*Hainuwele. Volkserzählungen von der Molukken-Insel Ceram*, Frankfurt am Main 1939; *Das religiöse Weltbild einer frühen Kultur*, Stuttgart 1948; Id., *Mythos und Kult bei Naturvölkern*, Wiesbaden 1951.)

those of Eleusis and Samothrace, to those of a more recent date, like the mysteries of Isis and Osiris, of Cybele and Attis, or of Mithras?

Only in this second case could we appeal to that "disintegration" of polytheism which took place in late Antiquity and which might account for a radical change of perspective owing to which polytheistic deities conceived as the custodians of order and cosmic functioning, and thus "non-saviours" by definition, became "saviour gods", i.e. the agents of man's escape from that order and those cosmic rhythms of which they were the privileged divine expression.

But does this type of solution do justice to the historical reality? Suffice it to consider the case of Eleusis: can we deny a "soteriological" character to the Eleusinian mysteries, which already appear in the 7th-6th century B.C. in the *Hymn to Demeter*, when they proclaim as ὄλβιος the man who has seen the sacred rites and who will consequently enjoy a special destiny in this life and the next (πλοῦτος at his own hearth, a special αἶσα when he goes to the "dark shades")?

And yet the rites of Eleusis do not imply an "escape" from the normal conditions of existence (unless we take this to mean—but in an entirely different perspective—the parenthesis of sacred time in which the ceremonies themselves are performed). At least in the Classical period, moreover, these rites were an "official" cult of the Athenian state which expected well-being and prosperity from their celebration. The Homeric Hymn, furthermore, attributes to Demeter the foundation of the mysteries. It sees it as an act that sanctions once and for all her activity as a goddess guaranteeing the order of agricultural rhythms after the dramatic crisis, entailed by the wedding of her daughter, which induced her to retire from the very office due to her in a polytheistic system regulated by the law of the specific divine "responsibilities" for the various cosmic departments. Nor are there any grounds for claiming that the Eleusinian ideology underwent substantial transformations in a late period. Even Cicero still indicates the double benefit of the mysteries in bestowing the fundamental principles which adorn human life, both in the *laetitia vivendi* and in the *spes melior moriendi* (*de leg.* II,14, 36).

A positive prospect in the hereafter, raising the question of soteriology, does not therefore imply a depreciation or a rejection of the conditions of present existence. Indeed, the mystery cult, in conformity with the polytheistic structure on which it is based, actually guarantees these conditions.

Where each of the mystery cults, whether Greek or Oriental, is concerned we should therefore avoid all preconceived ideas and uncalled for generalisations and try to identify its peculiarity. At the same time we should bring to light any analogy or element it might have in common with the others. Only thus will it be possible to solve the problem of the soteriological character of the ancient mysteries and their divine protagonists and to define the specific

significance of the soteriology pertaining to such cults; by clarifying one of its
fundamental aspects, we will be in a better position to formulate the historical
and phenomenological question of the mysteries and to tackle it without the
intrusion of facile comparisons or extraneous problems.

The present research on the cult of Cybele is intended as an approach to this
vast topic through the study of a particular environment. It is in relation to
this environment, moreover, that we shall encounter, in all their urgency and
complexity, the many problems briefly outlined here.

This study arose from a specific interest in the dissemination of the Oriental
cult in the West during the Hellenistic-Roman period (also the subject of
earlier works of mine). It matured at time of the research project on the mystic
and soteriological aspects of such cults directed by Prof. Dr. U. Bianchi,
Professor of the History of Religions at the University of Rome—a project
which has borne fruit in two international Colloquia on the "Religio-
historical character of Roman Mithraism with particular reference to the
documentary sources of Rome and Ostia" (Rome-Ostia 28-31 March 1978)
and on "The soteriology of the Oriental cults in the Roman Empire" (Rome
24-28 September 1979). These Colloquia, and the exchange of experiences and
comparison of methodologies which ensued, have contributed greatly to the
enrichment of the specific field of my research. I am therefore grateful to all
my colleagues who took part in these meetings, displaying their own learning
and personal commitment to the discussion and study of the subject in question. In the first place my thanks are due to Prof. U. Bianchi, the former
"mystagogue" of my initiation into religious historical studies, a
knowledgeable and perceptive master who has continued to offer me fresh
stimulation.

The results of these two Colloquia were published in the EPRO series of
Prof. Dr. M. J. Vermaseren, under whose patronage the second Colloquium
was held. Every scholar is indebted to his learning and to his fundamental
contributions to our acquaintance with Oriental cults in general and with the
cult of Cybele in particular. He is, of course, erecting a perennial monument
to the latter with the invaluable *CCCA*, supplemented by his *Cybele and Attis,
The Myth and the Cult* (London 1977), in which he records the results of more
than fifty years of research on the subject since the "classic" work by H.
Graillot, and which is now an indispensable book of reference.

I have been privileged to enjoy his friendship ever since the far-off years
when I wrote *I culti orientali in Sicilia* for that same series (EPRO 31) and I
owe to his generosity numerous subsidiary bibliographical references
necessary for the completion of this study. Thanks to him, the present work,
first published in a series of the Istituto di studi storico-religiosi of the
University of Messina (1979), now appears, with numerous additions and

revisions, in an English translation in the series of EPRO—the best possible place for a new edition.

I therefore take pleasure in expressing my deep gratitude to a friend and master, and I would also like to thank Mrs M. E. C. Vermaseren-Van Haaren, Dr M. B. de Boer and Dr J. J. V. M. Derksen who have been so kind and prompt in satisfying my requests for bibliographical material.

INTRODUCTION

The deity referred to in Greek sources of the 5th century B.C. under the title of Μήτηρ Μεγάλη or Μήτηρ θεῶν appears in actual fact to have been the Phrygian goddess Cybele[1] who received numerous toponymical nicknames in her Anatolian homeland, frequently derived from those mountains over which she rules in a particularly privileged manner.[2] The close connection between the goddess and the mountains emerges, moreover, from the attribute of ὀρεία which characterises her.[3]

Often identified with Rhea, the mother of the Olympic gods according to Hesiod's Theogony, and sometimes associated with Demeter,[4] the Phrygian goddess seems, in these sources, to have already been partially Hellenized by way of a process undoubtedly inaugurated by those Greeks from Asia who were the first to come into contact with the divinity.

According to Will[5] it was precisely in the Greek colonies of Asia Minor that there developed the iconographical type of the goddess veiled and seated, with a small lion on her knees, sometimes inside a *naiskos* which, at any rate from the 6th century B.C. onwards, represented Cybele. It was probably on the basis of this ancient model that Agoracritus of Paros elaborated, for the Athenian Metroon, the cult image of the goddess with tympanum and patera,

---

[1] For this problem see the observations in my "Connotazioni metroache di Demetra nel Coro dell' 'Elena' (vv. 1301-1365)", M. B. De Boer-T. A. Edridge (eds.), *Hommages à Maarten J. Vermaseren*, Leiden 1978 (EPRO 68), vol. III, 1154-1158.

[2] H. Graillot, *Le culte de Cybèle Mère des Dieux à Rome et dans l'Empire romain*, Paris 1912, 346-411; F. Cumont, *Les religions orientales dans le paganisme romain*, Paris 1929⁴, 45ff.; H. Gressmann, *Die orientalischen Religionen im hellenistisch-römischen Zeitalter*, Berlin-Leipzig 1930, 56-63; M. J. Vermaseren, *Cybele and Attis. The Myth and the Cult*, London 1977, 24-32.

[3] See the sources listed on p. 1165 of my article quoted above (n.1). This is one of the most frequent titles of the Phrygian goddess. It is sometimes used on its own to designate her since she is "the Mountain One" *par excellence*. Cf., for example, the Athenian inscription of the goddess Belela, where the ἱέρεια 'Ορείας διὰ βίου is mentioned (*IG* III³, 2361 = *SIG*³ 1111, line 70). Another cult title of the goddess was probably *despoina*. Cf. A. Henrichs, "Despoina Kybele: ein Beitrag zur religiösen Namenkunde", HSPh 80 (1976), 253-286.

[4] On the details of the relationship between the Phrygian goddess and Demeter, variously attested both on a mythical and on a ritual level, see art. cit. in n. 1, 1148-1187.

[5] E. Will, "Aspects du culte et de la légende de la Grande Mère dans le monde grec", *Éléments orientaux dans la religion grecque ancienne*, Colloque de Strasbourg 22-24 mai 1958, Paris 1960, 95-111. For M. J. Mellink, on the other hand, it was the Phrygians who created the type of Cybele within the *naiskos*, with musical attributes and accompanied by lions ("Early Cult-Images of Cybele in Asia Minor", *AJA* LXIV, 1960, 188). According to this author certain Anatolian rock monuments with an image of the goddess like the type described go back to the 8th century B.C. The Phrygian prototypes were later reproduced in the Aeolic and Ionic monuments. On the problem of dating the so-called Phrygian rock-façades cf. below.

seated on a throne among lions,[6] which was to become the "canonical" representation of the Mother of the Gods for the rest of her history.

Aside from the iconographical evidence we are still left with the difficulty of appreciating fully the effects of that process of Hellenisation on the nature of the Phrygian goddess and the procedure of her cult. For it is impossible to resort to a direct comparison with contemporary documents concerning the Phrygian—or, in a broader sense, the Anatolian—world in order to establish the quality and degree of the possible transformations undergone by the character of the divine Mother and her mythical-ritual complex as a result of her encounter with the Greek religious sphere.

Admittedly it now seems possible to reconstruct a sort of Anatolian "prehistory" of the goddess thanks to the highly advanced study of Assyrian, Mitannish, Khurrish and Hittite documents which have yielded the name of a goddess, Kubaba, who can almost certainly be fitted into a line of development leading to the Phrygian Cybele.[7] Nevertheless little to nothing is known about the nature and attributes of this goddess and the character of her cult.

---

[6] A. von Salis has shown that the attribution of the Athenian statue of *Meter* to Agoracritus proposed by Pliny (*Nat. Hist.* XXXVI, 17) is more likely than the attribution to Phidias suggested by Pausanias (*Descr.* I, 3, 5) and Arrian (*Periplus Ponti Eux.* 9) ("Die Göttermutter von Agorakritos", *JdI* XXXVIII, 1913, 1-26). It is on this iconographical scheme, with a few variations, that the numerous statuettes of the goddess within the *naiskos* at the Athens Museum are based. Cf. J. N. Svoronos, *Das Athener Nationalmuseum*, vol. I, Athen 1908, 622-626, nos. 266-317; vol. II, Taf. CXVI-CXX; vol. III, Taf. CLXXXXVIII; CCXXXIX-CCXL. In some of the pieces, however, the goddess is represented standing. For the typology of the goddess accompanied by beasts see H. Möbius, "Die Göttin mit dem Löwen", *Festschrift für W. Eilers*, Wiesbaden 1967, 449-468; C. Christou, *Potnia Theron. Eine Untersuchung über Ursprung, Erscheinungsformen und Wandlungen der Gestalt einer Gottheit*, Thessaloniki 1968 (esp. for Cybele among the lions 46ff.; 79f.; 174; 191f.)

[7] Cf. W. F. Albright, "The Anatolian Goddess Kubaba", *AOF* V (1928-29), 229-231; H. G. Güterbock, "Carchemish", *JNES* XIII (1954), 102-114, esp. 109ff. where he discusses the results of L. Woolley's excavations (*Carchemish: Report on the Excavations at Jerablus on Behalf of the British Museum*, Part III, *The Excavations in the Inner Town*) which brought to light on the acropolis a temple attributed to Kubaba, defined by some sources as "the queen of Carchemish". And indeed, she appears to have been the principal divinity of the city. See also A. Göetze, *Kulturgeschichte des Alten Orients*, Bd. III, 1 *Kleinasien*, München 1957², 80: a goddess *Kubabat* in the Cappadocian documents; p. 133: Kubaba amongst the Khurrish deities; 201-206: Cybele in Phrygia. Cf. also H. Otten, "Zur Kontinuität eines altanatolischen Kultes", *ZA*, N.F. XIX (= 53) (1959), 174f.; Id., "Die Religionen des alten Kleinasien", *Handbuch der Orientalistik*, I Abt., Bd. VIII, Absch. I, Leiden 1964, 118-120. For a vast bibliography on the problem see W. Fauth, s.v. *Kybele*, K. Ziegler-W. Sontheimer (eds.), *Der kleine Pauly*, Bd. III, Stuttgart 1969, 383-389.

For the Aramaean inscription found in Cilicia and which mentions a *Kubaba* connected with a locality (Kaštabalay) that can probably be identified with the Καστάβαλα familiar to the Greek sources, cf. A. Dupont Sommer, "Une inscription araméenne inédite de Cilicie et la déesse Kubaba", *CRAI* (1961), 19-23; Id., "Une inscription araméenne et la déesse Kubaba"; A. Dupont Sommer-L. Robert, *La déesse de Hiérapolis-Castabala (Cilicie)*, Paris 1964, 7-15.

On the figure of a great goddess in the Near East ever since the prehistoric era cf. J. Mellart, "Excavations at Çatal-Hüyük 1962, Second Preliminary Report", *AS* XIII (1963), 43-103; W. Helck, *Betrachtungen zur Grossen Göttin und den ihr verbundenen Gottheiten*, München-Wien

What still remains valid, at all events, are the conclusions of Laroche who, after an attentive scrutiny of all aspects of the problem, acknowledged that the elements peculiar to the Phrygian Cybele as she appears in Western sources, in other words the orgiastic character of the cult and the association with Attis, can in no way be applied to the Anatolian Kubaba.[8] Both these elements would seem to be the result of an encounter between the ancient local tradition concerning Kubaba and a foreign religion with orgiastic and ecstatic tendencies completely alien to the Hittite religious world. The chronological period in which this "syncretism" would appear to have taken place can be situated between the 12th and the 6th centuries B.C. The Balkan area can be regarded as the probable homeland of that type of religion[9] since it was around 1000 B.C. that, to our knowledge, the Thracian-Phrygian tribes migrated to the Anatolian peninsula.

The circumstances and the details of such an encounter defy historical investigation. The Phrygian rock monuments are of no use to us, especially since we should accept the attribution to the 7th-6th century B.C. recently made by R. D. Barnett[10] rather than the very early dating suggested by W. Ramsay.[11] In some of them we get the figure of the Great Goddess occasionally accompanied by the lion and her name in the form MATAP KYBIΛEZ....[12] Even if we share Barnett's conclusions as to the cultic, rather than the funerary, character of such monuments and their probable relationship with streams of water, we cannot infer anything precise about the details of the cult practised and the specific attributes of the deity. All we can say for sure is that, as in the Western documents, it is her maternal quality which is emphasised.

Neumann has identified as Cybele the goddess with a tall *polos* and naked bust, accompanied by two small male figures playing the flute and the lyre respectively in the sculptural group discovered in a cultic niche near Büyük-

---

1971, esp. 90-94 and 243-268 for the great Anatolian goddess; M. J. Vermaseren, *op. cit.*, 13-24; G. Sanders, "Kybele und Attis", M. J. Vermaseren (ed.), *Die orientalischen Religionen im Römerreich (OrRR)* (EPRO 93), Leiden 1981, 264ff.

The theory of a relationship between the Phrygian goddess, by way of the Anatolian Kubaba, and the Sumerian Baba, formulated by Albright and others, is illustrated by D. M. Cosi, "La simbologia della porta nel Vicino Oriente. Per una interpretazione dei monumenti rupestri frigi", *AFLPad*, I (1976), 113-152. A divinity with the name of Kubaba has been identified in Minoan documents by L. Deroy ("Kubaba, déesse cretoise", *Minos* II, 1952, 34-56).

[8] E. Laroche, "Kubaba, déesse anatolienne, et le problème des origines de Cybèle", *Éléments orientaux*, cit., 113-128.

[9] E. Laroche, art. cit., 127f.

[10] "The Phrygian Rock Façades and the Hittite Monuments, Plates VIII-X", *BiOr* X, 3/4 (1953), 78-82.

[11] "Studies in Asia Minor I. The Rock Necropoleis of Phrygia", *JHS* III (1882), 1-32; Id., "Some Phrygian Monuments", *ibid.*, 256-263; "Sepulchral Customs in Ancient Phrygia", *ibid.* V (1884), 241-251.

[12] See nos. 3, 5 and 13 of Barnett's list.

kale.[13] The monument is dated at the end of the 7th or the beginning of the 6th century B.C. and may well be the earliest image of the Phrygian goddess accompanied by two divine attendants (the Idaean Dactyls). It is also an attestation that her cult was characterised by music, albeit of a less "orgiastic" type compared to the music later known to the Greeks.[14]

Nevertheless it is impossible to be sure about the legitimacy of this identification since the iconography of the figure does not contain any of those elements which distinguish the image of Cybele after the 6th century.

Indeed, the triadic pattern of the goddess with two attendants is extremely widespread.[15] It can be connected also with the iconography of Cybele in different times and in different situations, with specific details which cannot here be illustrated but which do not coincide with the type of monument in question.[16]

Equally hypothetical is the identification of Cybele with the figure with the tall *polos* represented in a bas-relief from Ankara which goes back to the 6th century B.C. suggested by R. Temizer.[17] Nor, finally, are the arguments, primarily of a linguistic nature, used by Barnett to illustrate the continuity between the mythical Phrygian complex referring to Cybele and Attis as it was received by the Greeks, and the Anatolian traditions,[18] either completely convincing or always sufficiently documented.

However this may be, we must keep in mind the highly composite context in which the figure of the Great Mother Cybele was undoubtedly situated at the time when the Greeks from Asia learnt to know and revere her. From within this context the Greeks of Asia chose a number of elements which they carried to their homeland and to the Western colonies[19] thus building a divine image and a cult which bear clear and deep signs of Hellenisation.

---

[13] "Die Begleiter der phrygischen Muttergöttin von Boğazköy", *NAWG* VI (1959), 101-105. For such an identification see K. Bittel, "Untersuchungen auf Büyükkale. b. Das phrygische Burgtor", *MDOI* XCI (1958), 61-71, Abb. 59-66. Cf. E. G. Suhr, "The Phrygian Goddess of Bogazkoy", *AJA* LXIV (1960), 188f.; M. J. Vermaseren, *op. cit.*, 20f., fig. 10.

[14] G. Neumann, art. cit., 101-105.

[15] Cf. Ch. Picard, "ΠΟΤΝΙΑ "ΑΝΔΡΩΝ ΤΕ ΘΕΩΝ ΤΕ". Note sur le type de la Déesse-Mère entre deux assesseurs anthropomorphes (Pl. I-III)", *RHR* XCVIII (1928), 60-77; F. Chapouthier, *Les Dioscures au service d'une déesse*, Paris 1933.

[16] We need only recall the triad constituted by the *Meter* accompanied by the torch-bearing girl and the boy with *oinochoe*, sometimes identified with Hermes; that formed by the goddess with Hermes and a bearded figure on the reliefs from Ephesus or by the Great Mother between the Dioscuri or between Hermes and Attis. For a brief survey of the monuments in which these various iconographical schemes recur cf. G. Sfameni Gasparro, *I culti orientali in Sicilia*, Leiden 1973 (EPRO 31), 135-144.

[17] "Un bas-relief de Cybèle découvert à Ankara", *Anatolia* IV (1959), 183-187.

[18] R. D. Barnett, "Ancient Oriental influences on Archaic Greece", S. S. Weinberg (ed.), *The Aegean and Near East. Studies presented to Hetty Goldman*, New York 1956, 222-226. Cf. Id. "Some Contacts between Greek and Oriental Religions", *Éléments orientaux cit.*, 143-153.

[19] A first tendency of the cult of Cybele to expand towards the West can be connected with the earliest phases of colonisation, as emerged from the discovery of archaic *naiskoi* in Marseilles, a

The extent of this Hellenisation can be at least partially perceived if we examine the cult of the Mother of the Gods in Classical Greece, the currents of Cybele's religiosity which start to come to the surface in certain circles in the Hellenistic age and then the late forms of the myth and the ritual in the Roman Empire which appeal explicitly to the "Phrygian" tradition.[20]

The reason for the differences, often considerable, between these various religious expressions could perhaps be sought in the transformations which the cult of the goddess underwent under Greek influence—an influence which is particularly deep and decisive in certain periods and circles, but which recedes at other moments in the face of genuinely Phrygian components.

Yet, because of the difficulty of assessing precisely the original consistency of these components, we must appeal to them with the utmost caution. From a methodological point of view the ideal approach is historical. Aware of the variety and complexity of the elements which compose the cult of Cybele, we could then tackle directly the available documentation in order to define its specific peculiarities in the course of its development in time and space. For the time being, however, we must first see whether mystic aspects and soteriological prospects actually exist and assess their effect on the general context of the cult of the Great Mother.

I shall here be using the term "soteriology" in a broad sense, to mean the mass of benefits and guarantees which the worshipper expected from the celebration of the cult of Cybele. A detailed analysis of the documentation relating to the various periods and circles in which that cult was practised should clarify the specific quality of these benefits and allow us to ascertain whether they are limited to man's condition on earth or whether they also extend to his future life.

Phocaean colony (cf. A. Conze, *AA* 1866, 303-306; É. Espérandieu, *Recueil général des bas-reliefs de la Gaule romaine*, Paris 1907, vol. I, 48-52, n° 49, 1-21) and some terracottas with the figure of the goddess with a small lion on her knees at Gela and at Selinunte, in archaeological contexts of the 6th century B.C. (cf. G. Sfameni Gasparro, *op. cit.*, 115-119, Cat. n° 330 Pl. CV, fig. 146 and n° 330 bis). There is a fragment of pottery from Locri Epizefiri with an inscription bearing the name ϙυβαλας and ascribable to the end of the 7th century or, at the latest, the early 6th century B.C. The figure seems to have arrived in the city via Siri, a colony of Colophon (M. Guarducci, "Cibele in un'epigrafe arcaica di Locri Epizefiri", *Klio* LII, 1970, 133-138; "Il culto di Cibele a Locri", *AlmC* 1972-73, 25-29).

[20] The cult of Cybele as it was received in Rome from Pessinus, via Pergamum (cf. Varro, *De lingua lat.* VI, 15; H. Graillot, *op. cit.*, 38-51) was itself Hellenized, as we see from the fact that the liturgical hymns in honour of the Great Mother were composed in Greek. According to Servius, unlike the songs in honour of other deities which could be expressed in the particular language of each people, "*hymni vero matris deum ubique propriam, id est graecam, linguam requirunt*" (*Comm. in Verg. Georg.* II, 394).

See also G. Wissowa, *Religion und Kultus der Römer*, München 1902 (1912²), 320 n. 3; P. Boyancé, "Une exégèse stoïcienne chez Lucrèce", *REL* XIX (1941), 149 n. 6 (= *Études sur la religion romaine*, Rome 1972, 207 n. 6).

In this study I shall use the term "mystic" in a very specific sense, to characterise certain aspects and modes of the mythical-ritual complex gravitating round the Phrygian goddess. I shall base myself on that meaning of the term which on the one hand takes into account its historical origin and the semantic root connecting it with μυστήριον, and on the other embraces a wide religious historical typology exceeding the confines of the Greek world with which the term itself is linguistically connected.

If μυστικός is the adjective referring to that particular religious "form" constituted in Greece by the μυστήρια, of which Eleusis is the best known and most complex "type",[21] it can express the various aspects peculiar to such a structure, i.e. the ritual esoteric-initiatory component and the specific content, the latter viewed in the light of both the character of the divine being object of the cult and of the particular relationship which develops between deity and worshipper.

In order to give a still more flexible definition of a religious historical typology I shall use the term "mystery" (to which the adjective *mysterikós* also refers, not unknown to the Greek language even though it is rarely attested,[22]) to define that structure in its entirety. I shall reserve the term "mystic", on the other hand, for a broader category of religious phenomena in which we can detect precise analogies with that aspect of the "mysteries" which concerns the particular type of divinity worshipped and the quality of the relationship created between the divinity and the worshipper—an aspect which, together with the initiatory-esoteric institution, characterises such religious phenomena.

So, if the term mystery defines a mythical-ritual complex of the Eleusis type, in the organic interaction of all its aspects, precedence is given in this definition to the ritual component, with initiation and esotericism, practised within a sanctuary, by a specialised body of priests, which would appear to be wholly peculiar to the μυστήρια.

The term "mystic" can then be used to define those cults which, both inside and outside the Greek world, do not necessarily present an esoteric-initiatory structure but are centred round a superhuman figure with characteristics which are substantially analogous to the god of the mysteries and (/or) tend to give rise to a type of relationship between man and deity similar to the one established in the "mystery". Here, in fact, the nature of the god and the situation of man appear to be intimately connected in a special relationship,

---

[21] For the problem of the religious historical definition of the "category" of mysteries see my contribution, "Il mitraismo nell'ambito della fenomenologia misterica", U. Bianchi (ed.), *Mysteria Mithrae, Atti del Seminario internazionale su "La specificità storico-religiosa dei misteri di Mithra con particolare riferimento alle fonti documentarie di Roma e Ostia", Roma e Ostia 28-31 Marzo 1978* (EPRO 80), Roma-Leiden 1979, 299-337.

[22] Cf. Aristophanes, *Acharn.* v. 747.

so that the condition of the worshipper is defined in virtue of his participation in a cult which celebrates the vicissitude of the deity.

Religious historical analysis, however, can indeed distinguish between these two elements and define on the one hand the "type" of the "mystic god" and on the other the type of a "mystical experience", or rather of an experience religiously defined within the cult which entails an "interaction" between the human level and the divine one analogous, in its modes and aims, to that brought into being by the mystery cult.[23] This "interaction" is characterised in particular by the sense of familiarity between the worshipper and the deity, based on a similarity of experience, on a *sympatheia*, since man participates, through the rite, in the *pathos* of the divine vicissitude.

The distinction between "mystery" and "mystic", and the conjunction in the latter of the "objective" element, constituted by the particular quality of the deity celebrated in the cult as the god subject to vicissitude and the "subjective" element concerning the specific character of the religious experience achieved in this cult, is particularly useful for the analysis of the mythical-ritual complex of Cybele—a remarkably composite phenomenon with different manifestations in time and space.

---

[23] On the religious historical typology of the "mystic" and the "mystery" cf. U. Bianchi, *The Greek Mysteries*, Leiden 1976, 1-8; Id., *Prometeo, Orfeo, Adamo*, Roma 1976, 59ff., 71-94, 129-143, 188ff., 259ff. and the *Prolegomena* to the international seminary mentioned above (3-60). See also my "Riflessioni ulteriori su Mithra 'dio mistico' ", *ibid.*, 397-408.

For a different use of the terms "mystic" and "mysticism", understood as expressing the notion of an "escape from the worldly sphere", see D. Sabbatucci, *Saggio sul misticismo greco*, Roma 1965 (1979²). According to this interpretation the Eleusinian initiation would imply "a brief escape into otherness" by whoever decides to adapt himself to worldly existence, in its systems and civil and religious institutions, for the rest of his life (*ibid.*, 132).

CHAPTER ONE

THE MYSTIC CULT OF CYBELE IN CLASSICAL GREECE

While the earliest testimonies concerning the cult of the Great Mother sometimes attest to her association with a nocturnal[1] and a mountain[2] environment, they emphasise above all the presence of songs and the sounds of sacred instruments (cymbals, tambourines, flutes, bull-roarers) which were liable to arouse a state of sacred exaltation in the celebrants.

If the "Homeric" hymn *To the Mother of the gods* shows us the goddess enjoying the κροτάλων τυπάνων τ' ἰαχὴ σύν τε βρόμος αὐλῶν,[3] the other sources, from Pindar[4] to Diogenes Tragicus[5] and Euripides,[6] provide a lively description of her cult celebrated by groups, largely of women, to the sound of cymbals, crotala and tambourines in an atmosphere of the utmost religious enthusiasm.

As far as the nature and quality of the cult of Cybele in the Classical period is concerned, however, Euripides' report in the *Bacchae* is particularly significant since the rites of the "Great Mother Cybele" appear to be intimately associated with the Dionysiac ones, likewise called ὄργια.

The relevance of the term ὄργια and of the religiosity which it expresses to the "mystic" cults does not need to be demonstrated. Suffice it to recall that, while in its broader sense it means "rites", "sacrifices",[7] the "Homeric" hymn to Demeter refers to ὄργια founded by the goddess in both the passages where there is an explicit mention of the very special relationship which establishes itself between Demeter and the centre of her cult in Eleusis[8] in

---

[1] Cf. Pindar, *III Pyth.*, vv. 77-79: at night (ἐννύχιαι) the κοῦραι together with Pan celebrate the goddess near the poet's door; Herodotus, *Hist.* IV, 76: the Scythian Anacharsis performs a παννυχίς in honour of the Mother of the gods, as he saw it celebrated amongst the Cyzicenes (text in H. Hepding, *Attis, seine Mythen und sein Kult* (RGVV 1), Giessen 1903, 6).

[2] Anacharsis retires to a mountainous region, amongst thick woods, to celebrate the "sacred wake" for Cybele to the sound of tambourines (Herodotus, *loc. cit.*). Cf. Euripides, *Cretans* fr. 472 Nauck².

[3] Vv. 3-4 ed. J. Humbert, *Homère. Hymnes*, Paris 1967, 197. For the date cf. *ibid.*, 195f.; T. W. Allen-W. R. Halliday-E. E. Sikes, *The Homeric Hymns*, Oxford 1936², 394f.

[4] *Dithyr.* II, fr. 70 b ed. B. Snell, *Pindari Carmina cum fragmentis*, Leipzig 1964³, vol. II, 74f.

[5] Fragment from *Semele* (in Athenaeus 14, p. 636 A) in Nauck², 776f.: "And yet I hear that the turbanwearing women of Asian Cybele, the daughters of the rich Phrygians, with drums and bull-roarers and booming of bronze cymbals in their two hands make loud din...celebrating her who is the wise minstrel of the gods and healer as well" (translation by Ch. B. Gulick, *Athenaeus, The Deipnosophists*, vol. VI, London-Cambridge 1950, 431ff.).

[6] *Helena* vv. 1301-1365, for a comment on which see my work quoted above, Introduction n. 1.

[7] Cf. for example, Aeschylus, *Seven against Thebes*, v. 179f.; Sophocles, *Antigone* v. 1012f., *Trachiniae* v. 765ff. See also L. Ziehen s.v. *orgia, PWRE* 35 (1939), 1026-1029.

[8] Vv. 237f.: "ὄργια δ' αὐτὴ ὑποθήσομαι, ὡς ἂν ἔπειτα / εὐαγέως ἔρδοντες ἐμὸν νόον ἱλάσκοισθε"; vv. 476f. (ed. J. Humbert, 50 and 57).

virtue of the dramatic vicissitude to which she was subjected together with her daughter.

The use of ὄργια to designate the Eleusinian rites, the μυστήρια *par excellence*, continues also at a later period, from Euripides[9] to Aristophanes[10] and to the epigram of the hierophant Glaucus (2nd-3rd century A.D.) who recalls having shown ὄργια πᾶσιν .... βροτοῖς φαεσίμβροτα Δηοῦς.[11]

In Herodotus the term in question alternates with μυστήρια to denote the rites celebrated at Samothrace.[12]

At all events we see that in the course of the 5th century the term acquires an ever more precise meaning, being applied preferably to ritual complexes of a cathartic type[13] or to cults with a reserved or frankly esoteric character. Thus, for example, Herodotus speaks of the ὄργια of Demeter Achaean whose sanctuary and cult were reserved for the Gephyraeans, the other Athenians being excluded;[14] Aristophanes calls the Thesmophoric festivals ὄργια σεμνά,[15] typically esoteric rites exclusively reserved for women, and he uses the same term to define the rites of the Muses[16] which Strabo was later to associate with the cults of Dionysus, Apollo, Hecate and Demeter, as those to whom were due τὸ ὀργιαστικὸν πᾶν καὶ τὸ βακχικὸν καὶ τὸ χορικὸν καὶ τὸ περὶ τὰς τελετὰς μυστικόν.[17]

Finally the σεμνὰ ὄργια of the Thracian goddess Cotyto are evoked in Aeschylus' *Edonians* as rites celebrated in a context of extreme religious enthusiasm, to the sound of tympana and bull-roarers.[18]

In fact the term in question is used as early as the 5th century preferably to denote the Dionysiac rites characterised by similar manifestations of

---

[9] *Hercules* v. 613: to the question of Amphitryon who asks him if the capture of Cerberus has taken place "after fighting or as a gift of the goddess", Heracles replies: "Μάχη · τὰ μυστῶν δ' ὄργι' εὐτύχησ' ἰδών".

[10] *Frogs* v. 384f.: the chorus of the Eleusinian *mystai* invokes: "Δήμητερ, ἁγνῶν ὀργίων / ἄνασσα".

[11] *IG* II², 3661, 3. Cf. also the Eleusinian inscription in G. Kaibel, *Epigr. graec.*, Add. 97 a, line 3, 518: the hierophant τελέτας ἀνέφηνε καὶ ὄργια πάννυχα μύσταις; Arrian *fr.* 107 in Eustath. *Od.* ε 125, 1528, 14 ed. Jacoby, *FHG* II B, 871.

[12] *Hist.* II, 51: "ὅστις δὲ τὰ Καβείρων ὄργια μεμύηται, τὰ Σαμοθρήικες ἐπιτελέουσι ..... οὗτος ὡνὴρ οἶδε τὸ λέγω". Further on, recalling the *hieros logos* recounted by the Pelasgians with regard to Hermes, he says: "τὰ ἐν τοῖσι ἐν Σαμοθρήικῃ μυστηρίοισι δεδήλωται (text in N. Turchi, *Fontes historiae mysteriorum aevi hellenistici*, Roma 1930, 103, n° 156).

[13] Herodotus, discussing the significance of the prohibition for the Egyptian priests to introduce woollen garments into the sanctuaries or to be buried with such garments, notes the similarity with the behaviour of the Orphics, Pythagoreans and Bacchantes and concludes that οὐδὲ γὰρ τούτων τῶν ὀργίων μετέχοντα ὅσιόν ἐστι ἐν εἰρινέοισι εἵμασι θαφθῆναι (*Hist.* II, 81).

[14] *Hist.* V, 61.

[15] *Thesmoph.* v. 948; cf. vv. 1148-1152.

[16] *Frogs* v. 356.

[17] *Geogr.* X, 3, 10.

[18] *Fr.* 57 Nauck² p. 20. Cf. Ch. A. Lobeck, *Aglaophamus*, vol. II, Königsberg 1829, 1014-1039; R. Pettazzoni, *I misteri*, Bologna 1924, 25f.

enthusiastic religiosity.[19] It thus assumes a precise meaning, indicating a ritual complex which takes place under the sign of divine μανία, expressed in dances, songs, and sounds of sacred instruments.

Such is the picture offered by Euripides' tragedy which, quite apart from the problems of interpretation which it entails,[20] undoubtedly provides a lively view of Dionysiac religiosity and practices. It is of interest to us here since, in a moment of decisive importance for the understanding of the religious historical significance of that religiosity and cultic practice, the divine Bakchos is connected, on a mythical and ritual level, with the Phrygian Great Mother.

Such a connection, already familiar to Pindar[21] and emphasised elsewhere by Euripides himself,[22] is a fairly constant item in the Cybele's tradition, both in the Greek world[23] and in the Latin West.[24] Without wishing to overestimate

[19] Euripides, *Bacchae*, v. 34; 262; 415 (ὀργιάζειν); 470-76; 842; 1080.

[20] Cf. H. Grégoire, *Euripide*, vol. VI, *Les Bacchantes*, Paris 1961, 207-237. Of the many critical editions and commentaries suffice it to mention those of E. R. Dodds, *Euripides, Bacchae*, Oxford 1960² and of J. Roux, *Euripide, Les Bacchantes*, vols. I-II, Paris 1972.

[21] *Dithyr.* II fr. 70 b Snell, 74f. Strabo, to whom we owe the quotation of the fragment of Pindar, emphasises the analogy between the Dionysiac ritual and the Cybele's one which the poet brought out in his work (*Geogr.* X, 3, 13: τὴν κοινωνίαν τῶν περὶ τὸν Διόνυσον ἀποδειχθέντων νομίμων παρὰ τοῖς Ἕλλησι καὶ τῶν παρὰ τοῖς Φρυξὶ περὶ τὴν Μητέρα τῶν θεῶν συνοικειῶν ἀλλήλοις). Indeed, Pindar's passage referred to the ritual of Cybele celebrated with the typical musical instruments (cymbals, crotala) by torch light, and thus similar to the Bacchic one (σοὶ μὲν κατάρχει / Ματέρ<ι> πάρα μεγάλα ῥόμβοι κυμβάλων, / ἐν δὲ κέχλαδον κρόταλ', αἰθομένα τε / δαῒς ὑπὸ ξανταῖσι πεύκαις).

[22] *Palamedes*, fr. 586 Nauck², 545 where Dionysus is described in the act of enjoying the loud sound of the tympana "on the Ida, with his dear Mother", who, Strabo assures us (*Geogr.* X, 3, 13), can be identified as Cybele. Cf. E. R. Dodds, *Bacchae*, cit., 76f. *Cretans* fr. 472 Nauck², 505f. for which see below. The Chorus of *Helena*, in which Demeter assumes some aspects peculiar to Cybele, concludes with the evocation of the nocturnal mystic rites sacred to the goddess, amongst which we can undoubtedly detect the Eleusinian rites. Nevertheless they are intimately connected with the Bacchic celebrations with their "flecked fawnskins", the "green ivy crowning the sacred caskets", the "circular bull-roarer which rotates whipped by the air" and finally "the Bacchic tresses shaken for Bromius" (vv. 1358-1365; tr. after H. Grégoire, *Euripide, IV Hélène-Les Pheniciennes*, Paris 1950, 106; cf. R. Kannicht, *Euripides-Helena*, Heidelberg 1969, vol. II, 357).

The insistence on the aspects typical of the Dionysiac ritual has led me to acknowledge that the association of the two cults was made by the poet in the "Cybele's" perspective which dominates the entire passage rather than under the "Eleusinian" sign of Iacchus (G. Sfameni Gasparro, art. cit., 1152f., 1162-1165 wherein are quoted some examples of the Cybele-Dionysus relationship in the literary and figurative tradition).

[23] Besides the examples given in the article quoted in the preceding note we can recall the Hellenistic relief of Lebadeia which shows Dionysus in the act of presenting a veiled character (a male or female "initiate") to the Great Mother. See below.

Cf. also W. Fuchs, "Dionysos aus dem Metroon-Giebel?", *AM* 71 (1956), 66-73, Abb. I, Beilagen 44-46.

[24] A statue of Dionysus has been brought to light in the shrine of Attis in the sanctuary of the Great Mother at Ostia; Attis himself is represented with Dionysiac attributes in another statue from the same place. Cf. R. Calza, "Sculture rinvenute nel santuario", *MemPontAcc* VI (1942), 219f. n° 12, fig. 21 (Dionysus) and 218f. n° 11, fig. 20 (Attis); M. Floriani Squarciapino, *I culti*

the testimony of Euripides, we can nevertheless claim that the poet reflected a real situation [25] when he presented his spectators with the *orgia* of Cybele as a religious "form" profoundly similar to the Bacchic rites.

Therefore, even if the rites of Cybele do not constitute the primary object of the tragedy, the intimate relationship which unites them—in the general perspective of the work—to the Dionysiac religion permits us to attribute to them certain specific features of this religion. This applies above all to the long choral passage which opens the dramatic action, presenting the new religious message carried by the *thiasos* led by the divine βάκχος.

Festugière's penetrating analysis [26] has brought to light a typically liturgical structure in this *parodos*, in the metre, the language, and in the religious content. It is a hymn to the god which proclaims his nature, the εὑρήματα and above all the benefits obtainable from the practice of his cult. It is here that we find also that association with the figure of Cybele which effectively applies to the entire complex of the Dionysiac phenomenon as defined in the *parodos* itself.

---

orientali ad Ostia, Leiden 1962 (EPRO 3), 11. A statue of Attis at the Museum of Constantinople has an ivy leaf sculpted on the front of the foot (Th. Macridy Bey-Ch. Picard, "Attis d'un Métrôon(?) de Cyzique, Pl. XIV-XVII", *BCH* XLV, 1921, 436-470). A large shrine with a mask of Dionysus appears in the fresco with a Cybele's procession in Via dell'Abbondanza in Pompeii (V. Spinazzola, *Pompei alla luce degli scavi nuovi di Via dell'Abbondanza (Anni 1910-1923)*, Roma 1953, vol. I, 223-242, fig. 250 and 266, Tav. XIV). A wall painting in the house of Octavius Primus, also in Pompeii, is described by Fiorelli as representing a "shrine of Cybele with the herm of bearded Bacchus" (*ibid.*, 633 n. 213). The fragment of an antefix shows Cybele on a throne with a thyrsus on her right (Vermaseren, *CCCA* III, 10 n° 11, Pl. XX).

Finally there is Proclus' hymn to Helios (vv. 24ff. in H. Hepding, *op. cit.*, 73), the hymn used by the Naassenes (Hippolytus, *Philos.* V, 9 *ibid.*, 35) and the syncretistic oracle familiar to Socrates, the historian (*Hist.Eccl.* III, 23, *ibid.*, 71f.), all texts which identify Attis with Dionysus.

For the Dionysus-Attis relationship see Ch. Picard, "A travers les Musées et les sites de l'Afrique du Nord. Recherches archéologiques: I Maroc", *RA* S. VI, XXVII, 1 (1947), 229-233; Id., "Dionysos-Pais et Attis enfant", *AEph* I (1953-54) (1955) *[Memorial G. P. Oikonomou]*, 1-8. Cf. also R. Turcan, *Les sarcophages romains à représentations dionysiaques. Essai de chronologie et d'histoire religieuse*, Paris 1966, 394-399; 478; 547; 555-557.

[25] The famous red-figured volute crater of the necropolis of Spina, ascribable to the 5th century B.C., seems in particular to illustrate a cult of the type evoked in the *Bacchae* (Vermaseren, *CCCA* IV, 88f. n° 213, Pls. LXXXIII-LXXXV). If the two deities sitting within the *naos* are indeed Dionysus and Cybele (cf. G. Sfameni Gasparro, *art. cit.*, 1179f. where the relevant bibliography is quoted), they would appear to be the objects of a common cult, characterised by the elements typical of Bacchic orgiasm. We see the Maenads dancing to the sound of tambourines, cymbals and double-flutes, their heads wreathed by snakes which they manipulate in the excitement of the dance. A boy clashes the cymbals and a bearded male figure, with a long robe and crown of ivy, plays the flute, while a woman bears on her head the *liknon* covered by a cloth. She stands by the altar, opposite the two gods, thus conferring on the representation on the faces of the bowl the rhythm of a *pompé* directed towards the divinities seated in the sacred area of the cult. The complex of the Dionysiac ritual thus becomes an expression of Cybele's religiosity, as in Euripides' tragedy.

[26] "La signification religieuse de la Parodos des Bacchantes", *Eranos* LIV (1956), 72-86 repr. in *Études de religion grecque et hellénistique*, Paris 1972, 66-80.

The *thiasos*, and the god who inspires it, come "from the land of Asia, from the hallowed Tmolus" (vv. 64f.), a region sacred to the Great Mother, already evoked by Dionysus himself in connection with the sacred instruments wielded by the Bacchae;[27] shortly afterwards she is introduced as the object of the Bacchic cult in the exhilarating *makarismos* which proclaims the happiness of man who, "happy as the gods" (μάκαρ) and "divinely favoured with blessedness" (εὐδαίμων) "τελετὰς θεῶν εἰδὼς / βιοτὰν ἀγιστεύει καὶ θιασεύτει ψυχάν, / ἐν ὄρεσσι βακχεύων / ὁσίοις καθαρμοῖσιν· / τά τε ματρὸς μεγάλας ὄρ/για Κυβέλας θεμιτεύων / ἀνὰ θύρσον τε τινάσσων / κισσῷ τε στεφανωθεὶς / Διόνυσον θεραπεύει".[28]

Together with Festugière we should note the specific relevance of the language used here to the sphere of the mystery cults. To the announcement of the worshipper's "happiness", which has an obvious parallel in the Eleusinian ὄλβιος,[29] we can add the reference to the immediate knowledge emerging from the experience of "seeing", so typical of those cults,[30] to which the designa-

---

[27] Vv. 55-59 where the deity, addressing the women of the thiasos who have left the Tmolus to follow him, tells them to sound "the tambourines from Phrygia, invented by Rhea, the Great Mother" and by himself (αἴρεσθε τἀπιχώρι' ἐν πόλει Φρυγῶν / τύμπανα, 'Ρέας τε μητρὸς ἐμά θ' εὑρήματα).

For the function of music in the mystery and orgiastic rituals cf. G. Quasten, *Musik und Gesang in den Kulten der heidnischen Antike und christlichen Frühzeit* (Liturgiegesch. Quellen u. Forsch. 25), Münster i. West. 1930, 45-58.

[28] Vv. 72-82. Festugière translates: 'O fortuné comme les dieux, celui qui, divinement favorisé d'une bonne part, instruit des mystères des dieux, se comporte, par son genre de vie, en consacré, et devient, quant à l'âme, un vrai membre du thiase, communiant, sur la montagne, avec Bacchos par des saintes purifications. Heureux qui, selon le rite, célèbre les saints mystères de Kybélé, la Grande Mère, qui, brandissant le thyrse et couronné de lierre, vit au service de Dionysos" (art. cit., 67). See also the paraphrase by E. R. Dodds, *op. cit.*, 75: "O blessed is he who, by happy favour knowing the sacraments of the gods, leads the life of holy service and is inwardly a member of God's company".

[29] *Hymn to Demeter* vv. 480-482; Pindar, *fr.* 137 Schroeder; Sophocles, *fr.* 753 Nauck (texts in Turchi, *Fontes*, 79f. n° 114; 97f. nos. 151-152).

[30] *Hymn to Demeter, loc. cit.*: "ὄλβιος, ὃς τάδ' ὄπωπεν ἐπιχθονίων ἀνθρώπων"; Pindar: "ὄλβιος ὅστις ἰδὼν κεῖν' / εἶς ὑπὸ χθόν' "; Sophocles: "ὡς τρὶς ὄλβιοι /κεῖνοι βροτῶν, οἳ ταῦτα δερχέντες τέλη / μόλωσ' ἐς "Αιδου".

In connection with the experience of "seeing" at Eleusis, as it emerges from the definition of the final grade of initiation as ἐποπτεία and from the priestly office of the ἱεροφάντης, we can also refer to the transposition of mystery images and language to the hyperuranian vicissitude of the soul, performed by Plato in the splendid myth of *Phaedrus* (250 b-c), where the insistence on the "vision" is central. Cf., finally, the μυστικὰ θεάματα mentioned by Dio Chrysostomus in connection with the parallel between initiation and philosophy (*Olympicus* XXI, 33) and the *simulacra* to which Seneca refers in a similar context (*Ep. to Lucilius* XIV, 28). Cf. for these texts P. Boyancé, "Sur les mystères d'Éleusis. A propos d'un livre récent", *REG* LXXV (1962), 469ff.

The very special quality of the initiatory experience is expressed in an effective synthesis in Aristotle's famous definition according to which τοὺς τελουμένους οὐ μαθεῖν τί δεῖ ἀλλὰ παθεῖν καὶ διατεθῆναι γενομένους δηλονότι ἐπιτηδείους (*In Synes.Dion*, 48 in Turchi, *Fontes*, 53 n° 87). Cf. J. Croissant, *Aristote et les mystères*, Paris 1932, 137-157 where a text by Psellus has been quoted, also borrowed from the Aristotle's *Peri philosophias*, which mentions the θεωρία from which the initiate receives those deep impressions that qualify his religious experience (*ibid.*, 145f.).

tion of the rites as τελεταί[31] and the insistence on their cathartic aspect[32] also refer.

The Bacchic cult, described in its specific details (*oreibasia*, thyrsus, crown of ivy) is at the same time an expression of Mother's religiosity, since the θεμιτεύειν the *orgia* of Cybele, is parallel to the Διόνυσον θεραπεύειν. The common provenance of the two deities from the Asiatic areas, the common invention and possession of musical instruments intended to arouse the sacred *mania* are further elements which characterise the whole and point to the substantial homogeneity of the two cults. The bliss promised to whomever performs the rite of the Bacchants on the mountains "with sacred purifications" is an internal condition. It is the acquisition of a status religiously defined and expressed by the image of "becoming inwardly a member of a thiasus" (θιασεύεται ψυχάν) which implies a "sacred" life, holy and pure.

In its typical enthusiastic-orgiastic forms the ritual experience achieves that "interaction" between the divine and human levels, *via* the cosmos,[33] which is one of the aspects peculiar to the "mystic" sphere. The Dionysiac cult, in the early form of the thiasoi described by Euripides, and the cult of Cybele do not imply the re-evocation of a divine vicissitude, but rather the participation of

---

[31] This is no place in which to tackle the problem of the religious historical characterisation of the Greek rites called *teletai*, a term which has been all too frequently translated into modern languages by the somewhat reductive word "initiation". Thus, for example, J. E. Harrison, "The Meaning of the Word ΤΕΛΕΤΗ", CR XXVIII (1914), 36-38. See the various positions of H. Bolkestein, *Theophrastos' Charakter der Deisidaimonia als religionsgeschichtliche Urkunde* (RGVV 21, 2), Giessen 1929, 52-63; O. Kern, s.v. *Telete, PWRE*, ZR., IX Hb. (1934), 393-397; C. Zijderveld, ΤΕΛΕΤΗ, Diss. Utrecht, Purmerend 1934; F. Sokolowski, "A propos du mot ΤΕΛΕΤΗ", *Charisteria G. Przychocki a discipulis oblata*, Warsaw 1934, 272-276; P. Boyancé, *Le culte des Muses chez les philosophes grecs. Études d'histoire et de psychologie religieuses*, Paris 1936, esp. 40-59.

[32] On the importance of the cathartic aspect of the *teletai* see the works quoted in the preceding note; of these it is above all the analyses of Bolkestein and Sokolowski which emphasise the rôle of the cathartic component in the ritual complexes so denominated. The category of the τελεταί also includes the mysteries themselves, as we see from numerous sources and the explicit affirmation of Aristotle who defines τὰ ... μυστήρια πασῶν τιμιωτάτη τελετή (*Retor.* B, 24 p. 1401, 14f. rec. E. Bekker, Berlin 1960²).

There is no point in insisting on the function of the κάθαρσις in the Eleusinian initiatory *iter* (cf. P. Foucart, *Les mystères d'Éleusis*, Paris 1914, 284-296; 297ff.; 314-17; P. Roussel, "L'initiation préalable et le symbole éleusinien (Pl. II)", *BCH* LIV (1930), 51-74; G. E. Mylonas, *Eleusis and the Eleusinian Mysteries*, Princeton 1961, 237-285) and in the Orphic τελεταί. Suffice it to recall how the various definitions of the scheme common to the mysteries proposed by ancient authors give pride of place to the "purifications": Theon of Smyrna (ed. Hiller 14); Olympiodorus *in Plat. Phaed.*, 120f. ed. Norvin; Clement of Alexandria, *Strom.* VII, 27, 6 ed. Stählin 20 and VII, 68, 4 *ibid.*, 49, on whom see F. Pfister, *PhW* LX (1940), 105ff.

[33] The mountain setting of the Dionysiac rite which takes place outside the cultivated environment of urban society, the direct contact between the believer and an animal and vegetal sphere that gives rise to a sort of symbiosis which allows the Bacchante to manipulate wild animals as he likes and to dominate nature, are expressions of that direct relationship with the divine sphere, mediated through the cosmic level, which characterises the "mystic" moment of Dionysiac religion.

the adept in a rite which puts him, through the sacred possession to which he yields submissively, in immediate relationship with the deity. This relationship, expressed in the Dionysiac context by the presence of the term βάχχος to define the adept and his god,[34] is perceptible in the cult of Cybele in the denomination κύβηβος conferred on the man "possessed" by the Mother of the Gods.[35]

The capacity to infuse sacred *mania* is in fact one of the specific prerogatives of the great Phrygian goddess. From Euripides, who, in *Hippolytus*, evokes the Μῆτερ ὀρεία amongst the deities capable of rendering man ἔνθεος,[36] to Menander where, in connection with the experience of the θεοφορεῖν, we have an allusion to the obsession effected by the Mother of the gods,[37] up to the late lexicographers who record the word κύβηβος and say that

---

[34] Of the many examples we need only recall the famous "saying" quoted by Plato: "many are those who wield the thyrsus, few the Bacchantes" (*Phaedo* 69c = O. Kern, *Orphicorum Fragmenta*, Berlin 1922, F. 5, 84).

[35] Cratinus Θράτται in Photius, *Lexikon* s.v. Κύβηβον: Κρατῖνος Θράτται. τὸν θεοφόρητον. Ἴωνες δὲ τὸν μητραγύρτην καὶ γάλλον νῦν καλούμενον. οὕτως Σιμωνίδης (ed. A. Meineke, *Fragmenta poetarum comoediae antiquae*, Berlin 1840, vol. II, 65). Photius himself, s.v. Κύβηβος says: ὁ κατεχόμενος τῇ μητρὶ τῶν θεῶν, θεοφόρητος (*Lexikon* ed. S. A. Naber I, 355; cfr. Hesychius, *Lex.*, s.v.). Cf. Festus, s.v. *Cybebe Mater, quam dicebant Magnam, ita appellabatur quod ageret homines in furorem, quod Graeci* κύβηβον *dicunt* (ed. W. M. Lindsay, Leipzig 1913, 45).

[36] When faced with the melancholy behaviour of Phaedra the chorus of women from Troizen exclaim: "Are you not perchance possessed (ἔνθεος), o daughter, by Pan or by Hecate or by the terrible Corybantes or by the mountain Mother?" (vv. 141-144).
On the phenomenon of Corybantism, whose relationship with the cult of Cybele ought to be studied further, see I. M. Linforth, "The Corybantic Rites in Plato, *UCPCPh* XIII, 5 (1946), 121-162; "Telestic Madness in Plato, Phaedrus 244 DE," *ibid.*, XIII, 6, (1946), 163-172 (cf. the review by A. J. Festugière, *REG* LIX, 1946-47, 493-495); E. R. Dodds, *The Greeks and the Irrational*, Berkeley-Los Angeles 1951; H. Jeanmaire, *Dionysos. Histoire du culte de Bacchus*, Paris 1951, 131-138. I do not share the latter's interpretation when he identifies the Corybantic *mania* with pathological madness and attributes to Corybantism an exclusively cathartic function where mental illness is concerned. Admittedly the cathartic aspect is present in the Corybantic rites; but these also have an important initiatory component which ends in the acquisition of a state of essentially religiously possession.

[37] *Theophorumene* v. 25ff. (ed. A. Koerte, *Menander Reliquiae*, vol. I, Leipzig 1957, 101). In this text too possession by Cybele and the Corybantes appear to be connected. If the relationship of the Corybantes with the Great Goddess is a fairly frequent phenomenon in the mythical tradition which presents the former as "demons" in the train of Cybele (cf. for example, *Schol. in Vespas* 9; Strabo, *Geogr.* X, 3, 12. All the sources are collected in J. Poerner, *De Curetis et Corybantibus*, Halis Saxonum 1913), a passage in Diodorus Siculus, inspired by the canons of euhemerism, presents Corybas as a human character who, having gone to Phrygia, "conveyed ... the sacred rites of the Mother of the gods". He is the "son" of Cybele, who is also treated euhemeristically; it is worth noting, however, that the historian says that "Corybas gave the name of Corybantes to all who, in celebrating the rites of the Mother, acted like men possessed" (*Bibl.* V, 49, 3: "...τὸν δὲ Κορύβαντα τοὺς ἐπὶ τοῖς τῆς μητρὸς ἱεροῖς ἐνθουσιάσαντας ἀφ᾽ ἑαυτοῦ Κορύβαντας προσαγορεῦσαι". Transl. by C. H. Oldfather, *Diodorus of Sicily*, vol. III, London-Cambridge 1952, 233ff.).
There follows an identification between the Corybantes and the worshippers of Cybele, based on the essential analogy between their respective behaviours and the state of possession which characterises both of them. Similarly cf. also Ovid, *Fasti* IV, 209-214; Lucian, *Deor. Dialog.* XII.

the very name of the goddess, in the form Κυβήβη, is derived ἀπὸ τοῦ ἐνθουσιασμοῦ, which the goddess causes in the "initiates",[38] the sources unanimously emphasise this faculty of Cybele.

The theme of the μανία inflicted by the goddess as the punishment of an impious attitude on the part of man characterises the vicissitudes of Meander and Sagaris as they are recounted by the Pseudo-Plutarch.[39] The same author says that the goddess drove Scamander mad by appearing to him during the celebration of the rite;[40] an identical effect was produced on those performing the rites of Cybele by the sight of the stone called Μάχαιρα which is found on Mount Berecynthius, sacred to the Mother of the Gods, since it takes its name from the first of her priests.[41] Cybele, however, liberates whomever turns to her from the madness contracted by contact with the σώφρων herb which grows in the waters of the Meander.[42]

All these accounts are connected with the basic theme of "possession" as a condition characteristic of the cult of Cybele and which, induced and sought in the ritual context, can appear, outside it, as a terrible punishment inflicted by the goddess. Moreover, this theme, in its double significance (μανία beneficial if produced ritually and destructive "madness" which afflicts the guilty) defines the entire mythical vicissitude experienced by Attis, in its "Phrygian version", and the ritual complex of the Galli, to which I shall be returning later.

For the time being we should observe that, apart from that mythical-ritual complex which does not appear in the sources of the Classical period, the personality of the Phrygian *Meter* and her cult seem, in these sources, to be decisively characterised by the motif of divine possession which constitutes one of the aspects of the "mystic" sphere.

The connection with the Dionysiac sphere which seems to absorb the religion of Cybele entirely in Euripides' tragedy, is therefore revealing. It is to this religion that we can probably attribute, at least in the consciousness of the poet and his spectators, those "soteriological" prospects announced by the chorus in the urgent invitation to the city of Thebes to participate in the βακχεύματα.[43] These prospects consist, as we have seen, in reaching a state of inner bliss achieved through the practice of a cult with strongly cathartic connotations which entails a pure life and membership of a religious community.

---

[38] *Etymologicon Magnum* s.v. κυβήβειν. Cf. Suidas, *Lex.* s.v. Κυβήβη where we read: "αἰτία γὰρ ἐνθουσιασμοῦ τὸ μυεῖσθαι γίνεται". Cf. above n. 35.

[39] *De fluv.* IX, 2 and XII, 1 ed. F. Dübner, Paris 1876, 87 and 89.

[40] *Ibid.* XIII, 1 ed. Dübner 90.

[41] *Ibid.* X, 5 ed. Dübner 88.

[42] *Ibid.* IX, 3 ed. Dübner 87.

[43] Cf. v. 40 where the god announces his intention of introducing to the city whether it likes it or not, the power of his cult, ἀτέλεστον οὖσαν τῶν ἐμῶν βακχευμάτων.

That condition of intimate happiness which characterises the "true member of the thiasus" is then attained within this community.

There is no escatological projection of the εὐδαιμονία of the Bacchante in Euripides' text.[44] Admittedly the famous inscription from Cumae (5th century B.C.) which forbids burial in the place indicated εἰ μὲ τὸν βεβαχχευμένον[45] and above all the golden lamina of Hipponion, in which μύσται καὶ βά(κ)χοι are evoked who leave "in glory" along the sacred path which leads to the abode of the blessed,[46] clearly attest the existence of a link between the condition of the Bacchante and the prospect of an afterlife. Nevertheless these are documents from that Magna Grecia where, thanks to Orphic and Pythagorean ideologies, preoccupation with the future life of the soul were felt especially keenly. In all probability they reflect the concepts of Dionysiac circles strongly influenced by Orphism.[47]

Euripides himself refers to a circle of this type in the fragment of the *Cretans*, which combines in a single complex perspective the cult of Zeus *Idaios*, the "thunderbolts of Zagreus who wanders by night" and the torches wielded for the Mother ὀρεία.[48] Also in this context the poet insists on the purity of life of the believer, here called an "initiate" (μύστης) as well as βάκχος, but the reference to the "white robes", to the rejection of procreation and of ἔμψυχα, as well as the prohibition to have any contact with graves,[49] clearly illustrates a religiosity of an Orphic type which cannot be lumped together with the Dionysiac worship of the thiasoi or the cult of Cybele which Euripides so frequently assimilates with it.

---

[44] So also E. R. Dodds, *Bacchae*, cit., 75.

[45] D. Comparetti, "Iscrizione arcaica cumana", *Ausonia* I (1906), 13-20. According to M. P. Nilsson it is "a precious testimony to Bacchic initiations and their connection with the belief in the Underworld" (*The Dionysiac Mysteries of the Hellenistic and Roman Age*, Lund 1957, 12).

[46] G. Foti-G. Pugliese Carratelli, "Un sepolcro di Hipponion e un nuovo testo orfico", *PP* CLIV-CLV (1974), 103-126. The lamina can be dated in the late 5th or early 4th century B.C. and can thus be considered the earliest example of the well-known series of funerary documents on whose connection with one or other of the principal "mystic" circles of the Greek world (Eleusis, Orphism, Dionysiac cult) there has been so much discussion. Cf. amongst the many studies, W. K. C. Guthrie, *Orpheus and Greek Religion*, London 1952², 171-187; M.-J. Lagrange, *Introduction à l'étude du Nouveau Testament, IV, Critique historique, I Les mystères: l'orphisme*, Paris 1937, 137-148; P. Boyancé, *Le culte des Muses*, cit., 77-80; 381ff.; G. Zuntz, *Persephone. Three Essays on Religion and Thought in Magna Grecia*, Oxford 1971, 275-293.

[47] On the relationship between Bacchic cult and Orphism and the necessity of distinguishing between the two phenomena see esp. A.-J. Festugière, "Les mystères de Dionysos", *RBi* XLIV (1935), 192-211; 366-381 repr. in *Études*, cit., 13-47.

[48] Fr. 472 Nauck² 505f.: ἁγνὸν δὲ βίον τείνων ἐξ οὗ / Διὸς Ἰδαίου μύστης γενόμην, /καὶ νυκτιπόλου Ζαγρέως βροντὰς / τοὺς ὠμοφάγους δαῖτας τελέσας /μητρί τ' ὀρείῳ δᾷδας ἀνασχὼν / καὶ κουρήτων / βάκχος ἐκλήθην ὁσιωθείς (vv. 9-15).

[49] Vv. 16-19: πάλλευκα δ' ἔχων εἵματα φεύγω / γένεσίν τε βροτῶν καὶ νεκροθήκης / οὐ χριμπτόμενος τήν τ' ἐμψύχων / βρῶσιν ἐδεστῶν πεφύλαγμαι.

For an analysis of Euripides' fragment cf. M. Croiset, "Les Crétois d'Euripide", *REG* XXVIII (1915), 217-233; M.-J. Lagrange, *op. cit.*, 61-65.

Such testimonies, therefore, do not entitle us to claim that the Dionysiac cult of the Classical period invariably included the idea of future bliss for the believer which no other contemporary sources mention. We can consequently accept Festugière's conclusion that the efficacy of the Dionysiac cult was limited to the ritual act, and that the benefits obtained by the Bacchante consisted in reaching the state of divine possession, in the liberating joy of music and ecstatic dances.[50]

We are all the more entitled to apply a definition of this type to the cult of Cybele, so close to the Dionysiac religion of the thiasoi in its orgiastic manifestations, since no source allows us to presuppose the existence of eschatological prospects for the worshipper.

As for the procedure of the rite, even if the evidence examined allows us to recognise its mystic quality, there are no elements which reveal any initiatory and esoteric structure amongst the groups practising the orgiastic cult of Cybele. If we turn once again to the Dionysiac milieu, as to the phenomenon which offers the most specific analogies with that cult, we will see that, despite the presence in Euripides' tragedy of some indications pointing to a broadly "initiatory" practice in the Bacchic thiasoi,[51] there is no sign of the structure typical of the "mysteries" which includes a definite centre of the cult, a series of ritual acts intended for the religious qualification of the adept, and the specific esotericism which protects this ritual practice.[52] With regard both to

---

[50] *Les mystères de Dionysos*, 17f. On the cathartic and liberating function of the Dionysiac "festivals", characterised by "orgiastic" joy, see P. Boyancé, *Le culte des Muses*, 81-91.

[51] Cf. P. Boyancé, "Dionysiaca. A propos d'une étude récente sur l'initiation dionysiaque", *REA* LXVIII (1966), 33-60. The scholar sees a precise allusion to the "dressing" of the *mystes* in the episode of Pentheus' "disguise" (vv. 825-944). See also along these lines C. Gallini, "Il travestismo rituale di Penteo", *SMSR* XXXIV (1963), 211-228. A further indication of the reserved character of the rite has been detected in the dramatic conversation between the king of Thebes and Dionysus, when the former questions the "prophet" of the new cult about the origin and nature of the Bacchic *orgia* (vv. 471-474). These are indeed defined by the god as ἄρρητ' ἀβακχεύτοισιν εἰδέναι βροτῶν. Here the ἄρρητον typical of the mystery religiosity intervenes, which does not refer to a mythical tradition or a doctrine but rather to the concreteness and reality of the rite which becomes comprehensible, in all its religious virtue, only to him who celebrates it with the requisite internal disposition and in the prescribed manner. Dionysus expresses himself in the same obscure and deliberately allusive style in reply to Pentheus' further question about the utility, for man, of the Bacchic rites: "οὐ θέμις ἀκοῦσαί σ', ἔστι δ' ἄξι' εἰδέναι".

We should note the insistence, in both passages, on the immediate, "visual" experience, of the "knowing" reserved for the Bacchante. Finally, a certain esotericism of the ritual seems to transpire from some of the expressions of Agave who, in a state of divine possession, sees in her son a beast come to spy on the Maenads and tells them to capture him "so that he should not divulge the secret dances of the god" (vv. 1106-1109).

[52] On the performance of the orgiastic rites of the Bacchantes in a public context we need only recall the episode of Skylas (Herodotus, *Hist.* IV, 79) whose participation in the Dionysiac *teleté* aroused the violent reaction of his subjects. On the non-esoteric character (in a strict sense) and on the non-initiatory character of the Dionysiac cult of the Classical period see Nilsson (*The Dionysiac Mysteries, passim*) and Festugière (*Les mystères de Dionysos*, cit., 17).

the Dionysiac worship of the thiasoi and the *orgia* of Cybele it would be better to speak of a "seclusion" which protects those groups who celebrate the cult of the god, or rather of the Great Mother, in a state of mystic exaltation, from the indiscreet curiosity of the non-participants.

CHAPTER TWO

MYSTERIES IN THE HELLENIZED CULT OF CYBELE

The highly individual esotericism and above all the specifically mystic connotation of the ritual of Cybele can account for the use, in certain later
sources, of an obviously mystery terminology to designate it.

A scholium of the Hellenistic period to Pindar's 3rd Pythian Ode explains
the term ἐννύχιαι used by the poet by the fact that "the mysteries are performed at night" in honour of the goddess.[1] The same scholiast, recalling the
episode of the foundation of the little temple dedicated by Pindar to the
Mother of the gods, says that in it the goddess is honoured with τελεταί.[2]
Equally the scholiast of Sophocles' *Philoctetes* comments on the term by
which the "Gaia One who feedest all" (v. 391) is invoked, saying that "her
mysteries are performed on the mountains".[3]

The mountain setting and the nocturnal character of the cult are the two
elements which are stressed in these sources that define the rites of Cybele as
μυστήρια. While they confirm the mystic connotation of such rites, however,
they add no new elements to the picture which emerges from the earliest
testimonies: the mountainous and nocturnal context of the goddess'
"mysteries" actually reminds us of the cult of Cybele known to the sources of
the 5th century B.C. The terms τελεταί and μυστήρια are applied to it without
implying a reference to a ritual complex of an Eleusinian type, in other words
to a religious institution tied to a sanctuary and organised according to the
initiatory-esoteric scheme. It is in this sense that we could interpret the allusion to the μύσται who frequent the Dindymon in an ode in the Anthologia
Palatina,[4] but it does not seem right to attribute to the term the technical
meaning of "initiates",[5] since the text in question evokes the orgiastic cult of

---

[1] *Schol. in v.* 140 (= 79): "ἐννύχιαι δὲ, ἐπεὶ νυκτὸς αὐτῇ τὰ μυστήρια τελεῖται" (ed. A. B.
Drachmann, *Scholia vetera in Pindari Carmina*, vol. II, *Scholia in Pythionicas*, Leipzig 1910, 81).

[2] *Schol. in v.* 137 b (= 77) ed. Drachmann, vol. II, 81: "ἐκεῖσε τιμᾶν τὴν θεὸν τελεταῖς".

[3] *Schol. in v.* 391: "ἐν δὲ τοῖς ὄρεσι τὰ μυστήρια αὐτῆς γίνεται" (ed. P. N. Papageorgius, *Scholia in
Sophoclis Tragoedias vetera*, Leipzig 1888, 362). The Oriental character of the deity evoked in
Sophocles' tragedy is clearly apparent from the circumstance of her living near the Pactolos, a
river of Lydia, and from the mention of the "bull-killing lions" over which she presides (vv.
391-400). This is confirmed by the commentator who says that the passage refers to the goddess
"worshipped by the Phrygians" (*loc. cit.*).

[4] *Ant. Pal.* VI, 51 in H. Hepding, *op. cit.*, 8. The epigram opens with the invocation: "Μῆτερ
ἐμὴ Γαίη, Φρυγίων θρέπτειρα λεόντων,/Δίνδυμον ἧς μύσταις οὐκ ἀπάτητον ὄρος".

[5] It is to the widespread use at a late period of a generally mystery terminology that we can attribute the recurrence of the term μυεῖν, referred to the vicissitude of the *metragyrtes* with which
the foundation of the Athenian Metroon is connected, in the Lexicons of Suidas (ed. A. Adler,
vol. III, 1933, 391 s.v. Μητραγύρτης) and of Photius (*Lex.* s.v. Μητρῷον ed. S. A. Naber, vol. I,
1864-65, 422: "μητραγύρτης ἐλθών τις εἰς τὴν Ἀττικὴν ἐμύει τὰς γυναῖκας τῇ μητρὶ τῶν θεῶν").

the goddess, celebrated to the sound of cymbals, flutes and tympana in the typical condition of μανία.[6]

Nevertheless some sources of the Hellenistic period attest the existence of religious associations organised according to a structure of a mystery type who practise the cult of the Great Mother.

An inscription from Troizen, which can be dated in the second half of the 3rd century B.C., mentions the τελεστῆρες [τᾶς μεγάλας Ματρό]ς, i.e. "those who perform initiation", or the "*mystai*" of the Great Mother.[7]

At Argos a heavily mutilated inscription of uncertain date records a κοινὸν τῶν μυστῶν in connection with the Mother of the Gods.[8] The "community of the initiates" has a "priest-for-life" and assembles in its θρησκεία various deities whose identity is unknown to us.[9] Mention is also made of a garden and a dwelling (οἰκία), the object of the donation to the community recorded in the document.

Again, a decree of Minoa of Amorgos, dated in the 1st century B.C., provides some interesting information about the performance of the cult of Cybele, reorganised after the intervention of a certain Hegesarete.[10] The festival as a whole is called Μητρῷια and in it, besides ceremonies of a public nature and banquets, initiatory rites were also celebrated. A priestess is mentioned whose duty it was to perform the τελετή (B, line 11), or, as emerges from the context, "the initiation"; and we see that the πελανός i.e. the sacrificial offering ("obolus") paid by the initiates was considered sacred: "ὁ πελαν[ὸς ὁ ....]/δόμενος ὑπὸ τῶν τελουμένων ἱε[ρὸ]ς ἔστω "(line 11 ff.).[11] Further on we read of the "price of the initiation" (τὰ τέλεστρα, line 17).

We know that at Eleusis, as in other mysteries, the candidates had to give a certain sum to the priests in charge of the initiation. The existence of this

---

[6] The ode accompanies the dedication to the goddess of the sacred instruments of the cult by the Gallus Alexis (θῆλυς Ἄλεξις), who re-evokes the typical forms of orgiasm in which he has participated in the course of his life and which now, in his old age, he can no longer practise. Cf. also *Schol. in Aristoph. Aves* v. 877 ed. F. Dübner, Paris 1877, 230: "ἐν δὲ τοῖς μυστηρίοις τῆς Ῥέας μαλακοὶ πάρεισι", where the mention of the "eunuchs" makes it appear as if the scholiast is referring to the orgiastic procedure of the cult of the Galli, defining it μυστήρια. See also p. 77 on the use of a mystery terminology to characterise the practices peculiar to the Galli. Cf. *Etym. Magnum*, s.v. κυβήβειν :....αἰτία (*sc.* the Goddess) γὰρ ἐνθουσιασμοῦ τοῖς μύσταις γίνεται".

[7] K. D. Mylonas, Ἐπιγραφὴ ἐκ τῆς Τροιζῆνος, *BCH* X (1886), 141, lines 10-12 and 145; S. Wide, *De sacris Troezeniorum, Hermionensium, Epidauriorum Commentatio Academica*, Uppsala 1888, 65f.; Vermaseren, *CCCA* II, 150 n° 479.

[8] *IG* IV, 1, 659; Vermaseren, *CCCA* II, 146 n° 469.

[9] Cf. *ibid.*, line 13 and 16 where θεοί are mentioned. We should note that in the first mutilated line we read θεοὺς μεγάλους.

[10] *IG* XII, 7, 237 b = F. Sokolowski, *Lois sacrées des cités grecques*, Paris 1969, 196-199, n° 103 where the relevant bibliography is listed. Cf. Vermaseren, *CCCA* II, 205-208 n° 650.

[11] On the meaning of πελανός in Greek religious language see P. Stengel, ΠΕΛΑΝΟΣ, *Hermes* XXIX (1894), 281-289; R. Herzog, "Zu ΠΕΛΑΝΟΣ", *ibid.*, 625f.; L. Ziehen, s.v. *Pelanos*, *PWRE*, vol. 39, 246-250; P. Amandry, *La mantique apollinienne à Delphes*, Paris 1950, 86-103; M. J. Jameson, "The vowing of a Pelanos", *AJPh* LXXVII (1956), 55-60.

obligation in the ritual illustrated by the inscription in question confirms the fact that the cult of the Mother of the Gods had assumed, at Minoa, the institutionalised form of the mysteries in so far as they were rites implying an initiation regulated by precise norms and guaranteed by persons sacramentally qualified. A striking feature is that the performance of the priestly function is entrusted to a woman who practises the τελετή.

We should finally recall the Hellenistic bas-relief from Lebadeia which provides us with a scene of undoubtedly mystery connotation.[12] The reference to the cult is expressed in the four figures of worshippers who, in accordance with the conventions of Greek art, are represented in reduced proportions on the extreme right hand side of the marble slab, near a large table on which stand unidentifiable objects (bread, fruit?).

The figures, lined up facing outwards in a continuous series which ends on the left with the image of Cybele, seated on a throne in profile and flanked by the lion,[13] are on a larger scale and can undoubtedly be identified as deities, characterised by special attributes.

The Dioscuri with the typical pileus are followed by three Corybantes with broad shields, then comes a bearded figure, bare to the waist, with cornucopia and snakes, beside whom is a young woman with two long torches.[14] Pan comes next, playing the syrinx, and then Dionysus, recognisable from the thyrsus, leading by the hand a veiled figure who is also being led, on the right, by a woman with a large key which allows us to identify a priestess with initiatory functions.

The interpretation of the scene as the presentation of a *mystes* to the Great Mother is confirmed by the detail of his being veiled, a detail which recurs in the Greek mystery cults.[15]

---

[12] O. Walter, ΚΟΥΡΗΤΙΚΗ ΤΡΙΑΣ, *JÖAI* XXXI (1939), 59-70, figs. 23-24; M. P. Nilsson, *Geschichte der Griechischen Religion*, vol. II², München 1961, 642 Taf. 10, 3; M. J. Vermaseren, *op. cit.*, 36 and fig. 27; Id., *CCCA* II, 131f. n° 432, Pl. CXXVII.

[13] The presence of the animal permits us to identify as the Asiatic Great Goddess the figure represented in the relief of Lebadeia who, according to Walter, corresponds to Demeter-Europa, nurse of Trophonios (art. cit., 62).

[14] Walter suggests that the male figure is the local hero of Lebadeia Trophonios, whose chthonic connections and iconographical affinities with Asklepios are well-known. The torch-bearing girl would then be Herkyna, associated with the former in the cult (art. cit., 60f.). Nilsson, on the other hand, leaving out of consideration the reference to local cults, observes that the two figures could be identified with Pluton and Persephone.

[15] Cf. M. Bieber, "Der Mysteriensaal der Villa Item", *JdI* XLIII (1928), 317 n. 3; Nilsson, *op. cit.*, 642 n. 5. Walter thinks, rather, of a ritual connected with the consultation of the oracle of Trophonios, for which a particular costume was required, and suggests the existence of a mystery cult of the type celebrated at Crete for Zeus Idaeus, with whom the same hero had been identified (art. cit., 63-67). Such a complex hypothesis is not necessary, however, since the central figure of the entire scene, the one towards whom the whole representation is pointing, is undoubtedly the Great Goddess, to whom the "*mystes*" is presented.

Numerous other monuments, from the 4th century B.C. to the 2nd century A.D., show that the city was a flourishing centre of the cult of Cybele. Besides a dedication [Ματίρι Μιγάλ]η(ι) and an

We can agree with M. P. Nilsson in seeing in the relief of Lebadeia the transposition on a divine level of an initiatory ritual as it recurs in the Eleusinian milieu in relation to the initiations of Heracles and the Dioscuri even though we known nothing of the existence of a corresponding myth in connection with Cybele.

What should now be emphasised is the presence of an initiatory practice in this cult which, as far as we can see from the multiple divine associations, maintains the "orgiastic" characteristics typical of the "mystic" forms already analysed (Corybantes, torch-bearing girl, Pan, Dionysus), even if we also have new figures (Hades or Trophonios, the Dioscuri).[16]

Although we have noted the adoption by the cult of Cybele in the Hellenistic period of institutional elements of a mystery type, in a sense typologically analogous to the mysteries of Eleusis (at least as far as the practice of an initiation is concerned), we cannot provide any solution to the problem of possible guarantees offered to the initiate by the practice of the cult itself. The few documents in our possession—which I have analysed above—do not contain any elements which might point to such a solution. Even if we are entitled to formulate the hypothesis that, by establishing a closer degree of familiarity between the initiate and the goddess, the mystery cult procured for the initiate certain special benefits, it would not be correct from a methodological point of view to say anything about the nature of these benefits of which we do not even know the exact consistency.

Still less does the existence of Cybele's "mysteries" entitle us to project the guarantees and special benefits possibly offered to the initiate into an eschatological perspective. A procedure of this sort would imply the identification of the "form" of the mysteries with the Eleusinian rites, to which the eschatological perspective is fundamental, in the context of a cult which also guarantees an abundance of goods and a security in this world.[17]

---

altar dedicated θεῷ ῎Αττει (A. D. Keramopulos, Θηβαϊκά, *AD* III, 1917, 421 n. 2; Vermaseren, *CCCA* II, 130f. nos. 428-429), a further three inscriptions with dedications to the Great Mother have come to light, two of which were attached to the base of the statue of the goddess. Three examples of statues, partly mutilated, have also been found in the city. Cf. J. Jannoray, "Nouvelles inscriptions de Lébadée", *BCH* LXIV-LXV (1940-41), 40-48; O. Walter, "Archäologische Funde in Griechenland von Frühjahr 1940 bis Herbst 1941", *JdI, AA* 1942, 114f. The term Πηαωνία which appears on one of the marble bases, formerly interpreted as an epithet of the goddess as a helpful healer, is more likely to be a patronym (J. Jannoray, "Inscriptions de Lébadée. Erratum", *BCH* LXX, 1946, 262). Cf. Vermaseren, *CCCA* II, 131 n° 430f., 133 nos. 433-435.

[16] For the association of Cybele with the Dioscuri cf. G. Sfameni Gasparro, *I culti orientali in Sicilia*, cit., 141ff.

[17] On the double Eleusinian perspective see above all the *Hymn to Demeter* (vv. 480-489) and Cicero's passage which indicates the precious gifts bestowed by Athens, on the whole of humanity at the passing from bestial life to cultured life, marked by the knowledge of the agricultural techniques, in other words in the *laetitia vivendi*, and in the *spes melior moriendi*, conferred by the mysteries (*De leg.* II, 14, 36 in Turchi, *Fontes*, 98 n° 154). Cf. also Isocrates, *Paneg.* 28 in

The principal obstacle would seem to me to be the circumstance that a cultic complex which cannot be denied the character of "mysteries", such as that of Samothrace, familiar enough to us from literary[18] and monumental[19] testimonies which illustrate its secular history, does not appear to provide any specifically eschatological prospects. The "soteriology" connected to the cult of the *Megaloi theoi* of Samothrace does indeed entail a safeguard against dangers,[20] and particularly against dangers from the sea, but it can also be expressed in Diodorus' formula according to which the initiates simply thought they would become "more pious and more just, and better from every point of view".[21]

This is confirmed, moreover, by the formula of the dedicatory inscriptions, a large number of which have been found in the sanctuary of Samothrace, where the *mystai* call themselves εὐσεβεῖς or *pii*.

The benefit obtained by the initiation was not subject to the esoteric prohibition of being divulged; on the contrary, as is attested by Eleusis itself, it constituted the main argument in favour of the religious "propaganda" of the mystery cults (cf. the Dionysiac μακαρισμός of the *Bacchae*). It would consequently be hard to explain why the documents do not retain any trace of an eschatological prospect at Samothrace if the mysteries celebrated there had actually offered one.[22]

In any case, judging from the sources which have come down to us, we must admit that one of the earliest Greek religious complexes which displays the

---

Turchi, *Fontes*, 53 n° 86. On the meaning of the eschatological ἀγαθὴ ἐλπίς at Eleusis see F. Cumont, *Lux Perpetua*, Paris 1949, 401-405; U. Bianchi, Ο ΣΥΜΠΑΣ ΑΙΩΝ, *Ex orbe religionum. Studia Geo Widengren Oblata*, Leiden 1972, vol. I, 277-286.

[18] A complete collection in Naphtali Lewis, *Samothrace I, The Ancient Literary Sources*, New York 1958.

[19] Cf. P. M. Fraser, *Samothrace 2, I, The Inscriptions on Stone*, New York 1960; K. Lehmann, *Samothrace 2, II, The Inscriptions on Ceramics and Minor Objects*, New York 1960; Id., *Samothrace, The Hall of Votive Gifts*, New York 1962; K. Lehmann-D. Spittle, *Samothrace 4, II, The Altar Court*, New York 1964; K. Lehmann-Ph. Williams Lehmann, *Samothrace 3, The Hieron*, I-III, Princeton 1969.

[20] Cf. Aristophanes, *Peace* vv. 276-279; *Schol. in Pacem* v. 277 (ed. Dübner 179); Diodorus Siculus, *Bibl.* V, 49, 5: "διαβεβόηται δ'ἡ τούτων τῶν θεῶν ἐπιφάνεια καὶ παράδοξος ἐν τοῖς κινδύνοις βοήθεια τοῖς ἐπικαλεσαμένοις τῶν μυηθέντων".

[21] *Bibl.* V, 49,6: "γίνεσθαι δέ φασι καὶ εὐσεβεστέρους καὶ δικαιοτέρους καὶ κατὰ πᾶν βελτίονας ἑαυτῶν τοὺς τῶν μυστηρίων κοινωνήσαντας". Cf. also *Schol. in Pacem* v. 278: "δοκοῦσι δὲ οἱ μεμυημένοι ταῦτα (δίκαιοί τε εἶναι καὶ) ἐκ δεινῶν σώζεσθαι καὶ ἐκ χειμώνων".

[22] The identification of the four "Cabiri" of Samothrace with Demeter, Hades and Persephone, as well as with Hermes, as suggested in a scholium to the *Argonautica* of Apollonius Rhodius (*In Argon.* I, 917 in Turchi, *Fontes*, 107 n° 163), and the evident Eleusinian influence perceptible in the distinction of the two initiatory grades of *mystes* and *epoptes* (mentioned in inscriptions ever since the 1st century B.C.), lead one to suspect the possibility that an eschatological prospect of an infernal type, analogous to that of Eleusis, was not altogether extraneous to the mysteries of the Island, at least as from the late Hellenistic period. Judging from the complete silence of the sources, however, this cannot have been a specific cause of "attraction" for the mysteries themselves nor, consequently, the primary advantage of their celebration.

esoteric-initiatory structure of the μυστήρια and which probably entailed the ritual re-evocation of a divine "vicissitude",[23] in other words the cult of Samothrace, offers no support to the theory which establishes a necessary and indispensable relationship between the religious form of the "mysteries" and the existence of an eschatological prospect for the individual. The individual undoubtedly had a specific "soteriological" prospect, but its details and contents must be studied and defined case by case, without undue preconceptions.

To return to the cult of Cybele, we can say that in the sources examined hitherto the Phrygian Great Goddess has appeared as the sole object of a cult which, although submitted to a more or less deep process of Hellenisation, retains certain individual characteristics. It expresses a religiosity of a mystic type which, in some cases, assumes the institutionalised forms of the "mystery". As from the 4th century B.C.,[24] however, it is possible to follow another line of development of the cult of Cybele, the one connected to the figure of Attis who, albeit of a subordinate status, occupies a religiously significant position together with the goddess.

---

[23] See also the accounts of Clement of Alexandria (*Protr.* II, 19, I in Turchi, *Fontes*, 111 n° 173) and of Firmicus Maternus (*De err. prof. relig.* 11 in Turchi, *Fontes* 113f., n° 177), which do not, however, refer specifically to Samothrace but to "mysteries" of the Cabiri celebrated in Thessalonica, connected with a primeval blood crime.

A scholium to Euripides attests the presence of the "search" for Harmony in the ritual of Samothrace (*in Phoen.* 7 in Turchi, *Fontes*, 115 n° 180) which might suggest a further Eleusinian influence. On the spread of the cult of the Cabiri see B. Hemberg, *Die Kabiren*, Uppsala 1950. The problem of the Cabirian mysteries, both at Samothrace and in other centres (Lemnos, Imbros, Thebes) should be reconsidered.

[24] Apart from a brief mention of Attis in the lost comedy of Theopompus "The Hostesses" (text in H. Hepding, *op. cit.*, 6), in a fragment of Neanthes of Cyzicus (*ibid.*, 27; see below) and in Theocritus (*Id.* XX, 40 *ibid.*, 7) we can recall the ritual cry of the participants in the mysteries of Sabazius described by Demosthenes (*De corona* 259-260: "ὕης ἄττης, ἄττης ὕης").

It is at the end of the 4th century or at the beginning of the 3rd that we can date a marble stele found at the Piraeus with a figurative representation accompanied by an inscription. There appear two figures, a youth in Oriental dress seated on a rock and in front of him a female figure standing,with a tympanum in her left hand and a flower (?) in her right, turned towards the youth who makes the gesture of receiving it. The inscription identifies the figures in question as Attis and Agdistis. *IG* II², 4671: "'Ἀνγδίστει/καὶ "Ἀττιδι/Τιμοθέα/ὑπὲρ τῶν παίδων/κατὰ πρόσταγμα". Cf. B. Schröder, "Erwerbungen der Antiken Sammlungen in Deutschland", *AA* XXXIV (1919), 109 n° 28; M. J. Vermaseren, *The Legend of Attis in Greek and Roman Art* (EPRO 9), Leiden 1966, 22f. Pl. XI; Id., *CCCA* II, 92f. n° 308, Pl. LXXVIII.

Amongst the numerous figures surrounding the Great Mother in a rock relief from the island of Paros (4th century B.C.), placed as an ex-voto from the Odryses Adamas, we also have Attis as a young boy according to O. Walter (art. cit., *JÖAI* XXXI, 1939, 70 and fig. 25). This would then be the earliest representation of this character (cf. Ch. Picard, *Manuel d'archéologie grecque. La sculpture IV, Période classique-IVe siècle* (Deuxième Partie), Paris 1963, 1249 and fig. 486 on p. 1243). *Contra*: E. Will, *art. cit.*, 104 and 110.

CHAPTER THREE

MYSTIC ASPECTS IN THE
"PHRYGIAN" MYTHICAL-RITUAL CYCLE

a) *Attis the "mystic god" and the mythical theme of the androgyne.*

The relatively late appearance of Attis in Greek sources[1] does not mean that the myth and the ritual connected with him were a late creation, but rather that the Greeks who had come into contact with the cult of Cybele adopted the figure of the Great Goddess, partially Hellenising her by assimilating her with Demeter or, more often, by identifying her with Rhea, but at first rejected the figure of Attis. For he was at the centre of a mythical tradition and of a cultic practice which appeared alien, not to say frankly repugnant, to the Greek mentality of the Classical era.

Even in the Hellenistic and Roman Imperial period, moreover, the practice of eunuchism, performed by the Galli who used it as a means of dedicating themselves completely to Cybele, met, as we know, with considerable resistance in the Greek and Roman world.[2]

Such a practice appears to have been closely connected with the person of Attis from two different, but complementary, points of view. On the one hand it had its mythical basis in the act which, according to the so-called Phrygian version, was a prelude to the death of the divine personage. On the other hand Attis appeared in a vast documentary tradition as the prototype of the Gallus, or rather as the worshipper who celebrates the mystic-orgiastic cult of Cybele and, in a fit of total devotion to the goddess, under the influence of the *mania*, dedicates his own virility to her.

The sources thus present the figure as one who, having betrayed his loyalty to the Great Mother, inflicts a terrible punishment on himself in a state of madness and mutilates himself. This act becomes the mythic *aition* of the cultic practice of the Galli.

---

[1] Herodotus (*Hist.* I, 34-45), who does indeed testify to the existence of the myth of the death of Attis, says nothing about his superhuman quality and his association with the Great Goddess. We read of the vicissitude of Atys, son of Croesus, King of the Lydians, who is killed unintentionally by the Phrygian Adrastus during a boar hunt. The comparison with some later sources, which present Attis as having been killed by a boar, shows that Herodotus actually knew and recounted a euhemeristic version of the myth, in the so-called "Lydian" tradition. Cf. also Diodorus Siculus, *Bibl.* IX, 29.

For the literary sources see the collection of Hepding, to whom we owe the distinction between two mythical traditions, Lydian and Phrygian, back to which the entire documentation concerning Attis can be traced (*op. cit.*, 98-122).

[2] Cf. H. Graillot, *op. cit.*, 287-319; J. Carcopino, "La réforme romaine du culte de Cybèle et d'Attis, II. Galles et Archigalles", *Aspects mystiques de la Rome païenne*, Paris 1942[6], 76-109.

It is in this light that the episode of Attis is recounted in Ovid's *Fasti*, where the *phryx puer*, who "bound the goddess with chaste love" when he was living in the woods, did not live up to the absolute devotion and chastity which the Goddess demanded of him[3] but went off with the nymph *Sangaritis*. In a moment of folly Attis took a sharpened stone and mutilated himself, the mutilation being represented as the punishment deserved by his infidelity.[4]

At this point Ovid's report ends: only interested in "explaining" the behaviour of the Galli,[5] Ovid says nothing about the consequences of Attis' gruesome deed. So even if the latter is presented as the prototype of the eunuch of Cybele, it is still not possible to conclude from this source, of markedly "aetiological" inspiration, that the theme of Attis' death was unknown or that it was introduced into the mythical cycle concerning him after the theme of mutilation, by way of a contamination by the myth of Adonis or according to the canons of euhemerism, as Lagrange suggests.[6]

The theme in question, moreover, is amply developed in Catullus 63rd *carmen* where Attis is deprived of all superhuman connotations and simply appears as a devotee of Cybele—who, in an outburst of orgiastic exaltation, performed the brutal mutilation which dedicates him to the goddess irremediably.[7] Even the poems of the Anthologia Palatina often represent the figure of the Gallus overcome by *mania* and, in at least one case, Attis appears as the goddess' devoted eunuch, her θαλαμηπόλος.[8]

---

[3] *Fasti* IV, 221-244 in H. Hepding, *op. cit.*, 18f.; v. 225f.: *"hunc sibi servare voluit, sua templa tueri,/ et dixit 'Semper fac puer esse velis' "*.

[4] *Ibid.*, vv. 237-240: *"Ille etiam saxo corpus laniavit acuto,/ longaque in inmundo pulvere tracta coma est,/ voxque fuit 'Merui: meritas do sanguine poenas./ Ah pereant partes, quae nocuere mihi.' "*

[5] In Ovid, of course we get a dialogue between the poet and the Muse. The latter, induced to narrate the episode of Attis by a precise question about the behaviour of the Galli (*ibid.*, v. 221f.: " *'Unde venit' dixi 'sua membra secandi/impetus*?' "), concludes her account with the words: *"Venit in exemplum furor hic, mollesque ministri/ caedunt iactatis vilia membra comis"*. Cf. Fr. Bömer, *P. Ovidius Naso. Die Fasten*, vol. II, Heidelberg 1958, 220-239.

[6] "Attis et le christianisme", *RBi*, NS XVI (1919), 419-480, esp. 438-450.

[7] Text in H. Hepding, *op. cit.*, 13ff. For Catullus' dependence on a composition by Callimachus, already noted by Wilamowitz-Moellendorff ("Die Galliamben des Kallimachos und Catullus", *Hermes* XIV, 1879, 194-201), see A. Klotz, "Zu Catullus", *RhMus*, NF. LXXX (1931), 350-355; O. Weinreich, "Catullus Attisgedicht", *AIPhO* IV, 1 (1936) [Mélanges Fr. Cumont], 463-500; J. P. Elder, "Catullus' Attis", *AJPh* 68 (1947), 394-403. On the poet's attitude towards the Oriental cults which attracted proselytes in Rome cf. L. Herrmann, "Catulle et les cultes exotiques", *NC VI* (1954) [*Mélanges Roger Goossens*], 236-246. A literary and psychological analysis of Catullus' *Carmen* in P. Oksala, "Catulls Attis-Ballade über den Stil der Dichtung und ihr Verhältnis zur Persönlichkeit des Dichters", *Arctos*, N.S. III (1962), 199-213; Id., "Das Geschlecht des Attis bei Catull", *ibid.*, N.S. VI (1969), 91-96. Cf. P. Numminen, "Severa Mater", *ibid.*, N.S. III (1962), 143-166.

[8] Dioscorides, *Anth. Pal.* VI, 220 in H. Hepding, *op. cit.*, 7f.: "ἁγνὸς "Ατυς, Κυβέλης θαλαμηπόλος", where we should note the qualification of "pure" given to Attis. Cf. A. S. F. Gow, "The Gallus and the Lion. Anth. Pal. VI, 217-20, 237", *JHS* LXXX (1960), 88-93, Pl. VIII, I.

The myth and the cult of Attis, as we shall see, do not end in the practice of eunuchism, so it is not possible to conclude, as has so often been done,[9] that the mythical complex concerning him has a purely "aetiological" value, the character being no more than the "prototype" of the Gallus, Cybele's eunuch. At the same time, while such a conclusion proves inadequate because it neglects the other significant aspects of the figure of Attis, it leaves open the problem of the true religious historical meaning of the practice itself, for which the many explanations advanced by scholars are, for various reasons, unsatisfactory.

There is no precise evidence for the hypothesis that eunuchism was connected at a late date with the cult of Cybele by the Semitic world and that a cultic custom originally alien to Attis[10] was transferred onto the mythical level pertaining to him. Nor does it appear very likely in view of the central position adopted by eunuchism in the Phrygian mythical-ritual complex. It would seem, rather, that such a cultic custom was expressing a basic component of this complex. After all, for many centuries it remained unchanged, outside its original ethnic and cultural habitat, retaining its typically archaic procedure.[11] It survived, furthermore, in the face of profound changes in historical and spiritual conditions, and despite the open hostility and contempt of Western environments who regarded it as "barbarous" and alien to their own religious habits and cultural premises.

The requirement of ritual purity achieved in its most definitive and irrevocable form by way of mutilation[12] may indeed have owed a debt to those

---

[9] Cf. F. Cumont, s.v. *Gallos, PWRE* XIII (1910), 675. According to this scholar "Attis ist ein einheimischer Gott, und seine Fabel ist nichts anderes als eine ätiologische Erklärung des Kultgebrauches, aus dem sie erwachsen ist".

For the complex problem of the origin and significance of the practice cf. *ibid.*, 681f. Fracassini, too, states that the myths of Attis, in their various forms, are only aetiological where the practice of the Galli is concerned (*Il misticismo greco e il cristianesimo*, Città di Castello 1922, 123-128).

[10] Cf. Hepding, according to whom the practice is derived from the Semitic world and in particular from the cult of the goddess Syria (*op. cit.*, 217f.; cf. also H. Graillot, *op. cit.*, 290f.). He appeals to an observation by Rapp (s.v. *Kybele*, Roscher, *Myth.Lex.*, II, 1, 1657) who says that Herodotus' silence about the presence of the Galli in the cult of Cybele at Cyzicus proves that at that time the rite of mutilation had not yet been introduced into it. On the significance of this rite see also H. Hepding, *op. cit.*, 160-165; A. Loisy, *Les mystères païens et le mystère chrétien*, Paris 1914, 97-103; M.-J. Lagrange, art. cit., 422-436. Finally cf. the wide survey in G. M. Sanders, s.v. *Gallos, RAC* VIII, Fasc. 63 (1972), 984-1034, esp. 1025-1031.

[11] The mutilation of Attis takes place *acuto...silice* (Catullus, *Carmen* 63) or *saxo...acuto* (Ovid, *Fasti* IV, 237), while Martial recalls the *Samia...testa* (*Epigr.* III, 81, 3 in H. Hepding, *op. cit.*, 24). The archaic character of the rite, evident from the use of the fragment of terracotta or the stone, has been emphasised by Pettazzoni (*op. cit.*, 107).

[12] A. D. Nock, "Eunuchs in Ancient Religion", *ARW* XXIII (1925), 25-33 repr. in *Essays on Religion and the Ancient World*, Oxford 1972, vol. I, 7-15; P. Boyancé, "Une exégèse stoïcienne chez Lucrèce," cit., 215f. According to Graillot it is a votive offering, a rite which substitutes the sacrifice of life to the deity (*op. cit.*, 293f.). Cf. 128f. where the author sees in self-castration "the highest grade of Phrygian catharsis", even though the practice did not originally have a purificatory, but a substitutive, character.

cathartic preoccupations which are not extraneous to the cult of Cybele, but it does not provide a completely satisfactory explanation for such a singular and violent practice.

To interpret it as a rite aimed at promoting the fertility of the earth[13] runs up against several objections.[14] And besides, such an aim, considered outside an organic religious structure which might provide adequate grounds for this type of behaviour, hardly justifies the choice of so gruesome a method.

The significance of eunuchism in the cult of Attis, then, cannot be explained rationalistically. It can only be understood in the light of the religious context in which the practice has a concrete "function" and of which, as I said, it is an essential component. We must therefore proceed to a direct examination of this context in order to establish the position occupied by this particular theme in the mythical and ritual complex gravitating round the figure of Attis.

Numerous elements in the sources concerning the myth and the ritual in honour of Attis emphasise the character's profound and multiple connections with a sphere of vegetal fertility. He would therefore come under the category of the so-called "fertility gods", significant examples of whom are provided by the mythologies and cults of the Near East, and who appear to be involved variously in an alternating situation of presence and absence.[15]

---

[13] R. Pettazzoni, op. cit., 105ff.; J. G. Frazer, The Golden Bough. A Study in Magic and Religion, vol. IV, Adonis, Attis, Osiris, I, London 1936³, 268-271; Id., Publii Ovidi Nasonis Fastorum Libri Sex. The Fasti of Ovid, vol. III, Commentary on books III and IV, London 1929, 217-224. M. Delcourt emphasises the positive value of the motif of androgyny in the mythical-ritual complex of Agdistis but also thinks that the practice of castration fundamental to it tended to stimulate fertility (Hermaphrodite. Mythes et rites de la bisexualité dans l'antiquité classique, Paris 1958, 47-50).

[14] Cf. A. Loisy, op. cit., 99f.

[15] For the typology of the so-called "fertility cults", with special reference to Tammuz and Adonis cf. U. Bianchi, "Initiation, mystères, gnose (Pour l'histoire de la mystique dans le paganisme gréco-oriental)", C. J. Bleeker (ed.), Initiation, Leiden 1965, 154-171. The complexity of aspects present in the figure of Tammuz has been underlined by L. Vanden Berghe ("Réflections critiques sur la nature de Dumuzi-Tammuz", NC VI, 1954 [Mélanges Roger Goossens], 298-321). Cf. also O. R. Gurney, "Tammuz reconsidered: some recent developments", JSS VII (1962), 147-160; T. Jacobsen, Toward the Image of Tammuz and other Essays on Mesopotamian History and Culture, Cambridge (Mass) 1970.

For the interpretation of the mythical-ritual complex concerning Adonis see the note by P. Lambrechts, "La résurrection' d'Adonis", Mélanges Isidore Levy, AIPhO XIII (1955), 1-34, and more recently the conclusions of W. Atallah, Adonis dans la littérature et l'art grecs, Paris 1966, 268-273. It is outside the traditional interpretative schemes which emphasise the connections of this mythical-ritual complex with the sphere of vegetal fertility that we must place the latest research of M. Detienne (Les jardins d'Adonis, Paris 1972) and G. Piccaluga ("Adonis, i cacciatori falliti e l'avvento dell'agricoltura", B. Gentili-G. Paioni (eds.), Il mito greco. Atti del convegno internazionale, Urbino 7-12 maggio 1973, Roma 1977, 33-48; cf. Ead., "La ventura di amare una divinità", Minutal. Saggi di storia delle religioni, Roma 1974, 9-35).

This is not the place to examine the polemic between the two scholars (cf. G. Piccaluga, "Adonis e i profumi di un certo strutturalismo", Maia XXVI, 1974, 33-51; M. Detienne, "Le chasseur malheureux", QUCC XXIV, 1977, 7-26) or to express a judgement about the objective

Despite this definition which recalls Frazer's formula, I do not intend to accept the interpretation of such characters proposed by the English anthropologist in so far as it implies their insertion in a pattern of death and resurrection.[16] I wish, rather, to emphasise their undoubted connections with the sphere of fertility and their quality as deities typically subject to vicissitude.

For similar superhuman figures we can consequently employ a terminology better suited to the methodological premises I outlined at the beginning of this study and use the definition of "mystic gods". They can, after all, be situated typologically in a fairly homogeneous religious historical category which includes the same divine protagonists of the mystery cults in so far as they too are gods subject to vicissitude.

It is hardly necessary, moreover, to stress the chthonic references and the connections with the sphere of fertility in the vicissitude of Demeter and Persephone as it is celebrated in the Eleusinian mysteries. We must therefore examine the function and significance of Attis in connection with the Cybele's tradition in order to see whether we are entitled to situate the character in the category of the "mystic gods" in the sense elucidated above.

This is all the more necessary since Lambrechts has objected violently to the common definition of Attis as a "god of vegetation" who "dies and rises"

---

value of their respective conclusions. If, however, Frazer's scheme is insufficient for defining the figure of Adonis, who has a number of aspects which the scholars cited have contributed to bring to light, the divergence, not to say the incompatibility, of the results which they have reached stresses the need to avoid giving precedence to a single aspect at the expense of all the others. Once this need has been satisfied, on the other hand, we cannot deny that a significant component of the myth and the cult of Adonis includes a pattern of presence and absence and a series of associations, of varied importance, with the vegetal world.

[16] *Op. cit.*, Pars IV, vols. I-II. Frazer's scheme of the "dying and rising god" has been accepted by numerous authors, such as A. Loisy (*op. cit.* in n. 10); J. Leipoldt (*Sterbende und auferstehende Götter*, Leipzig 1923); R. Reitzenstein (*Die hellenistischen Mysterienreligionen*, Leipzig 1927³); E. Briem (*Zur Frage nach dem Ursprung der hellenistischen Mysterien*, Lund-Leipzig 1928).

The definition of the god of the mysteries as a "resurrected" god continues to be adopted in learned literature without adequate proof (cf. A. Benoit, "Les Mystères païens et le christianisme", F. Dunand et alii, *Mystères et syncrétismes*, Paris 1975, 71-91), despite the criticisms that have been advanced from various sides. Cf. M.-J. Lagrange, art. cit., *RBi*, N.S. XVI (1919), 420-446; *Attis ressuscité? ibid.*, XXIV (1927), 561-566; E. B. Allo, "Les dieux sauveurs du paganisme gréco-romain", *RSPh* XV (1926), 5-34; L. De Grandmaison, "Dieux morts et ressuscités", *RechSR* XVII (1927), 97-126; W. Goossens, *Les origines de l'Eucharistie. Sacrament et sacrifice*, Paris 1931, 256-291; G. C. Ring, "Christ's Resurrection and the dying and rising Gods", *CBQ* VI (1944), 216-229; L. Bouyer, "Le salut dans les religions à mystères", *RSR* XXVII (1953), 1-16; K. Prümm, "I cosiddetti 'dei morti e risorti' nell'Ellenismo", *Gregorianum* XXXIX (1958), 411-439.

See finally the extensive survey of the various attitudes to the problem in G. Wagner, *Das religionsgeschichtliche Problem von Römer 6, 1-11*, Zürich 1962 (eng.tr., *Pauline Baptism and the Pagan Mysteries*, Edinburgh-London 1967).

and offers his adepts some hope of immortality.[17] If the Belgian scholar's criticism of Frazer's scheme of the "dying and rising god" is fully acceptable,[18] the same cannot be said of his refusal to acknowledge the originally superhuman nature of Cybele's young paredros and his connections with the sphere of fertility. According to Lambrechts, he was a mere human being, a devotee of the goddess who only achieved a divine rank in the 2nd century A.D. when, in order to check the victorious advance of Christianity, he was made into a god who overcomes death.

Although I shall develop all my arguments in the course of the present study I should here point out that one of the elements on which Lambrechts bases his interpretation is constituted by the terracottas in the Museum of Istanbul which come from Cyprus and Cos.[19] They represent a goddess seated on a throne,[20] holding in her lap a child identified with Attis on account of his typically Phrygian headdress. Lambrechts, who dates these statuettes approximately in the Roman Imperial period, deduces that in this late period the "legend" of Attis was still particularly fluid since the character appears neither as a devotee of the goddess nor as a deity equal to her, but as a "son".

This observation seems to contradict Lambrechts' basic hypothesis according to which Attis was not originally a divinity but rather a "human" worshipper of the Great Mother. For if the figure is conceived as the "son" of the goddess, he clearly leaves the human sphere and enters a divine one.

The notion of Attis as the "son" of Cybele, furthermore, can be situated coherently in the "Phrygian" mythical version which recounts the birth of Attis from a girl fecundated by the fruit of a tree born from the blood of the hermaphrodite Agdistis, and which thus presents the character as the latter's son.

This same tradition also specifies Agdistis' "maternal" care of the child.[21]

On the other hand the Attis' superhuman nature is in no way impaired by

---

[17] *Attis, van Herdersknaap tot God* (avec un résumé français par G. Sanders), Brussel 1962. Cf. the reviews by Ch. Picard (*RA*, 1964, II, 211-215), F. L. Bastet (*BiOr* XXII, 3/4, 1965, 201-203), J. A. North (*JRS* LV, 1965, 278f.) and J. Ter Vrugt-Lentz (*Mnemosyne*, S. IV, XVIII, 1965, 448f.) For the other works by the Belgian scholar on the same subject see below.

[18] With the reservation that in my opinion one cannot talk of Attis' "resurrection"—as Lambrechts does—even in connection with the later developments of the religious complex pertaining to him.

[19] *Op. cit.*, 45f., Pls. 8-11. Cf. M. J. Vermaseren, *The Legend of Attis*, 10 and Pl. I, 1 who believes that the items can be dated in a far earlier period. Cf. Id., *CCCA* II, 222-227, nos. 695-720, Pls. CCVIII-CCXIV: sixth-fifth century B.C.

[20] In one piece the goddess bears the mural crown (Inv. nr. 3590; P. Lambrechts, *op. cit.*, 46 and Pl. 8) while in two others the throne is flanked by lions (Inv. nrs. 3494 and 3517, loc. cit., Pls. 10-11). These typical attributes of Cybele allow us to identify the goddess with certainty.

[21] See below. For the relationship between Attis and the Great Mother as that between "son" and "mother" we can recall, together with Vermaseren (*op. cit.*, 8f.), a scholium to *Iuppiter tragoedus* v. 8 of Lucian (in H. Hepding, *op. cit.*, 28) and the inscription of the statue dedicated by Valentilla in a cave in Lydia near Hamam, in which Attis is described as Μητέρος ἀθανάτων

the fact that he does not appear in the sources as a personality of equal rank to the Great Mother. In actual fact, in accordance with the typology of the so-called "fertility gods", he is an inferior deity, but connected to Cybele by profound bonds in a relationship at once intimate and ambivalent.

A recent exegetical study of the documentation relating to Attis has denied the original and specific nature of his association with fertility.[22] Colpe, for example, rejects the "naturalistic" interpretations of the myths concerning Attis suggested by modern authors on the basis of ancient sources which stress the character's vegetal connections. Such sources would seem to have submitted those myths to an interpretation in the light of the "physical" theory, in other words of the fairly widespread notion in late Antiquity of the correspondence between divine entities and natural phenomena.

Colpe bases his own analysis on the mythical version recounted both by Pausanias (VII, 17, 10-12) and Arnobius (adv. Nat. V, 5-7)[23] and takes the central theme of these accounts to be the myth of the primeval Androgyne, with specifically chthonic characteristic.

Agdistis, having lost her bisexuality through mutilation, tends to reacquire it through the connection with Attis who represents the male counterpart. The crisis of this relationship leads to the mutilation of Attis which should not be seen as a reduction of the character to a female category but as a means of overcoming the polarity of the sexes. Castration would thus reconstitute the "totality" of the primeval androgyne.

The principal telluric significance of this mythical theme, which Colpe deduces from certain details of the account (the earth or the rock Agdos fertilised by Zeus, etc.), is expressed in the conclusion according to which Attis (who would correspond to the Great Mother as an androgyne, identifying himself with her on the one hand and constituting her male counterpart on the other) and Cybele "stehen nicht zur vegetative Fruchtbarkeit, sondern zur tellurischen Erdkraft in Beziehung, als deren Manifestation man sich etwa den Magnetismus oder die Strahlungen vorstellen kann, welche die alten Prospektoren das Wasser oder das Erz im Stein finden liessen".[24]

Aside from the psychological elements stressed in the mythical complex in question,[25] Colpe, of course, is proposing a "physical" interpretation more

---

Φρύγιον θάλος ἀγλαόν. Cf. J. Keil-A. von Premerstein, Bericht über eine zweite Reise in Lydien (Denkschriften der Kais. Akad. d. Wiss. in Wien, Phil.-hist. Kl., Bd. LIV, II), Wien 1911, 122-124, Abb. 72-74; P. Hermann, Ergebnisse einer Reise in Nordostlydien (Denkschr. Oest. Akad. Wien, Phil-Hist. Kl., Bd. LXXX), Wien 1962, 43f. n° 36 and Pl. XI, 1.

[22] C. Colpe, "Zur mythologischen Struktur der Adonis-, Attis- und Osiris-Überlieferungen", W. Röllig (ed.), "lišān mithurti, Festschrift Wolfram Freiherr von Soden zum 19.VI.1968 gewidmet von Schülern und Mitarbeitern, Neukirchen-Vluyn 1969, 23-44.

[23] The texts in H. Hepding, op. cit., 37-41.

[24] Art. cit., 43.

[25] For a psychological interpretation of the myth of Cybele and Attis see also M. Meslin, "Réalités psychiques et valeurs religieuses dans les cultes orientaux (Ier-IVe siècles)", RH DXII

radical than the one in the ancient sources and, to some degree, than the one in the modern literature on the subject. But be that as it may. We shall now proceed to a direct analysis of the mythical and ritual traditions of Attis. For this alone can authorise a religious historical definition of the personality in question.

After having related Hermesianax's statement containing the so-called "Lydian version" of the myth of Attis,[26] Pausanias introduces a different account which, in his own words, constituted the ἐπιχώριος λόγος of Pessinus. The parallel but far more extensive account in Arnobius confirms the close connection between this second mythical version and the city sacred to the Mother of the Gods; it also reveals its own status as a "sacred discourse" within the cult of Pessinus.[27]

No doubt the account given by Arnobius is the product of various stratifications and elaborations whose sources and age cannot be identified with any certainty.[28] In any case the attempt to confer a Hellenized garb on the myth is perfectly obvious with the introduction of characters like Themis, Pyrrha and Deucalion, and Dionysus-*Liber*. Nevertheless it retains certain authentically Phrygian features which emerge from a comparison with other sources and which were due above all to its close connections with the ritual practice, usually more stable and conservative compared to the sometimes even considerable variations in the mythical accounts.

(1974), 289-314; Id., "Agdistis ou l'androgynie malséante", *Hommages M. J. Vermaseren*, cit., vol. II, 765-776.

[26] *Descr.* VII, 17, 9-12. See below.

[27] As we know, the Christian polemicist indicates his own source in that "Timotheus not ignoble among the theologians" usually identified as the Eumolpid Timotheus who, together with the Egyptian Manetho, collaborated in the "foundation" of the Alexandrian cult of Serapis (Plutarch, *De Iside* 28; Tacitus, *Hist.* IV, 83. Texts in Turchi, *Fontes*, 188-191 nos. 243-244).

On this figure, who seems to have played a fundamental part in the religious life of early Hellenism, see esp. Th. Zielinski, "Les origines de la religion hellénistique", *RHR* LXXXVIII (1923), 173-192, repr. in *La Sibylle. Trois essais sur la religion antique et le christianisme*, Paris 1924, 59-96. At all events, the information gathered by Timotheus was obtained, according to his own testimony, from texts of great antiquity, pertaining to the Phrygian "mysteries" (...*origo haec sita est, ex reconditis antiquitatum libris et ex intimis eruta, quemadmodum ipse scribit insinuatque, mysteriis, Adv.Nat.* V, 5).

The reference to sacred texts going back to remote periods is one of the most widespread commonplaces of the Hellenistic-Roman era. Nevertheless it reveals a desire to be connected with an authoritative local tradition.

On the value of Arnobius' testimony, esp. in connection with the ritual, cf. H. Le Bonniec, " "Tradition de la culture classique". Arnobe témoin et juge des cultes païens", *BAGB* IV, 2 (1974), 201-222.

[28] According to Zielinski the Eumolpid Timotheus had a direct hand in this elaboration of the myth, introducing a "reform" in the Eleusinian sense in the cult of Cybele (art. cit.). Cf. also R. Pettazzoni, *op. cit.*, 119; F. Cumont, *Les religions orientales*, 223, nos. 16-17. *Contra*: L. Gernet-A. Boulanger, *Le génie grec dans la religion*, Paris 1932 (repr. 1970), 376f.

Kalkmann maintains that the two accounts go back to a single source which, he suggests, is Alexander Polyhistor (*Pausanias der Perieget*, Berlin 1886, 247-250; cf. Knaack, s.v. *Agdistis*, *PWRE*, vol. I, 767).

It should first be pointed out that Pausanias' account only has the figure of Agdistis as the protagonist of the vicissitude directly involving Attis, while Arnobius also presents the character of the Great Mother next to Agdistis. The Great Mother occupies a position which would seem on the one hand to be parallel to that of Agdistis (she too loves Attis and, after his death, joins Agdistis in the dirge) but on the other she displays a superior dignity and authority, appearing as an attentive supervisor of the entire vicissitude.[29]

It is not easy to appreciate the religious historical significance of this double divine "presence" in the religious complex in question unless we interpret it as a straightforward "doubling" of the character of the Great Mother, possibly due to the "Hellenizing" mythographer's intention to safeguard, in the crudity of the episode narrated, the dignity of the "Mother of the Gods" from the "barbarous" and coarse aspects of the hermaphrodite Agdistis.[30]

Indeed the figure of Agdistis occupied a special position in the traditions connected with the Cybele's religion. If, as we know, some literary and epigraphic sources identify the *Meter theon* with Agdistis, presenting the latter name as her epithet,[31] others prefer to distinguish between the two characters, mentioning the one next to the other in the same context.

Thus an inscription from Iconium invokes τήν τε Ἄγγδιστιν καὶ τὴν μ[ητέ]ρα Βοηθηνὴν καὶ θεῶν τὴν μητέρα among the gods regarded as σωτῆρες besides

---

[29] She feeds the young mother of Attis, condemned by her father to die of starvation; she enters the city where Attis' wedding is about to be celebrated in an endeavour to avoid the tragic outcome and, after Attis' death, she celebrates his funeral rite (see below).

[30] Cf. J. Toutain, "La légende de la déesse phrygienne Cybèle. Ses transformations", *RHR* LXI (1909), 299-308. Rapp claims that Arnobius has "confused" the mythical traditions and thus attributed to two different characters a series of vicissitudes which concerned a single deity (s.v. *Attis*, Roscher, *Myth. Lex.*, I, 1, 716).

[31] Thus Strabo, *Geogr.* X, 3, 12 gives the name of Agdistis as one of the numerous denominations of the goddess amongst the Phrygians. Cf. *ibid.* XII, 5, 3; Hesychius, s.v. Ἄγδιστις · ἡ αὐτὴ τῇ μητρὶ τῶν θεῶν. Of the inscriptions which give Agdistis as the epithet of the Mother of the gods see *CIG* IV, 6837, of uncertain provenance, with a dedication Μητρὶ θεῶν Ἀγγίστει; *CIG* III, 3886 from Eumeneia in Phrygia, where the reading Μητρὸς]/θεῶν Ἀνγδίστεω[ς proposed and confirmed by Keil ("Zur Mythologie aus griechischen Inschriften", *Philologus* VII, 1852, 199) seems preferable to the plural form θεῶν Ἀνγδίστεω[ν restored by Franz (*CIG, Addenda*) and accepted by Hepding (*op. cit.*, 78 n° 1), and numerous pieces coming from the so-called "City of Midas" in Northern Phrygia (W. M. Calder, *Monumenta Asiae Minoris Antiquae*, vol. VI, Manchester 1939, 137 n° 397: Μητρὶ θεῶν Ἀνγδίσσῃ; 136 n° 395 and 137 n° 398: Μητρὶ θεᾷ Ἄνδξι and Μητρὶ θεᾷ Ἀνδίσσῃ).

It is probably in this category that we can place the dedication Μητρὶ Ἀγγδίστει which accompanies a votive relief with the figure of the goddess between two male figures, identifiable as the Dioscuri, because of the epithet of "Mother" qualifying the personage (*Arch.-Epigr. Mitt. a. Oesterr.* VIII, 1884, 198, 19); cf. W. Drexler s.v. *Meter*, Roscher, *Myth. Lex.*, II, 2, 2851; F. Chapouthier, *op. cit.*, 71f., n° 63; E. Schwertheim, "Denkmäler zur Meterverehrung in Bithynien und Mysien (Taf. CLXXXVI-CXCVIII, Abb. 1-41)", S. Şahin-E. Schwertheim-J. Wagner (eds.), *Studien zur Religion und Kultur Kleinasiens. Festschrift für Friedrich Karl Dörner zum 65. Geburtstag am 28 Februar 1976* (EPRO 66), Leiden 1978, 829 n° 4.

A statuette of the type of Cybele found at Çarmiklar bears on the forehead a Greek inscription with the dedication Θεᾷ Ἀγγίστει (E. Schwertheim-S. Şahin, "Neue Inschriften aus Nikomedeia

Apollo and Artemis.[32] Of particular interest is an altar from Sizma, a village of Lycaonia situated near Iconium and Laodiceia, whose four faces bear reliefs representing deities and inscriptions. While sides A and C have dedications to Apollo Sozon and to Helios, side B has the inscription Ἄνγδισι ἐπ[η]κόῳ accompanied by a heavily damaged relief with the figure of horsemen. On side D, near the front view of a figure on a throne, we read the dedication Μητρὶ Ζιζιμμηνῇ.[33]

The epithet of Zizimene is frequently used to designate the Great Mother in various centres of Asia Minor;[34] according to Ramsay it is a dialectal form of Dindymene.[35] However that may be, in at least one case the Mother of the Gods is explicitly called Zizimene.[36] Consequently the altar of Sizma represents the Great Mother and Agdistis as separate characters.

In many more cases Agdistis appears alone. In addition to a figurative stele with an inscription from the Piraeus,[37] she is mentioned in Greece at Rhamnus where she had a sanctuary of her own.[38] We have a dedication Ἀγδίσσιδι from Methymna[39] and we read the name Ἀ]γδίστιος on a marble base found at Paros, ascribable to the 2nd century B.C.[40] The same island has yielded a dedication Μητρὶ θεῶν,[41] while a marble stele, also of the 2nd century B.C., records a ναός dedicated to the "Phrygian" goddess.[42]

---

und Umgebung", *ZPE* XXIV, 1977, 259f. n° 1; E. Schwertheim, art. cit., 798f. n° 9, Taf. CLXXXVIII, Abb. 8 a-b).

On the numerous variants of the name in question see F. Hiller von Gäertringen, "Eine verkannte Gottheit", *ARW* XXIV (1926), 169-170; R. Gusmani, ΑΓΔΙΣΤΙΣ, *PP* XIV (1959), 202-211.

[32] *CIG* III, 3993. Cf. *MAMA* VIII, 53, n° 297.

[33] W. M. Ramsay, "Lycaonian and Phrygian Notes. I. Zizima and the Zizimene Mother", *CR* XIX (1905), 367-369; D. M. Robinson, "The Discovery of a Prehistoric Site at Sizma", *AJA* XXXI (1927), 28f. and fig. 2.

[34] H. S. Cronin, *JHS* XXII (1902), 341 n° 64; 342 nos. 65 and 65A; W. M. Calder, "Inscriptions d'Iconium" *RPhLH* XXXVI (1912), 72-74, nos. 45, 45a, 46; Id., *MAMA* VII, Manchester 1956, n° 515 and XXXII-XXXVI. Cf. also *JHS* XXXVIII (1918), 170-72, 130ff., 138ff.

[35] "Laodiceia combusta and Sinethandos", *AM* XIII (1888), 237 n° 9; cf. P. Kretschmer, *Einleitung in die Geschichte der griechischen Sprache*, Göttingen 1896, 196.

[36] It is an inscription from Savatra in Lycaonia, placed by a slave of an Archigallus (J. G. C. Anderson, "Exploration in Galatia cis Halym, Part II", *JHS* XIX, 1899, 280 n° 163: "Δάδα Ἀττά/λου ἀρχιγάλ/[λ]ου θρεπτὴ/Μητρὶ Θεῶν/Ζιζιμμηνῇ εὐχήν"). Cf. J. Carcopino, *Aspects mystiques de la Rome païenne*, cit., 96 n° 14 who attributes the inscription to the Antonine period.

[37] Cf. above ch. 2, n. 24.

[38] This emerges from the copy of a public decree kept in the Metroon of Athens which gave a certain Zeno of Antioch the right to practise the cult of the goddess in the temple of Rhamnus. The date suggested is the 1st century B.C. (Cf. K. A. Rhomaios, IEPON EN PAMNOYNTI THΣ ΑΓΔΙΣΤΕΩΣ, Ἑλληνικά I, 1928, 233-243; P. Roussel, "Un sanctuaire d'Agdistis à Rhamnonte", *REA* XXXII, 1930, 5-8; J. Pouilloux, *La forteresse de Rhamnonte*, Paris 1954, 91; 139-141 n. 24; Vermaseren, *CCCA* II, 64f., n° 245.

[39] *IG* XII, Suppl. 524.

[40] *BCH* LXXV (1951), 122; *SEG* XIII (1956), 108 n° 445.

[41] *IG* XII, 5, 1, 239.

[42] *Ibid.*, 240: "Σοὶ τόνδε, ὦ Φρυ[γίη]/ναὸν περικαλλέα σεμν[ῶι] βήσης ἐν δαπέδωι". Cf. Vermaseren, *CCCA* II, 205 nos. 647-649.

The island of Paros was therefore a centre of the cult of Cybele. The Phrygian aspects of this cult were heavily accentuated, but it is impossible to tell whether the Mother of the Gods received the name of Agdistis or whether she was considered, as in the mythical version familiar to Arnobius, a character at least partially separate from her.

At Panticapaeum there was a dedication which Πλουσία ὑπὲρ τῶν θυγατέρων κατὰ πρόσταγμα Ἀγγίσσει ἀνέθηκε,[43] while in Egypt the priest Mochos, in the reign of Ptolemy Philadelphus, records the erection of a *naos* with its *temenos* Ἀγδίστει ἐπηκόωι.[44]

There are also numerous mentions of Agdistis on her own in the inscriptions of the "city of Midas",[45] although they are all fairly late. At Kandira, on the Black Sea, an inscription from the Antonine period placed on a small altar, contains the dedication of a *synodos* θεᾷ Ἀνγίστῃ;[46] another inscription from Viranköy, heavily mutilated, contains the words θεᾶς Ἀνδίσσεω[ς---.[47]

There are some far earlier documents, on the other hand, which come from various localities in Asia Minor. The decree of Philadelphia, which contains a number of ritual prescriptions for a religious community which venerated numerous gods, goes back to the 2nd or early 1st century B.C. The community was based at the sanctuary of Agdistis, defined as φύλαξ καὶ οἰκοδέσποινα of the sacred dwelling and the guarantor of the prescriptions themselves.[48]

In one of the votive bas-reliefs of the series studied by Conze, in which the *Meter* is attended by two male figures, one young, the other bearded,[49] the

---

[43] *I. G. OPEux*, II, 31.

[44] Dittenberger, *OGIS*, 28. The reconstruction Ἀγδίστι accepted by Preisigke (*Sammelbuch griechischer Urkunden aus Aegypten* n° 306; cf. F. Chapouthier, *op. cit.*, 239 n. 1) in an inscription of the 3rd century B.C. found in Egypt is very uncertain. Cf. *SEG* XXIV, 1969, n° 1174 where Ἀδω⟨ν⟩ι is suggested.

[45] W. M. Calder, *MAMA* VI, 135-137 nos. 390-394, 396 and 399. Cf. L. Robert, "D'Aphrodisias à la Lycaonie", *Hellenica* XIII (1965), 108; *SEG* XX (1964), 40.

[46] G. Mendel, "Inscriptions de Bithynie", *BCH* XXV (1901), 58 n° 203. Cf. Fr. Poland, *Geschichte des griechischen Vereinwesens*, Leipzig 1909, 573 B 418 e; H. Graillot, *op. cit.*, 379 n. 9 and 567; L. Robert, "Inscriptions de Bithynie", *REA* XLII (1940), 318; E. Schwertheim, art. cit., 798 n° 8.

[47] *MAMA* VIII (*Monuments from Lycaonia, the Pisido-Phrygian Borderland, Aphrodisias*), Manchester 1962, 70 n° 396. Cf. Robert, art. cit., *Hellenica* XIII (1965), 108.

[48] J. Keil-A. v. Premerstein, *Bericht über eine dritte Reise in Lydien und den angrenzenden Gebieten Joniens*, Denkschriften d. K. Akad. d. Wiss. in Wien, Philos.-hist. Kl., 57 Bd., 1 Abhand., Wien 1914, 18-21 n° 18; O. Weinreich, "Stiftung und Kultsatzungen eines Privatheiligtums in Philadelpheia", *SBHAW* XVI (1919), 1-68; the text is on pp. 4-6. Line 50ff. reads: "[Τὰ παραγγέλμα-]/τα ταῦτα ἐτέθησαν παρὰ Ἀγγδιστιν [τὴν ἁγιωτάτην]/ φύλακα καὶ οἰκοδέσποιναν τοῦδε τοῦ ο[ἴκου]".

Cf. R. Pettazzoni, *La confessione dei peccati*, vol. III, Bologna 1936, 77-80.

[49] A. Conze, "Hermes-Kadmilos (Tafel 1-4)", *AZ* XXXVIII (1880), 1-10. It is a shrine in the centre of which we have a front view of the goddess standing, with a tall *polos* from which descends a veil and a long draped robe; in her left hand she holds a broad tympanum and in her right an unidentifiable object. By her side squat two lions. It is therefore the usual iconographical scheme for representing the *Meter theon*. To the right of the goddess is a male figure with a short

representation of the deities is accompanied by an inscription of the 3rd century B.C. in which Keil reads the dative Ἀ]γδίστε[ι.[50]

Finally, we have an inscription from Sardis, recently published by Robert, who recognised it as the copy of a decree issued in the 4th century B.C. by the Persian governor of the city, in which there is mention of the "mysteries" of Agdistis amongst the rites which the priests of Zeus are forbidden to attend.[51]

The name of Agdistis, as a specific denomination of the deity connected with the mythical-ritual cycle of Pessinus, was therefore quite well-known in various parts of Asia Minor and the Greek mainland and islands, at least as far back as the 4th century B.C. It is not possible to establish whether this implied a specific acquaintance with that religious complex, including the peculiar theme of the character's originally hermaphroditic nature, or whether the name of Agdistis only appeared as one of many epithets of the Great Goddess whom the Hellenized world worshipped primarily with the title of *Mater theon*.

Indeed, the latter has various features in common with the Agdistis of Pessinus, such as the capacity to inspire μανία and the connection with Attis, but she also differs from her precisely where that aspect of her nature is concerned.

On the other hand the theme of the divine androgyne is present, too, in other Phrygian religious traditions.[52]

We can probably accept the conclusion of Gusmani who sees in Agdistis the Graecised form of the Phrygian name (possibly *Andisis*) of a primeval androgyne whose figure was partially superimposed at Pessinus on the one, with very different origins, of the Great Goddess.[53] This appears all the more likely in view of the fact that, in the myth of Pessinus, the androgyny of Agdistis does not express the notion of plenitude, but rather of disorder and confusion. It can thus be associated with the theme, recurrent in so many cosmogonical contexts in Greece and the Near East, of the chaotic and violent

---

chlamys holding the *oinochoe* in his right hand; to her right we can see the traces of another figure with a sceptre. On the left-hand anta of the shrine is carved the image of the torch-bearing girl.

If the figures of the young *propolos*, perhaps identifiable as Hermes, and of the girl with the torch are fairly common in association with the goddess, the singularity of the series is constituted by the presence of the bearded male figure sometimes holding the sceptre (cf. *ibid.*, 3f., nos. M-N, Taf. 3, 1-2).

[50] J. Keil, "Denkmäler des Meter-Kultes", *JÖAI* XVIII (1915), 73, L fig. 45. The *naiskos*, kept in the Museum of Vienna is of unknown provenance but can probably be attributed to a centre in Asia Minor on account of its substantial affinities with the reliefs of Ephesus and neighbouring localities (*ibid.*, 66-78). Cf. Vermaseren, *CCCA* VII, 49f. n° 175, Pl. CVI.

[51] L. Robert, "Une nouvelle inscription grecque de Sardes: Règlement de l'autorité perse relatif à un culte de Zeus", *CRAI* 1975, 306-330.

[52] Cf. A. Dieterich, "Die Göttin Mise", *Philologus* LII (1893), 1-12.

[53] R. Gusmani, art. cit., 206-209.

origins in which entities as yet amorphous and semi-personal, *archai* rather than deities clearly defined in their nature and functions, act.

This conclusion would seem to be confirmed by a more recent investigation performed by Fauth. Starting from a Khurrish ritual text which contains the name of *Kubaba* accompanied by that of *Adamma*, and basing himself on linguistic and etymological considerations, he succeeded in recognising in the latter the name of an ancient Anatolian deity with features both paternal and maternal.[54] Fauth concluded that the document in question does indeed confirm the presence in Anatolia of a divine maternal entity with androgynous connotations, but also provides an attestation of the process by which the goddess Kubaba, on entering Anatolia, was partially assimilated with this entity and assumed its name as an epiclesis.[55]

We cannot deny the value of studies of this type, even if it must be pointed out that the linguistic element does not exhaust all the aspects of a deity and its religious context; it would consequently be as well to avoid any definite conclusion about the religious historical meaning of a mythical or cultic figure based exclusively on etymological evidence.

As far as we are concerned this form of research can help us to interpret a figure like Agdistis and her complex myth, revealing the interaction of various elements and layers.

Besides, if the observations made by the scholars quoted are correct, the distinction established by Arnobius and other sources between the character of Agdistis and that of the Great Goddess shows that the same religious tradition had maintained some trace of the original diversity of the deities in question, or at least of the specific peculiarities of each one. In any case, as we shall see from a direct examination of the accounts in Pausanias and Arnobius, the significance of the deities and their cult goes way beyond the theme of the primeval androgyne, which would appear to be no more than a single component of a far more complex and flexible picture.

We read, then, that Attis was the son of Nana, the daughter of the king or the river Sangarius,[56] who had deposited in her womb the fruit of a tree, an almond (Pausanias) or a pomegranate (Arnobius), which had sprung in its turn from earth fertilised by the blood of Agdistis.[57] The vegetal and chthonic connections of the episode are emphasised by the circumstances of the birth of

---

[54] W. Fauth, "Adamma Kubaba", *Glotta* XLV (1967), 129-148. For the Khurrish text see A. Goetze, "The Ugaritic Deities pdgl and ʾibnkl", *Orientalia* IX (1940), 225.

[55] *Ibid.*, 146.

[56] Pausanias does not mention the girl's name, defining her "the daughter of the river Sangarius"; Arnobius speaks of *Nana...regis Sangari vel fluminis filia* (*adv. Nat.* V, 6).

[57] For the theme of Attis' birth from the fruit of the almond-tree see the syncretistic Hymn known to the Naassenes, reported by Hippolytus. Here the character is invoked as the "Flute-player whom the Fertile Almond brought forth" ("⟨τ⟩ὸν πολύχαρπος ἔτιχτεν ἀ/μύγδαλος ἀνέρα συριχτάν..." *Ref.* V, 9 in H. Hepding, *op. cit.*, 35).

the hermaphrodite Agdistis from the earth (Pausanias) or from a rock (Arnobius), fecundated by a heavenly being (Zeus-Juppiter).

The youthful mother of Attis is rejected by her father, imprisoned and starved. But the Mother of the Gods looks after her and feeds her with the fruits of a pomegranate and other provisions.[58] Later on Arnobius himself says that these were acorns and figs.[59]

Agdistis, reduced by mutilation to femininity, takes care of Attis who is fed on goat's milk[60] and grows up in the mountains amongst the beasts of the woods given by the goddess to her protégé.[61] Arnobius' version attributes to the Mother of the gods the same love for Attis.

The familiarity between the two characters comes to an end when the king of Pessinus decides to give his daughter in marriage to the youth. When Agdistis appears in a fury at the wedding ceremony and drives the guests mad, the setting of the myth presents a series of obvious references to the naturalistic environment and, particularly, to the sphere of arborescent and florescent vegetation. Attis, in a fit of *mania*, castrates himself under a pine-tree and dies. From his blood spring the violets which surround the tree. Arnobius, who gives us these details, notes that *inde natum et ortum est nunc etiam sacras velarier et coronarier pinos*.[62] The practice of the rite, based as it is on the myth, thus confirms the vegetal connections of the character and his vicissitude.

After having wrapped his body in strips of wool and celebrated the funeral dirge, Attis' bride also dies.[63]

Further on Arnobius, returning to the various episodes of the Phrygian

---

[58] *Adv. Nat.* V, 6: "*Tamquam vitiatam claudit pater et curat ut inedia moriatur: pomis atque aliis pabulis deum sustentatur a matre*".

[59] *Ibid.*, V, 13: "*Glandibus atque ficis alebat Berecyntia religatam*". On Cybele's relationship with the oak cf. Apollodorus in *Schol. in Apollonium Rhodium, Argon.* I, 1124 a (ed. C. Wendel, Berlin, 1958, 100): "ἡ γὰρ δρῦς ἱερὰ τῆς 'Ρέας, ὥς φησιν 'Απολλόδωρος ἐν γ' Περὶ θεῶν" (244 frag. 92 J).

It should be observed that, according to the testimony of Julian, the prohibited foods of the cult of Cybele include pomegranates and apples, while figs are allowed (*Orat.* V, 174 B: "καὶ σῦκα μὲν ἐσθίεσθαί φασι, ῥοιὰς δὲ οὐκέτι καὶ μῆλα πρὸς τούτοις). On the significance of these abstentions and on the special quality of the foods connected with that cult in Rome see A. Brelich, "Offerte e interdizioni alimentari nel culto della Magna Mater a Roma", *SMSR* XXVI (1965), 27-42.

[60] *Adv. Nat.* V, 6: the child, exposed on the orders of the king Sangarius, is found and fed on goat's milk. Hence his name, since goats were called *attagoi* by the Phrygians ("...*exponi Sangarius praecipit: repertum nescio quis sumit [formas], lacte alit hirquino et quoniam Lydia forma scitulos vocat, vel quia hirquos Phryges suis attagos elocutionibus nuncupant, inde Attis nomen ut sortiretur effluxit*".)

[61] *Ibid.*: "...*Acdestis...saltuosa ducens per nemora et ferarum multis muneribus donans*". These gifts, later defined as *silvestria*, are presented by Arnobius as *venatoria munera* (*ibid.*, V, 13).

[62] *Ibid.*, V, 7.

[63] *Ibid.* The author, basing himself on the authority of a *Valerius pontifex*, says that the name of the girl was Ia. This confirms the accuracy of the report by Arnobius who, in addition to the

myth in order to give a polemical emphasis to its unseemly and absurd features, adds another detail; before she died the girl cut off her breast.[64] We thus have a mutilation parallel to that of Attis as the prelude to death. Purple violets also spring from the blood of the girl and, after she has been buried by the Mother of the Gods, her tomb gives birth to the almond-trees.[65]

The behaviour of the goddess also recalls the ritual practice: she takes into her dwelling the tree beneath which Attis died and *sociatis planctibus cum Agdesti tundit et sauciat pectus pausatae circum arboris robur*. The reference to the March ceremonies connected with the cutting of the pine, to its ritual treatment as the symbol of dead Attis and to its introduction into the sanctuary of Cybele where it was the object of funeral dirges[66] is obvious.

---

work of *Timotheus theologus*, also used other written sources of value (*...quam Valerius pontifex Iam nomine fuisse conscribit*).

We should also note that even the theme of the woollen garments with which Ia covers Attis' body has a precise correspondence in the ritual, as Arnobius shows further on: "*Quid lanarum vellera, quibus arboris conligatis et circumvolvitis stipitem? nonne illarum repetitio lanarum est, quibus Ia deficientem contexit et teporis aliquid rata est se posse membris conciliare frigentibus?*" (*ibid.*, V, 16).

[64] *Ibid.*, V, 13: "*Si Midas rex offenderat, qui uxore adulescentulum vinciebat, quid admiserat Gallus, quid pelicis filia, ut ille se viro, haec mammarum honestate privaret?*". We need hardly recall that the theme of the amputation of the breast also exists in the mythical cycle of the Anatolian Amazons, connected with the Artemis of Ephesus (cf. Ch. Picard, *Éphèse et Claros. Recherches sur les sanctuaires et les cultes de l'Ionie du Nord*, Paris 1922).

[65] *Ibid.*, V, 7: "*...purpurantes in violas cruor vertitur interemptae. Mater suffodit † etas deum, unde amegdalus nascitur amaritudinem significans funeris*". Cf. M. Eliade, "La Mandragore et les mythes de la «naissance miraculeuse»", *Zalmoxis* III (1940-1942), 3-48; S. Ribichini, "Metamorfosi vegetali del sangue nel mondo antico", *Atti della Settimana di Studi "Sangue e antropologia biblica nella letteratura cristiana"*, Roma, 29 novembre-4 dicembre 1982, cur. F. Vattioni, Roma 1983, vol. I, 233-247.

[66] The interpretation of Lagrange, according to whom the cutting of the tree and the pertinent ceremonies in the Roman March ritual were originally intended to commemorate the mutilation of Attis and not his death (art. cit., 426f.), does not account for the liturgical motif of the funeral dirge that characterises that ceremony. If the myth of Attis is none other than an aetiological myth explaining the "foundation" of the practice of eunuchism, Attis being the Gallus *par excellence*, one cannot understand why the cult which, according to Lagrange, represents the primary and most authentic element of the entire religious complex in question, is essentially a funeral cult.

The mutilation points to the "consecration" of the worshipper, while Attis, both in the "Lydian" version which does not contain that theme and in the "Phrygian" one which puts it in evidence, is condemned to die. Admittedly the myth includes a special treatment and burial of the *vires* (Arnobius, *Adv. nat.* V, 7); this recals the practices of the Galli (cf. *Schol. in Nicandri Alex.*, v. 8 in H. Hepding, *op. cit.*, 9) and fits into the context of that close parallelism which exists between Attis and the goddess' devoted eunuch.

A further confirmation of the relationship of the pine, the object of the ceremony of the *arbor intrat*, with the person of Attis and his death, rather than with the theme of mutilation, can be seen in the custom of hanging his image on the branches of the tree. See, for example, the relief from Ostia which shows Attis dying beneath the tree near which stands a little image of himself (M. Floriani Squarciapino, *op. cit.*, 11f. and Pl. III; M. J. Vermaseren, *The Legend of Attis*, 35, Pl. XXI, 1; Id., *CCCA* III, 119 n° 384, Pl. CCXXXIX; Id., "L'iconographie d'Attis mourant", R. van den Broeck-M. J. Vermaseren (eds.), *Studies in Gnosticism and Hellenistic Religions*

The "Phrygian" authenticity of this ceremony, as it emerges from the testimonies which we shall return to later, entitles us to reach certain precise conclusions of a religious historical character concerning the nature of the divine protagonists of the myth and the cult, independently of any reservation about the "physical" interpretation of mythographers and ancient theologians.

The episode ends with Agdistis' request to Zeus to have Attis returned to life; the request is not granted but the youth's body is saved from dissolution: his hair will continue to grow and his little finger will be in constant motion.[67] Appeased by this concession, Agdistis "dedicated the body (of Attis) to Pessinus with annual ceremonies and honoured it with priestly orders".

In the somewhat strange and crude complexity of its details the myth here recounted helps to elucidate the multiple chthonic and vegetal connections of the religious complex of Cybele, the character of the superhuman personalities in action and the significance of the rite which appeals to the mythical vicissitude.

Agdistis, born from a rock or from the earth, is a divine being expressing the savage violence of the forces of nature, unbounded and uncontrolled. While the mutilation of this hermaphroditic figure defines her nature by concentrating and normalising her fertilising capacities in a manner which is no longer destructive and unbridled, it gives rise at the same time to a vegetal element typically charged with a vital force (the almond or the pomegranate tree).

Agdistis' connection with fertility is further emphasised by the extraordinary circumstances of the birth of Attis, generated by the fertilising power of the fruit of the tree produced by the earth in the manner described. Attis' vegetal connections, on the other hand, are stressed both by the circumstances of his birth and by those of his death (pine tree, violets).

We should also note that, as in the so-called "Lydian version"[68] of the myth, so too in the Phrygian one which we have examined, the conclusion of

presented to Gilles Quispel on the Occasion of his 65th Birthday (EPRO 91), Leiden 1981, 419-431).

The custom is also familiar to Firmicus Maternus (_De err. prof. rel._ XXVII, 1: "_In sacris Frygiis, quae Matris deum dicunt, per annos singulos arbor pinea caeditur, et in media arbore simulacrum iuvenis subligatur_").

[67] Thus Arnobius. Pausanias does not mention a request for "revival" but only Agdistis' "repentance" and the concession, by Zeus, of the incorruptibility of Attis' body (_loc. cit._: ""Ἄγδιστιν δὲ μετάνοια ἔσχεν οἷα Ἄττην ἔδρασε, καὶ οἱ παρὰ Διὸς εὕρετο μήτε σήπεσθαί τι Ἄττῃ τοῦ σώματος μήτε τήκεσθαι"). Elsewhere Pausanias himself says that at Pessinus, near the mountain which takes its name from Agdistis, it was possible to see Attis' tomb (_Descr._ I, 4, 5 in H. Hepding, _op. cit._, 29: "....ταύτην τε δὴ τὴν Ἄγκυραν εἷλον καὶ Πεσινοῦντα ὑπὸ τὸ ὄρος † τὴν Ἄγδιστιν, ἔνθα καὶ τὸν Ἄττην τεθάφθαι λέγουσι"). Cf. J. G. Frazer, _Pausanias' Description of Greece_, vol. II (repr. New York 1965), 74f.

[68] Cf. Hermesianax in Pausanias, _Descr._ VII, 17, 9-12 in H. Hepding, _op. cit._, 30; _Schol. in Nicandri Alex._ v. 8 _ibid._, 9. For the interpretation of these and other sources concerning the Lydian version see _ibid._, 100-103.

the vicissitude is tragic.[69] The goddess responsible for the dramatic epilogue of the episode is the first, moreover, to begin the dirge round the tree which commemorates the death of Attis.

Unlike the Lydian version, however, the accounts of Pausanias and Arnobius contain an attempt to modify this doleful conclusion by reviving Attis. Although this does not actually take place, a form of survival after death is indeed accorded to him: his body does not decay and his hair continues to grow while a finger remains in motion, a sign that Attis is not completely dead.

So if we cannot talk of the youth's return to life or "resurrection", the mythical tradition attested by the two authors has an outcome which, even if it is characterised by *pathos* and by mourning, guarantees a positive prospect for Attis, since he is saved from complete annihilation. In this manner the youth obtains a subsistence beyond death, or rather what we would be entitled to call a subsistence "in death". The presence of Cybele's young paredros in the religious practice is also guaranteed by the annual repetition of the rite in

---

[69] Admittedly according to some sources the mutilation does not entail the Attis' death. These, however, are mainly sources which establish a close parallelism between Attis and the figure of the Gallus, with whom he is even identified. Cf. for example, Catullus (*Carmen* LXIII), Lucian (*De Dea Syria* 15), Ovid (*Fasti* IV, 237ff.), Minucius Felix (*Octavius* XXII, 1) (cf. above p. 26f. and nos. 3-8).

As for the mysteriosophic interpretations of a Julian or a Sallustius (see below), we cannot deduce anything from their silence about the theme of the death of Attis. It is difficult to reconcile it with the premises of these Platonising exegeses which see in the protagonist of the myth the "symbol" of the divine intermediary principle, whose descent to the cosmic level concludes with generation. It is along these lines, on the other hand, that the theme of mutilation is stressed as something which puts an end to the process of becoming and to birth.

I do not feel I can accept Wagner's conclusions (*op. cit.*, 217f.). Basing himself on the interpretation of Lagrange (cf. above n. 66), Wagner attributes to the myth of Attis a fundamentally "initiatory" nature, since it is aetiological with regard to the practice of the Galli. This may be true of the theme of mutilation as such, yet, as we see from the same Phrygian version in which it acts as a prelude to the character's death and not to his "consecration" as a Gallus, it represents a second and complementary element with regard to the primary element of death which distinguishes the entire episode of Attis and the (funeral!) cult dedicated to him.

In other words, even if Wagner and Lagrange are right in rejecting the "death-resurrection" scheme as the means of interpreting the character and the cult of Attis (*op. cit.*, 208-256), Wagner's criticism goes too far when he denies that the theme of death is central to this religious complex.

On the other hand Lagrange himself admits that "cependant l'idée de la mort devait pénétrer assez naturellement, *si Attis était aussi et dès l'origine un génie de la végétation* assez semblable à Adonis" (art. cit., 441; my italics). For a critical discussion of Lagrange's theory see also K. Prümm, s.v. *Mystères, DB*, Suppl., fasc. XXX (1957), 113ff. The same scholar has amply emphasised the chthonic and vegetal connections of the cult of Cybele and of Attis in particular (*ibid.*, 88-115). Cf. Id., "Die Endgestalt des orientalischen Vegetationsheros in der hellenistisch-römischen Zeit", *ZKTh* LVIII (1934), 463-502 (esp. for Attis 491-499); *Religionsgeschichtliches Handbuch für den Raum der altchristlichen Umwelt*, Roma 1954, 255-263.

which the vicissitude is commemorated with ceremonies directly connected with the essential moments of the myth.[70]

b) *Attis' vegetal connections*

Before we come to these ceremonies both in their public aspect (above all in connection with the cycle of the March festivals celebrated in the Roman world) and in their private or truly mystery aspect, we should cast a glance at other testimonies which stress Attis' connection with arborescent and florescent vegetation. This will enable us to confirm the pertinency of the character with all his peculiar features, to the category of those superhuman figures whose vicissitude of presence and absence can be seen as a support and divine guarantee of the alternating rhythm of vegetation.

The stability typical of the Great Goddess, on the other hand, expresses rather the substantial immutability of fertile nature, beyond periodic change and seasonal alteration.

Even the quality of the relationship between Attis and the Great Goddess confirms these conclusions; it is a typically ambivalent relationship, of love and benevolence on the one hand, but on the other a source of destruction for the young paredros. This is how it appears both in the "Lydian" version of the myth, according to which Attis is killed by the boar set onto him by Zeus, jealous of the preference which Cybele displays for the young man, and in the "Phrygian" version in which the jealous and possessive love of Agdistis entails the death of the character whom she is then the first to bewail.[71]

A similar significance is assumed by the vicissitude of Attis in the clearly euhemeristic version known to Diodorus Siculus. Despite the essentially humanized setting in which the characters move[72] their principal features and their multiple and fundamental connections with the sphere of nature, both animal and chthonic, do indeed emerge. The mountainous setting, inhabited by beasts and shepherds with their flocks, shows up a fundamental aspect of

---

[70] In the polemical disquisitions which follow Arnobius' exposition of the myth, its connections with the ritual of March are indeed stressed. There also clearly emerges the notion of Attis' effective presence in the cult, especially in the final question which he puts to his pagan interlocutor: *"Cur ad ultimum pinus ipsa paulo ante in dumis inertissimum nutans lignum mox ut aliquod praesens atque augustissimum numen deum Matris constituatur in sedibus?"* (*Adv. Nat.* V, 16-17 in H. Hepding, *op. cit.*, 43).

[71] For this theme cf. Theocritus, *Id.* XX, 4 (in H. Hepding, *op. cit.*, 7): "Thou o Rhea, mournest for the shepherd" ("καὶ σὺ 'Ρέα κλαίεις τὸν βουκόλον").

[72] *Bibl. Hist.* III, 58, 1-59, 8 (only partially in H. Hepding, *op. cit.*, 16f.). Cybele appears as the daughter of Meïon, king of Lydia and Phrygia, and of a woman, Dindymê; at her birth, however, she is abandoned on Mount *Kybelon* from which she takes her name. After having been fed by wild beasts of the woods she is brought up by women grazing their flocks in the country and receives the attribute of "Mountain Mother". Living amongst beasts and on mountains, she displays a particular fondness for children and animals, whose illnesses she cures with καθαρμοί,

the personality of Cybele who, though presented as a girl, receives the typical epithet of μήτηρ ὀρεία and turns out to be gifted with medical and cathartic powers in relation to the invention of the sacred musical instruments typical of the orgiastic cult.

In the obviously romanticised picture of the marriage of Cybele and Attis-Papas there emerge the essential components of the myth already known to us: the bond between the two characters turns out to be disastrous for Attis who is subjected to death. What, in the "Lydian" version, was Zeus' jealousy at the evident preference displayed by the goddess for the young devotee, becomes, in Diodorus' euhemeristic account of the events, the wrath of the king whose vengeance strikes his daughter's clandestine bridegroom. The daughter's reaction to the death of Attis is in keeping with the common mythic tradition: "Raising loud cries and beating the tympanum, she wandered through the country alone, her hair loose".[73]

We therefore have a characteristic theme: that of dearth and plague which afflict the country as the result of Attis' death and the mourning of Cybele.[74]

If on the one hand it is a repetition of the familiar theme of flails which afflict a people marked by the killing of an innocent, on the other we cannot help noticing the coherence of such a theme with the general context of the vicissitude. As the convergence of so much evidence seems to demonstrate, it does indeed fit into the framework of a religiosity of a chthonic type, nature, of course, being seen as spontaneous vegetal rhythms or arborescent vegetation rather than in the Demetrian sense of regular, "cultivated" agrarian rhythms.

At the same time, however, the barrenness which strikes the country as the result of the death of Attis and the departure of Cybele turns out to be comparable to the situation in the analogous episodes of Ishtar-Tammuz and Demeter-Persephone. In both of these, as we know, the climax of the crisis, characterised by the momentary absence of the Great Goddess of nature, is marked by an animal and earth sterility which threaten the human race with extinction. In the case of Inanna-Ishtar, this is due to the temporary "death"

---

having also invented various musical instruments (the syrinx with several pipes, cymbals and tympana).

The goddess' celebrated relationship with the silenus Marsyas, defined here as a Phrygian of extraordinary wisdom and noted for his chastity (*ibid.*, 58, 3), is also represented in a euhemeristic form.

Attis is a local youth with whom Cybele contracts a secret marriage; recognised by her father and brought to the palace, she is the object of her father's wrath because of this bond. The king has Attis and Cybele's nurses put to death, and Cybele, maddened with grief, wanders through the country in the company of Marsyas.

[73] *Ibid.*, III, 59, 1.

[74] *Ibid.*, III, 59, 7: "Κατὰ δὲ τὴν Φρυγίαν ἐμπεσούσης νόσου τοῖς ἀνθρώποις καὶ τῆς γῆς ἀκάρπου γενομένης".

of the goddess caused by her descent into the infernal regions; or in the case of Demeter, to the voluntary cessation of the functions peculiar to the deity.[75]

It is difficult to decide on the "Phrygian" authenticity of the motif of sterility resulting from the death of Attis and the mourning of Cybele. We cannot exclude, any more than we can for other aspects of the cult of Cybele in its Hellenized forms, an "influence" of the Demetrian type, all the more likely in view of the complex and elaborate character of Diodorus' version. Even in this second event, however, we must admit that the theme in question fits coherently into the general context of the myth and the Phrygian cult: the disappearance of Attis, provoking the crisis and the removal of the great chthonic goddess from her functions (mourning as a state of withdrawal and inactivity), is directly reflected in the life of the country which turns out to be seriously affected and threatened by extinction.

The character is indeed connected with the Great Goddess of nature in an ambiguous manner, even if, in the light of the religious ideology in question, this manner is also perfectly coherent. Condemned to death precisely because of his relationship with the goddess, he is loved and bewailed by her, and his death is a source of sorrow and desolation for the entire country until his *pathos* is in some way redeemed and the goddess pacified.

In contrast to the Demetrian myth which knows the alternating situation of Persephone, the case of Attis knows neither a periodic "return" nor a form of "revival" of the character: he dies once and for all, as emerges from all the testimonies, with only a very few exceptions.

Nevertheless dead Attis is annually commemorated by the funeral rites of lamentation performed by the Phrygians before his image.[76] In this manner the character is felt to be present in a ritually effective way, and order returns after its disruption.

The establishment of the rite in which the moment of mourning is essential and characteristic in so far as it is a commemoration of the *pathos* of Attis together with the divine Mother, thus appears as the conclusive moment of the whole episode, the one which, repeated annually, guarantees in a stable and definite manner the regular rhythm of the seasonal cycle.

Amongst the many literary sources which attest the connections of Attis with the pine tree[77] and the functions of the pine in the ritual of Cybele, we

---

[75] Cf. the poem of *Ishtar's descent to the Nether World* vv. 76-80 in J. B. Pritchard, *Ancient Near Eastern Texts Relating to the Old Testament*, Princeton 1969³, 108; *Hymn to Demeter*, vv. 305-313; 450-453 ed. J. Humbert, 51 and 56.

[76] The oracle consulted by the Phrygians reveals that plague and famine will only end if the body of Attis is buried and Cybele worshipped "as a goddess". Since the body was lost, they "built an image of the youth, before which they celebrated his suffering with funeral rites at the right time and placated his wrath, for he had been punished unjustly". Altars are built and annual rites performed in honour of Cybele (*ibid.*, III, 59, 7-8).

[77] For the figurative monuments which variously stress Attis' vegetal connections see Ch. Picard, "Sur quelques documents nouveaux concernant les cultes de Cybèle et d'Attis: des

have Ovid who, in accordance with the general theme of his *Metamorphoses*, actually talks of the transformation of the *Cybeleius Attis* into the trunk of a pine-tree.[78]

In actual fact this tree is really an image of Attis, the sign of his presence in the practice of the rite, as is confirmed in a passage from the *Thebais*, evoking the behaviour of the Gallus of Cybele who, at the height of his religious enthusiasm, "shakes on his chest the sacred branches of the pine".[79] The commentator glosses this expression, underlining the holiness of the tree "venerated in the ceremonies of the Mother of the Gods, under which lay Attis, beloved" by the goddess.[80]

Certain Christian authors, appealing to the interpretations of the same learned pagans, try to prove that the naturalistic references in the myths and religious traditions of paganism are essential. Eusebius, for example, claims that Attis and Adonis display profound analogies with the fruits of the earth in their character and in their vicissitude. But, he adds, Attis is more the symbol of the flowers that bud in the spring and are picked before they reach their bloom; his mutilation is the sign of the fate of the flower which must fall in order for the fruit to ripen. Adonis, on the other hand, is "the symbol of the harvest of ripe fruits".[81]

Attis and Adonis would consequently be connected with the two successive moments of the flowering and the ripening of the fruit.

Even if we do not accept an interpretation which simply "reduces" the two deities to the naturalistic element, there is no doubt that, in the definition suggested by Eusebius, we have an item of evidence specifically connecting Attis with florescent vegetation.

The same connection between Attis and spring flowers, also present in the Phrygian version of the myth, is stressed by Augustine who appeals to the authority of Porphyry and elaborates a complex speculation around the equation of Attis with flowers, concluding that the significance of the character's mutilation must be seen in the fact that *flos decidit ante fructum.*[82]

Balkans à la Gaule", *Numen* IV (1957), 1-23. Of these an altar from Périgueux is particularly significant. On it a leafy pine emerges from Attis' head, the character's bust being represented above an altar (*ibid.*, 12-15, Pl. I). Cf. also the dedication *Arbori sanctae* on an altar from Osuna placed *ex visu* by a certain *Q. Avidius Augustinus* (A. Blanco Freijeiro, "Documentos metroacos de Hispania", *AEspA* XLI, 1968, 95ff. and fig. 3 and 5). As Freijeiro points out, the expression used here appears as an alternative form of the dedications *Attidi sancto* (cf. *ILS* II, 1, 4149 and 4117), in virtue of the intimate relationship between the phrygian god and the pine.

[78] *Metam.* X, 103-105 in H. Hepding, *op. cit.*, 18: "*et succincta comas hirsutaque vertice pinus,/ grata deum Matri: siquidem Cybeleīus Attis/ exuit hac hominem truncoque induruit illo*".

[79] Statius, *Thebais* X, 170-175 in H. Hepding, *op. cit.*, 22.

[80] *Lactantii Placidi qui dicitur commentarii*, v. 175 in H. Hepding, *op. cit.*, 23.

[81] *Praep. evang.* III, 11, 12 in H. Hepding, *op. cit.*, 47. The same notion is repeated by Eusebius in other parts of the work (III, 11, 15; III, 13, 14).

[82] *De civ. Dei* VII, 25 in H. Hepding, *op. cit.*, 69f.

A close parallelism between the vicissitude of Attis and the annual cycle of vegetation is also detected by Firmicus Maternus, who tries to prove that the Phrygian myth and rite arose on the one hand as a result of the divinisation of human beings in Antiquity and on the other reflect natural experiences connected with the agricultural rhythm. He thus appeals both to the canons of euhemerism and to the widespread tendency in cultivated pagan circles of the time to interpret the characters of the myth as "personifications" or "symbols" of natural phenomena or events.

After pointing out that of all the cosmic elements the Phrygians of Pessinus display a particular veneration for the earth, which they call "mother of all things", Firmicus says that, in order to have sacred rites with an annual recurrence, they instituted ceremonies of lamentation in honour of a queen who had caused the death of her young lover by her jealousy.[83]

At the conclusion of what is obviously an euhemeristic interpretation of the "Phrygian" version of the myth, the Christian polemicist says that the Phrygians *ut satis iratae mulieri facerent aut ut paenitenti solacium quaererent, quem paulo ante sepelierant revixisse iactarunt, et cum mulieris animus ex impatientia nimii amoris arderet, mortuo adulescenti templa fecerunt.*

There follows a parallelism between the lot of Attis and that of the crops. The relationship between the goddess and the young man is seen in the light of the relationship existing between the crops and the earth; the mutilation of Attis is thus equivalent to harvesting: *mortem ipsius dicunt, quod semina collecta conduntur, vitam rursus, quod iacta semina annuis vicibus redduntur.*

It is precisely the parallelism which the polemicist establishes between the youthful protagonist of the Phrygian myth and the fate of the *fruges*, not found elsewhere since Attis is invariably associated with arborescent and florescent vegetation,[84] which has induced the Christian author to talk of Attis' "rebirth" as well as of his death. The verb *"revivere"*, moreover, appears to have been borrowed by Firmicus from Christian terminology. Consequent-

---

[83] *De err. prof. rel.* 3 in H. Hepding, *op. cit.*, 47f.

[84] Attis is called "harvested Green ear of corn" in the syncretistic hymn known to the Naassene Gnostics, reported by Hippolytus (*Ref. omnium haer.* V, 9 in H. Hepding, *op. cit.*, 34f.). On this text see the long commentary by T. Wolberg, *Griechische religiöse Gedichte der ersten nachchristlichen Jahrhunderte*, Bd. I, *Psalmen und Hymnen der Gnosis und des frühen Christentums*, Meisenheim am Glan 1971, 60-75.

The pre-agrarian and pre-corn-growing character of the cultural and religious complex relating to Cybele has been emphasised by A. Brelich, who stressed the distinction, which sometimes turns into opposition, between this complex and that relating to *Ceres* in the Roman world. This was contrary to what happened in the Greek world where, as has so frequently been said, Cybele was associated with, and sometimes even assimilated by, Demeter; cf. art. cit., above p. 39 n. 59. Brelich also notes the lateness of the process which led to a similar partial assimilation in the Roman cult of Cybele (*ibid.*, 35f.). See below ch. 5 nn. 1-2.

ly the notion of a "resurrection" of Attis does not belong to the Phrygian mythical-ritual context.[85]

Despite the use of the verb in question, the resort to the concept of "resurrection" really does not seem suitable for defining Attis' vicissitude, even in the form in which it is presented by Firmicus Maternus. The idea of resurrection implies a definitive victory over death through the reconstitution of the psycho-physical integrity of the individual resurrected. The association between the vicissitude of the young Phrygian shepherd and the crops shows, rather, that in this perspective the lot of Attis is stabilised in an alternating rhythm of presence and absence, and does not include a definitive and total liberation from death.

On the other hand it would be going too far to say that Firmicus Maternus' account is nothing but the fruit of a personal interpretation by the author or of late speculations in a "physical" key on pagan myths, and that we should consequently reject the idea of a parallelism between the vicissitude of Attis and vegetation. For the chthonic and vegetal connections of the character appear evident from the documents examined, even if, as we have seen, they concern arborescent and florescent vegetation and not crops.

The very iconography of the character recalls this relationship with vegetal fertility when he is represented in the act of supporting a cornucopia or a basket full of fruit. Amongst the various examples of this type[86] there is a statue found in Athens close of the Stoa of the Attalids and ascribable to the 1st-2nd century A.D.[87] Displaying a significant correspondence with the mythical and ritual data examined earlier, it represents Attis with a basket in which, in addition to pine cones and pomegranates, we can distinguish a bunch of violets.

We must now see whether, aside from the mythical evidence which makes of the death of Attis the conclusive moment of the vicissitude, only redeemed, according to the Phrygian version, by a form of survival in death and physical incorruptibility, we can find further indications of Attis' connection with the

---

[85] M.-J. Lagrange, art. cit., 447-449. Attis' "resurrection" has been, and still is quite frequently mentioned, above all in connection with the festival of the *Hilaria* (see below).

[86] Suffice it to quote a bronze from the Museum of Madrid (H. Graillot, *op. cit.*, Pl. XI, 1) and another bronze from the British Museum (E.-J. Harris, *The Oriental Cults in Roman Britain* (EPRO 6), Leiden 1965, 101f.), a terracotta figurine from Cumae (A. Levi, *Le terrecotte figurate del Museo Nazionale di Napoli*, Firenze 1926, 115 n° 505; Vermaseren, *CCCA* IV, 4 n° 3, Pl. I), a statuette in the Capitoline Museum (C. Pietrangeli, *Musei Capitolini. I monumenti dei culti orientali*, Roma 1951, 15 n° 17) and one from Fianello Sabino (D. Facenna, "Rinvenimenti di un gruppo di sculture", *NSc*, Serie VIII, V, 1951, 68f. and fig. 13 b; Vermaseren, *CCCA* IV, 71f. n° 176, Pl. LXVIII). For all these types cf. M. J. Vermaseren, *The Legend of Attis*, 16 and 52, Pl. VI, 1-2 and XXXIII, 2.

[87] T. Leslie Shear, "The Sculpture found in 1933, Pl. IV-V", *Hesperia* IV (1935), 396f. fig. 23: 2nd century A.D.; Vermaseren, *CCCA* II, 39f. n° 135 and Pl. XXII.

cyclical rhythm of vegetation as it is expressed in the late testimony of Firmicus Maternus.

We should therefore examine a series of sources concerning the cult which associate Attis, in Greece and Rome, with the Great Mother, both in public forms and in those reserved for private or obviously esoteric communities, in a context of genuine "mysteries".

The public aspects of the cult of Attis provide elements useful for the religious historical characterisation of the personage and serve to elucidate the circumstances by which, in some circles and at certain periods of history, Attis, together with the Great Mother, came to be the centre of a mystery structure.

c) *The mystic cult of Cybele and Attis in the Greek world*

The earliest attestation of Attis as the object of a cult together with the Great Mother on Greek soil is provided, as we know, by the documents referring to the community of the ὀργεῶνες of the Metroon at the Piraeus.[88]

The inscriptions, consisting for the most part in honorific decrees for the priestesses who presided over the cult, fall into the period which runs from the middle of the 3rd to the beginning of the 1st century B.C.,[89] but numerous ex-votos also belong to the Roman Imperial period.[90]

Nevertheless, the earliest document which reveals the cult of the Mother of the Gods at the Piraeus is a decree of *thiasotai*,[91] a community of foreigners who were then to yield their own rights to the sanctuary to the citizens of Athens, thereby joining the religious association of the *orgeones*.[92]

The cult practised by this association, at all events, displays indubious Phrygian connotations evident from the presence of a ritual in honour of At-

---

[88] Cf. K. Fr. Hermann, "Die Verehrung der Göttermutter im Piräeus nach neuentdeckten Inschriften", *Philologus* X (1855), 293-299; P. Foucart, *Des associations religieuses chez les grecs. Thiases, Eranes, Orgéons*, Paris 1873, 84-101, inscr. nos 4-18; W. Scott Ferguson, "Attic Orgeones", *HThR* XXXVII (1944), 107-140; Vermaseren, *CCCA* II, 68-97 nos. 257-322, Pls. LIX-LXXXV.

[89] See the list of inscriptions, in chronological order, in W. Scott Ferguson, art. cit., 108: *IG* II², 1316 (246/45? B.C.); 1301 (220/19 B.C.); 1314 (213/12 B.C.); 1315 (211/10 B.C.) = H. Hepding, *op. cit.*, n° 9, 79f.; 1328 I (183/82 B.C.) = H. Hepding, *op. cit.*, n° 10, 80f.; 1327 (178/77 B.C.); 1328 II and 1329 (= H. Hepding, *op. cit.*, n° 11, 81), both of 175/74 B.C. and finally 1334 of 70 B.C.

[90] Cf. P. Foucart, *op. cit.*, 200f., nos 15-18; H. Graillot, *op. cit.*, 507f. For the history of the finds at the Piraeus see E. Michon, "Buste de Mélitiné prêtresse du Métroon du Pirée (Musée du Louvre)", *Mémoires de la Société Nationale des antiquaires de France* LXXV (1915-18), S. VIII, V, 91-129.

[91] *IG* II², 1273 perhaps ascribable to 284/83 B.C. Cf. K. Fr. Hermann, art. cit., 296f. Vermaseren, *CCCA* II, 70f. n° 258.

[92] This is the conclusion of Ferguson, who detects a trace of this passage in the *IG* II², 1316, the earliest which refers to the *orgeones*, and which, on the inside of the crown adorning the stele, has the term θιασωταί (art. cit., 107 n. 49 and 137-140).

tis: the priestess Krateia is praised for the piety with which she has tended the cult dedicated "to the goddesses" and for the preparation of the "bed" (κλίνη) εἰς ἀμφότερα τὰ 'Αττίδεια.[93] The inscription was made in the month of Μουνιχιών (April-May) and it is probable that the festival commemorated had been celebrated in the not too distant past. This, then, would be a springtime characterisation of the *Attideia*.

The significance and precise nature of the *Attideia*, however, remain largely problematical. Foucart's hypothesis, that it was a mystery ritual with two ceremonies, one of which commemorated the death of the personage and the other his return to life,[94] is open to various objections.[95] It should above all be kept in mind that our documentation does not confirm the hypothesis that Attis is at the centre of a mythical-ritual scheme entailing death followed by a "resurrection", as the stable and definitive recuperation of life. There is, rather, a survival of Attis "in death", in relation to the sphere of vegetal fertility, just as there is a religiously defined presence in the cult, characterised in its earliest forms chiefly by funeral dirges.

Lagrange, and other authors before him,[96] have thought that the mention of the κλίνη is an allusion to the rite of the *lectisternium*, which was recurrent in the normal Greek cult.[97] Finally, the reference to two ceremonies in honour of Attis has been understood as concerning a double celebration of the festival, one by the members of the community who were Athenian citizens and one by foreigners.[98] But none of these solutions are sufficiently well grounded to be accepted without reserve.

To conclude, while it is not possible to say anything definite about an ultimately mystery nature of the rites in question, there remains the significant evidence of a private association which, in the 3rd century B.C., knew and venerated, beside the Μήτηρ θεῶν, her young paredros, thereby showing a familiarity with the Phrygian forms of the myth and the cult of Cybele.

This is further emphasised by a dedication to "Artemis-Nana" in the museum of Athens, orginating from the Piraeus.[99] It is more than likely that it comes from the Metroon of the *orgeones*, thus revealing the complexity of the mythical picture familiar to them. If Νάνα is the Graecised form of the name

---

[93] *IG* II², 1315 = H. Hepding, *op. cit.*, 79f. n° 9; Vermaseren, *CCCA* II, 75f. n° 262. Attis' presence in the cult of the *orgeones* is confirmed by another decree (*ibid.*, 1327), which mentions θεοί in whom, in view of the context, we can recognise the Great Mother and her paredros.

[94] *Op. cit.*, 92-97.

[95] Both the rites require the preparation of a bed; it is difficult to account for its presence, however, at the time, suggested by Foucart, when the Attis' "resurrection" is being celebrated.

[96] H. Hepding, *op. cit.*, 136-138, where reference is made to Rohde's argument (*Psyche*, vol. I², Freiburg i.B., Leipzig-Tübingen 1898, 129f., n. 3) about the expression κλίνην στρῶσαι θεῷ as being pertinent to the θεοξένια.

[97] *Art. cit.*, 436f.

[98] W. Scott Ferguson, *art. cit.*, 112 and 140.

[99] *IG* II², 4696; cf. P. Foucart, *op. cit.*, 101 and 201 n° 19.

of an Elamite and Babylonian divinity, usually identified with the Persian Anahita assimilated in her turn by Artemis,[100] we must remember that, in the mythical version recounted by Arnobius, Nana is the name of the nymph or the youthful mother of Attis. Nor must we forget that it was also at the Piraeus that the above-mentioned relief with a dedication to Attis and Agdistis was discovered which, even if it does not appear to come from the Metroon, points to a circle venerating Cybele with decidedly Oriental and Phrygian features.

The existence of the mythical and ritual complex in its "Pessinuntic" form as transpires from the presence of Nana and Agdistis, may perhaps indicate a new solution, different from that proposed hitherto,[101] to the problem of the enigmatic plural "the goddesses" which recurs in two decrees of the *orgeones*.[102] Was the community of the Piraeus perhaps aware of the two aspects which coexisted in the character whom the commonest Hellenising tradition presented as the Great Mother of the gods? Did it distinguish, as in Arnobius' version, between two deities, both connected with Attis in an essentially unitary perspective? In either case a certain "duplicity" of the divine figure of the Mother seems to be reflected in the use, attested in certain examples of Attic *naiskoi*, of a double representation of the goddess,[103]

---

[100] Cf. Wagner, s.v. *Nana*, Roscher, *Myth. Lex.*, vol. III (1897-1902), 4f. U. von Wilamowitz-Moellendorf, *Der Glaube der Hellenen*, vol. II, Berlin 1932, 466; J. Duchesne-Guillemin, *La religion de l'Iran ancien*, Paris 1962, 147, 180f.

[101] Foucart concluded that the two goddesses were Cybele and Aphrodite Urania, in other words the Phoenician Astarte, who was the object of a dedication which, he believed, came from the Metroon (*op. cit.*, 99f., cf. inscr. n° 11 on p. 198). It has been proved, however, that the inscription (*IG* II², 337, 4636) comes, rather, from the sanctuary of the Cypriot Aphrodite (cf. W. Scott Ferguson, art. cit., 137f.). For other explanations of the plural θεαί see also H. Hepding, *op. cit.*, 138 n. 7.

[102] *IG* II², 1315, line 14f.: "εὐσεβῶς διετέλεσεν θεραπεύουσα τὰς θεάς"; cf. line 18 and 22; IG II², 1329, line 14.

[103] Besides the piece known to Foucart (*op. cit.*, 100 n° 1: it is an Attic relief published by Stephani in the *Mémoires de l'Académie des Sciences de Saint-Petersbourg*, VI S., vol. 8, 1855, Pl. 7, n° 2) there is the one published by A. Conze (art. cit., 3, n° 1, Taf. 2, 1), also from Attica. Hepding speaks of seven pieces (*op. cit.*, 138 n. 7). The National Museum of Athens has three examples of *naiskoi* with a double image of Cybele (J. N. Svoronos, *op. cit.*, I, 623, n° 283 Taf. CXVIII, 1540; n° 307 Taf. CCXL, 2; n° 277 Taf. CXVIII, 1921) while two others are kept at the Museum of the Acropolis (O. Walter, *Beschreibung der Reliefs im kleinen Acropolismuseum in Athen*, Athens 1923, nos. 127-128, 75ff.). Double *naiskoi* also come from Delos (Ph. Bruneau, *Recherches sur les cultes de Délos à l'époque hellénistique et à l'époque impériale*, Paris 1970, 433, Pl. VI, 2) and Corinth (S. S. Weinberg, "Investigation at Corinth 1947-1948", *Hesperia* XVIII, 1949, 151). For these and other reliefs of the same type see now Vermaseren, *CCCA* II, 31 n° 90, Pl. XIV; 46 n° 172, Pl. XXXVII; 49 n° 183, Pl. XXXVII; 52 n° 193, Pl. XXXIX; 62 n° 239, Pl. LIII; 63 n° 241, Pl. LV; 102 n° 341, Pl. XCIII; 114f n° 386, Pl. CXVI (Attica); 141f. n° 454, Pl. CXXXV (Isthmus); 144 n° 461, Pl. CXXXIX (Corinth); 150 n° 478, Pl. CLXIII (Trezene); 160 n° 509, Pl. CL (provenance unknown); 166 n° 521, Pl. CLVI (Corfu); 196 n° 611, Pl. CLXXVII (Delos). A similar piece is in the possession of the Museum of Belgrade (G. Seure, "Reliefs votifs inédits ou disparus", *REA* XXVI, 1924, 44f. n° 7; Vermaseren, *CCCA* VII, 5 n° 14, Pl. VI), another one, probably of Athenian origin, is kept at the Museum of Bonn (Ver-

according to a typology in which other religious contexts also participated.[104]

Besides the *Attideia* the *orgeones* of the Piraeus were acquainted with another ceremony which consisted in preparing "two thrones as beautiful as possible".[105] This entailed a general assembly of the community and was probably dedicated to the Mother of the gods and to Attis, in whose honour the thrones in question were prepared. Not even in this case, however, can we say anything precise about the nature of the rite or an ultimately mystery character.[106]

An indication of the particular quality of Attis and of the mythical-ritual complex in which he belongs is provided by a statement by Neanthes of

---

maseren, *CCCA* VII, 7 n° 21, Pl. XV). Still other examples, provenance unknown but probably Greek, are in the possession of various museums (cf. Vermaseren, *ibid.*, 19 n° 63, Pl. XLV; 41 n° 142, Pl. LXXXVIII).

[104] Cf. Th. Hadzisteliou Price, "Double and Multiple Representations in Greek Art and Religious Thought (Plates I-X)", *JHS* XCI (1971), 48-69, esp. for Cybele 53-56. See also V. K. Müller, "Die Zierndel aus dem III Mykenischen Schachtgrab", *AM* 43 (1918), 156-162; C. Christou, *op. cit.*, 46 f.

[105] *IG* II² 1328 line 10ff.: "[σ]τ[ρω]ννύειν θρόνους δύο [ὡς] καλλίστους"; cf. *ibid.*, 1329, 15. An inscription from Chios, ascribable to the 1st century B.C., records the dedication to the *Meter* by a certain Callisthenes of a στρωτή and καθέδραι (W. G. Forrest, "The Inscriptions of South-East Chios I", *ABSA* LVIII, 1963, 59 n° 9; Vermaseren, *CCCA* II, 180 n° 559).

Although the term στρωτή has been variously interpreted ("carpet": Hausollier in *BCH* III, 1879, 324 n° 11; "bed": H. Graillot, *op. cit.*, 367 n. 5; "floor": W. G. Forrest, *loc. cit.*) we cannot help noticing the very specific character of the votive offerings of Callisthenes and their close affinity with the cultic articles mentioned in the inscriptions from the Piraeus. If the καθέδραι recall the θρόνοι mentioned there, the στρωτή (probably "carpet" or "bed" rather than "floor") recalls the terminological context of the Attic decrees which use the verb στρωννύειν for the preparation both of the κλίνη and of the θρόνοι and talk of στρώσεις ἱεραί (*IG* II², 1329, 15).

It is of course impossible to know whether the στρωτή and the καθέδραι in the island of Chios were at the centre of a ritual analogous to that performed by the *orgeones* of the Piraeus. For the function of the throne in the cult of Cybele cf. Ch. Picard, "Le trône vide d'Alexandre dans la cérémonie de Cyinda et le culte du trône vide à travers le monde gréco-romain", *CArch* VII (1964), 1-17, Pls. I-V. According to E. Akurgal the Anatolian rock-thrones of the Phrygian period are to be linked to the cult of the Great Mother and Attis (*Phrygische Kunst*, Ankara 1955, 96-100. Cf. A. Archi, "Trono regale e trono divinizzato nell'Anatolia ittita", *Studi micenei ed egeo-anatolici*, I [Incunabula Graeca vol. XI], Roma 1966, 76-120).

[106] The term ἀγερμός which appears in both the inscriptions cited lends itself to various interpretations. Hepding thinks of a procession with the image of the goddess surrounded by the φιαληφόροι and by other members of the priesthood on which occasion, as was customary in Rome, gifts were collected (*op. cit.*, 137f.). Foucart reads ἀγυρμός and, in accordance with his mystery interpretation of the cult celebrated by the *orgeones*, he claims that this term indicates the day of the "mysteries". For this definition he appeals to Hesychius who, *sub voce* ἀγυρμός, records the following meanings: "ἐκκλησία· συγκρότησις· ἔστι δὲ πᾶν τὸ ἀγειρόμενον· καὶ τῶν μυστηρίων ἡμέρα πρώτη (*op. cit.*, 97).

Together with Hepding we can recall a passage from Dionysius of Halicarnassus (*Ant. Rom.* II, 19, 2) who, praising the orderliness of the religious practices of the Romans, lists a series of rites and habits alien to them. These include the ἀγυρμοί ("...οὐ θεοφορήσεις οὐ κορυβαντιασμούς, οὐκ ἀγυρμούς, οὐ βακχείας καὶ τελετὰς ἀπορρήτους"). We can deduce that this term indicates rituals of a "mystic" nature and, more precisely, of an enthusiastic-orgiastic nature, such as the ritual of Cybele.

Cyzicus, who claims that the mythical account concerning the figure is "mystic"—in other words that it is part of a religious context which must be surrounded with the utmost secrecy.[107]

This also emerges from the reservations advanced by Pausanias many centuries later at the very moment at which he is about to recount the mythical traditions relating to Attis: his nature constitutes an ἀπόρρητον, a religious secret, even if various stories have been told about him.[108]

In the account of the elegiac poet Hermesianax[109] the *orgia* celebrated by Attis in honour of the Mother of the Gods do not seem to have a mystery character, but should be identified rather with the enthusiastic-orgiastic rites typical of the earliest forms of the cult of Cybele. Nevertheless, we cannot deny the presence of a mystery connotation in the cult described by Nicander.

In the *Alexipharmakon* (vv. 6-8) the author evokes "the caves of Rhea Lobrine and the hall for the *orgia* of Attis" ('Ρείης Λοβρίνης θαλάμαι τε καὶ ὀργαστήριον "Αττεω). The scholiast explains the term θαλάμαι by saying that it applies to "sacred subterranean areas dedicated to Rhea" where the *vires* of those who celebrate the cult of Cybele and Attis are deposited.[110]

The *thalamai* mentioned by Nicander would then be places consecrated for the cultic practice of the Galli, which certainly cannot be identified with the entire complex of the Cybele's ritual or with the form of the "mysteries" which it sometimes assumes. In other words nothing permits us to identify the "mysteries" of Cybele with the mutilation of the Galli, which is only one aspect of the general picture of the cult of the Phrygian Great Goddess.

---

[107] Neanthes of Cyzicus in Harpocration, *s.v. Attis*: "μυστικὸς δὲ ὁ λόγος" (H. Hepding, *op. cit.*, 27).

[108] *Descr.* VII, 17, 9 in H. Hepding, *op. cit.*, 30: "'Αττης δὲ ὅστις ἦν, οὐδὲν οἷός τε ἦν ἀπόρρητον ἐς αὐτὸν ἐξευρεῖν".

[109] In Pausanias, *loc. cit.*

[110] H. Hepding, *op. cit.*, 8f: "Λοβρίνης θαλάμαι· τόποι ἱεροί, ὑπόγειοι, ἀνακείμενοι τῇ 'Ρέᾳ, ὅπου ἐκτεμνόμενοι τὰ μήδεα κατετίθεντο οἱ τῷ "Αττει καὶ τῇ 'Ρέᾳ λατρεύοντες". An ode in the Anthologia Palatina (VI, 220) records the dedication to the goddess by a Gallus of tambourines and the θαλάμη. The significance of this term, viewed in relationship with Nicander's scholium, seemed obscure to Gow since the context of the ode made it impossible to understand how the sacred eunuch could have offered to the goddess a "subterranean place" of the type described. Gow concluded that the θαλάμη referred to a sort of portable *naiskos*, of the type held on the chest of the Gallus in the statue of the Capitoline Museums (cf. art. cit., above p. 27 n. 8).

Nevertheless the significance of the dedication in question can be explained rather in the light of a scholium to Euripides' *Phoenissae* where, referring to v. 931 (δεῖ τόνδε θαλάμαις) the commentator explains: "καταδύσεις, θῆκαι, ἀγγεῖα κεράμεια, εἰς ἃ ἐμβάλλεταί τινα ἀπόρρητα καὶ εἰς γῆν τίθεται". Thus, in addition to being a subterranean place where the *vires* of the Galli were deposited, as the scholiast to Nicander will have it, the θαλάμη also constituted the receptacle in which they were placed before being committed to the earth.

This meaning of the term would also explain the mention of *t(h)alamas c(h)rionis* in two Spanish taurobolium inscriptions, in both of which they were entrusted to women (texts in R. Duthoy, *The Taurobolium. Its Evolution and Terminology* (EPRO 10), Leiden 1969, 36 nos. 74-75; A. Blanco Freijeiro, art. cit., 94 and figs. 1-2 on p. 92).

The commentator does not offer any explanation of the term ὀργαστήριον used by Nicander. It is difficult to decide whether the sacred rites celebrated in this "hall for the ὄργια" dedicated to Attis can be identified with the grim practice of the Galli or whether it is a mystery cult in the true sense, with the initiation of the believers and esotericism.

In reporting the essential characteristics of the myth which provides the basis for the cultic connection between Cybele and Attis the scholiast offers a further element which can contribute to the religious historical appreciation of the character and his rite. The mythical tradition to which he appeals can be traced back to the "Lydian" version, in which Attis is a shepherd, deeply devoted to Cybele who loves him in return. He dies because of the jealousy of Zeus who sets a boar onto him.[111] At the end of the episode the commentator of Nicander says that "the goddess buried him lamenting and the Phrygians bewail him in the spring".[112]

We have here the theme of the familiarity between the goddess and the young paredros. The familiarity, however, is the cause of Attis' ruin, in accordance with the typically ambivalent relationship between the great goddess and her companion in the context of cults aimed at promoting fertility, like the Babylonian cult of Ishtar and Tammuz.

A phenomenological analogy, and perhaps also an historical contiguity, with such a context emerges not only from the doleful and collective character of the cult, but also from its periodic recurrence: Attis is the object of annual rites of lamentation which, inaugurated by the goddess herself, are celebrated by the entire population at the arrival of the spring (κατὰ τὸ ἔαρ). The spring element of the rites confirms what we observed earlier about Attis' vegetal connections and, more precisely, about Attis' relationship with florescent vegetation.

Again in connection with Nicander's work, we have a testimony which illustrates the content of the rite performed in honour of Cybele and the young Phrygian shepherd. In the *Metaphrasis* to the *Alexipharmakon* Eutecnius Sophist says that "the sacred rites of Rhea persist amongst them (sc. the Phrygians), the marriage of Attis and all that follows, which is ritually performed by them".[113]

---

[111] *Schol. in v. 8* in H. Hepding, *op. cit.*, 9: "It is said that Attis was a Phrygian shepherd who, grazing (the flocks) and celebrating with songs the Mother of the Gods, was loved by her and that often (the goddess) showing herself (to him) thought him worthy of honour".

[112] *Loc. cit.*: "ἡ δὲ κατολοφυρομένη αὐτὸν ἔθαψεν, οἱ δὲ Φρύγες κατὰ τὸ ἔαρ θρηνοῦσιν αὐτόν".
For the spring recurrence of the Phrygian rites of lamentation over Attis see also Lucian, *Tragodopodagra*, vv. 30-53 in H. Hepding, *op. cit.*, 29 and 131f.: "πρώταις ἔαρος ἐν ὥραις" (v. 43), "'Ανὰ Δίνδυμον Κυβήβης/Φρύγες ἔνθεον ὀλολυγὴν/ἀπαλῷ τελοῦσιν "Αττῃ" (v. 30f.).

[113] Text in H. Hepding, *op. cit.*, 9: "καὶ τὰ τῆς Ῥέας ὄργια παρὰ τούτοις μένει, ὅ τε τοῦ "Αττεω γάμος καὶ τὰ ἐπὶ τούτοις, ὅσα παρά σφι τελεῖται".

These words give us a fairly clear image of a ritual which evokes cultically the moments of a divine vicissitude. Although we have no reason to suspect an initiatory-esoteric character in the participation in this rite, the quality of liturgical drama which characterises it expresses one of the aspects typical of the "mystery" in so far as it is a cult connected with a divine vicissitude ritually repeated in its most significant moments.

As for the content of this liturgical representation, the mention of the *gamos* does not refer to a hypothetical marriage between Attis and Cybele, about which, if we except a decidedly euhemeristic source,[114] our documentation says nothing,[115] but to the episode of the attempted marriage between the youth and a woman or nymph who, in the Phrygian version of the myth, is responsible for the crisis in his relationship with the Great Goddess and thus for Attis' death.

This episode is widely emphasised in the sources, from Ovid[116] to Apuleius[117] and Julian. The latter attributes a great importance to the union of Attis with the nymph in the context of his Sophic and Platonizing interpretation of the myth.[118]

The inscription βασιλεὺς Ἄττις νεόγα[μος] which appears on a statuette of Attis seated, with pastoral attributes[119] also seems to allude to this marriage.

According to the interpretation suggested by Ch. Picard, a bronze bowl from Alexandria provides a figurative representation of this dramatic episode in the story of Attis,[120] while P. Friedländer interprets the complex scene undoubtedly connected with Cybele's cult on a tapestry at the Metropolitan Museum of New York[121] along the same lines.

From these date it emerges clearly that the *gamos* of Attis ritually evoked by the "Phrygians" is no less than the tragic event which constitutes the climax of the whole vicissitude. The cause of the character's death, it is also the cause of his final return to the divine Mother. And indeed, as a result of that event the relationship between the two characters receives a precise ritual sanction

---

[114] Diodorus Siculus, *Bibl. Hist.* III, 58-59 in H. Hepding, *op. cit.*, 16f. See above.

[115] No importance should be attached, in this connection, to the heavily ironical allusions of Christian polemicists and pagan satirical authors to the unseemly passion of the mature "Mother of the Gods" for the youthful Attis. For the interpretation of the term *pastos* which recurs in the mystery formula cited by Clement of Alexandria see below.

[116] *Fasti* IV, vv. 221-244. Cf. above p. 27.

[117] *Metam.* IV, 26 in H. Hepding, *op. cit.*, 27: "*sic ad instar Attidis vel Protesilai dispestae disturbataeque nuptiae*".

[118] *Oratio* V, 165 c-d; 167 a-b. See below.

[119] H. Chadwick, "An Attis from a Domestic Shrine", *JThS*, n.s. III (1952), 90-92, Pls. I-II; M. J. Vermaseren, *CCCA* VII, 38 n° 132, Pl. LXXXIV.

[120] "La rencontre sur le mont Dindymon et la passion d'Attis: d'après un cratère de bronze hellénistique", *RA* 1960, II, 63-72.

[121] *Documents of Dying Paganism. Textiles of late Antiquity in Washington, New York, and Leningrad*, Berkeley-Los Angeles 1945, 27-46.

(the annual lamentation instituted by the goddess) which both guarantees the lot of Attis as the object of the cult and consecrates his presence, no longer endangered, next to the Great Mother.

d) *The mystic cult of Cybele and Attis in the Roman Empire*[122]

The funereal and doleful nature of the Cybele's rites commemorating the vicissitude of Attis also emerges from certain testimonies of Latin authors who confirm the public context of the manifestations of grief by the devotees of Cybele.

Thus, in Seneca's *Agamemnon*, we read of the *tristis turba* who, striking their breasts and lacerating their arms, "bewail the Phrygian Attis",[123] and Statius mentions the women of Phrygia who *non sua funera plorant*.[124] Suetonius recalls the day on which "the venerators of the Mother of the Gods begin to lament and weep",[125] while Arrian says that the Romans "worship the Phrygian Rhea who came to them from Pessinus" and then adds that "the bewailing of Attis according to the Phrygian custom is also practised in Rome".[126]

This *penthos* ends by bathing the image of the goddess in the waters of the Almo, in other words with the rite of the *lavatio*, known to us from numerous sources.[127] This rite constitutes, in the Roman ceremonial, the re-evocation of

---

[122] On the various details and phases of the introduction of the cult of the Great Mother in Rome see, besides Graillot's reconstruction (*op. cit.*, 25-69), the most recent studies by A. Bartoli, "Il culto della Mater deum magna idaea e di Venere genitrice sul Palatino", *MemPontAcc* VI (1942), 229-239; Id., "Tracce di culti orientali sul Palatino imperiale", *RendPontAcc* XXVIII (1954/55), 1956, 14-16; P. Lambrechts, "Cybèle, divinité étrangère ou nationale?", *BSBAP* LXII (1951), 44-60; M. Van Doren, "Peregrina sacra. Offizielle Kultübertragungen im alten Rom", *Historia* III, 4 (1955), 488-497; Th. Köves, "Zum Empfang der Magna Mater in Rom", *Historia* XII (1963), 321-347; F. Bömer, "Kybele in Rom. Die Geschichte ihres Kults als politisches Phänomen (Taf. 33)", *RM* LXXI (1964), 130-151; J. Bremmer, "The Legend of Cybele's Arrival in Rome", M. J. Vermaseren (ed.), *Studies in Hellenistic Religions* (EPRO 78), Leiden 1979, 9-22; J. Gérard, "Légende et politique autour de la Mère des dieux", *REL* LVIII (1980), 153-175.

[123] *Agamemnon*, vv. 686-690 in H. Hepding, *op. cit.*, 21. On Seneca's attitude to the cult of Cybele, and particularly to the phenomenon of eunuchism, cf. R. Turcan, *Sénèque et les religions orientales* (Coll. Latomus XCI), Bruxelles 1967, 25-38. L. Deroy's theory that the *cucurbitacea* in Seneca's *Apocolokyntosis* refers to Cybele's cult ("Que signifie le titre de l' 'Apocoloquintose'?", *Latomus* X, 1951, 311-318) seems most unlikely.

[124] *Silvae*, V, 3, 242-245 *ibid.*, 23.

[125] *Otho* 8 *ibid.*, 26.

[126] *Tactica* 33, 4 *ibid.*, 26f.: "καὶ γὰρ ἡ Ῥέα αὐτοῖς ἡ Φρυγία τιμᾶται ἐκ Πεσσινοῦντος ἐλθοῦσα, καὶ τὸ πένθος τὸ ἀμφὶ τῷ Ἄττῃ Φρύγιον ⟨ὂν⟩ἐν Ῥώμῃ πενθεῖται καὶ τὸ λουτρὸν δ' ἡ Ῥέα, ἀφ' οὗ τοῦ πένθους λήγει, τῶν Φρυγῶν νόμῳ λοῦται".

[127] The *Menologium rusticum Colotianum* (*CIL* VI 2305) and the *Menologium Vallense* (*CIL* VI, 2306), both of the mid-1st century A.D., mention the *lavatio* amongst the public festivals of the month of March.

the ritual bath to which the idol of Cybele was submitted when it arrived in the city.[128]

Even Martial[129] and Valerius Flaccus[130] allude to the *lavatio* as the conclusive moment of the Phrygian ritual, characterised by a funereal aspect. Nevertheless the text of the *Argonautica* introduces a new element with the mention of the "joy" of Cybele and of the *festae taedae*, with an obvious allusion to the manifestations of joy coming immediately after the grief.

We may then wonder what is the significance of this earliest statement of an explosion of joy amongst the participants in the rite of Cybele after the funeral celebrations. It is only in the 3rd and 4th century that we have various testimonies concerning a ceremony of a joyous nature, the *Hilaria*, which, celebrated after the lamentations, is in its turn followed by the *lavatio* which puts an end to the cycle of the March festivals in honour of the Mother of the Gods and Attis.[131]

The theory of Carcopino, who attributes to the emperor Claudius the institution of the entire series of Cybele's ceremonies, including the *Hilaria* as it is attested by the so-called Philocalian Calendar of 354 A.D.,[132] is opposed by Lambrechts.[133] The latter shows that, before the middle of the 3rd century,

---

[128] Cf. Ovid, *Fasti* IV, vv. 337-340 in H. Hepding, *op. cit.*, 19.

[129] *Epigr.* III, 47, 1f. *ibid.*, 24: "*Capena grandi porta qua pluit gutta/ Phrygiumque Matris Almo qua lavat ferrum*".

[130] *Argonautica* VIII, 239-242 *ibid.*, 22: "*sic ubi Mygdonios planctus sacer abluit Almo,/ laetaque iam Cybele festaeque per oppida taedae,/ quis modo tam saevos adytis fluxisse cruores/ cogitet? aut ipsi qui iam meminere ministri?*"

[131] Aelius Lampridius, *Vita Alexandri Severi* 37, 6 *ibid.*, 46; Flavius Vopiscus, *Vita Aureliani* 1, 1 *ibid.*; *CIL* I² p. 312 *ibid.*, 51; Julian, *Oratio* V, 169 d *ibid.*, 55; Sallustius, *De diis et mundo*, IV *ibid.*, 59; Dionysius the Areopagite, *Epist.* VIII, 6 and *Schol. S. Maximi ad hunc locum, ibid.*, 74; Macrobius, *Satur.* 1, 21, 7-11 *ibid.*, 63; Damascius, *Vita Isidori (apud Photium, cod.* 242) *ibid.*, 74.

[132] *CIL* I² p. 312. J. Carcopino, "La réforme romaine du culte de Cybèle et d'Attis I. L'introduction officielle à Rome du culte d'Attis", *Aspects mystiques de la Rome païenne*, cit., 49-75. The ancient source on which this attribution is based is the famous passage in Joannes Lydus (*de mensibus* IV, 59 in H. Hepding, *op. cit.*, 75) where we read: "Τῇ πρὸ δεκαμιᾶς Καλενδῶν 'Απριλίων δένδρον πίτυς παρὰ τῶν δενδροφόρων ἐφέρετο ἐν τῷ Παλατίῳ· τὴν δὲ ἑορτὴν Κλαύδιος ὁ βασιλεὺς κατεστήσατο".

[133] The attribution of the entire festive cycle to the Claudian reform (cf. H. Graillot, *op. cit.*, 115ff.; F. Cumont, *Les religions orientales*, cit., 51-54; 62ff.) was considered improbable by G. Wissowa (*op. cit.*, 322ff.) who ascribed to the mid-2nd century A.D. the constitution of the Phrygian ritual in the complete form described in the Philocalian Calendar.
A criticism of the Phrygian festival calendar suggested by Carcopino had already been advanced by C. Gatti ("Per la storia del culto della 'Magna Mater' in Roma", *RILomb* LXXXII, 1949, 253-262). Having rejected the theory of a single "reform" in the Claudian period the scholar also concluded by acknowledging a succession of attempts to reform the Roman cult of Cybele, the first of which can be attributed to Augustus and was in relation to the rite of the *lavatio*. The ritual complex of the cannophoria, the dendrophoria and the *dies sanguinis* entered the public cult in the time of Hadrian, while the *Hilaria* and the *Requietio* only appeared in the Antonine period. On the roman cult of Cybele cf. also S. Fasce, *Attis e il culto metroaco a Roma*, Genova 1978.

we have no certain attestations of a rite of joy in the March festival, since the *lavatio* follows immediately after the manifestations of mourning and concludes the annual ceremonies in honour of Cybele and Attis.[134]

He therefore distinguishes between two successive reforms in the Roman cult of the Mother of the Gods, the first of which, ascribable to Claudius, entailed the admission of the Phrygian ritual in its typically mournful form, with flagellations and orgiastic manifestations sometimes culminating in the practice of castration. In this first phase, then, we have the ceremony of the *dendrophoria* and the *dies sanguinis* which is followed by the *lavatio* at the end of the festival cycle.

Only later, perhaps owing to Antoninus Pius whose interest in the cult of Cybele is well known,[135] and anyhow in the period which runs from the reign of Hadrian to that of Alexander Severus, was there a second, more extensive "reform", with the introduction of the rite of the *Hilaria*.[136]

Even if the reconstruction proposed by Lambrechts seems quite probable[137] we cannot neglect the fact that, in the text of the *Argonautica*, we read of

---

[134] P. Lambrechts, "Les fêtes 'phrygiennes' de Cybèle et d'Attis", *BIBR* XXVII (1952), 141-170. The mention of the *Hilaria* in the *Vita* of Alexander Severus by Aelius Lampridius leads the earliest attestation of such a festival back to the first half of the 3rd century.

[135] It would seem to be to the Antonine period that we can ascribe the sanctuary of the Mother of the Gods at Ostia in its final and grandiose form, according to the conclusions of G. Calza, "Il santuario della Magna Mater a Ostia", *MemPontAcc* VI (1942), 183-205, plates I-III. R. Meiggs, however, suggests that the building of the sanctuary of Cybele at Ostia should be ascribed to the age of Hadrian (*Roman Ostia*, Oxford 1960, 364-366). Cf. M. Floriani Squarciapino *op. cit.*, 1-18. On the religious policy of Antoninus Pius see J. Beaujeu, *La religion romaine à l'apogée de l'Empire, I. La politique religieuse des Antonins (96-192)*, Paris 1955, 279-330. The author accepts and develops still further Lambrechts' theory about the decisive attempts at reforming the cult of Cybele by the emperor, with the institution of the complete cycle of March festival, the priestly office of the Archigallus and the introduction of the taurobolium (*ibid.*, 312-320). Cf. Id., "La religion de la classe sénatoriale à l'époque des Antonins", M. Renard-R. Schilling (eds.), *Hommages à Jean Bayet* (Coll. Latomus LXX), Bruxelles 1964, 54-75.

[136] For the evolution of the Cybele's ritual of March see also D. Fishwick, "The Cannofori and the March Festival of Magna Mater", *TAPhA* XCVII (1966), 193-202.

[137] This does not mean that I accept Lambrechts' conclusions about the personality of Attis and his rôle in the cult of Cybele in the first two centuries of the Empire (cf., by the same author, also "Attis à Rome", *Mélanges G. Smets*, Bruxelles 1952, 461-471; *Attis en het Feest der Hilariën* Med. Ned. Ak. Wett. Lett., N. Reeks, 30, n. 9, Amsterdam 1967 (which I have not consulted)). Romanelli's excavations in the sanctuary area of the Great Mother on the Palatine have yielded a large quantity of terracottas with the figure of Attis, ascribable to the 1st century B.C. Cf. "Lo scavo al tempio della Magna Mater sul Palatino e nelle sue adiacenze", *MonAL* XLVI (1962), 201-330; Id., "Magna Mater e Attis sul Palatino", M. Renard-R. Schilling (eds.), *Hommages à Jean Bayet* (Coll. Latomus LXX), Bruxelles-Berchem 1964, 619-626. Cf. also M. J. Vermaseren, *CCCA* III, 10-36 nos. 12-199, Pls. XXI-XCVII; Id., "Iconografia e iconologia di Attis in Italia", *Studi romagnoli* XXVII (1976), 46-62. A report of the new excavations on the area of the Metroon on the Palatine by P. Pensabene, "Nuove indagini nell'area del tempio di Cibele sul Palatino", U. Bianchi-M. J. Vermaseren (eds.), *La soteriologia dei culti orientali nell'Impero Romano*, Atti del Colloquio internazionale su La soteriologia dei culti orientali nell'Impero Romano, Roma 24-28 Settembre 1979 (EPRO 92), Leiden 1982, 68-108, Pls. I-X. This contradicts the theory that Attis did not arrive in Rome together with Cybele (cf. G. Showerman, "Was Attis

manifestations of joy, albeit after the *lavatio*. This would suggest that in a fairly remote period, and anyhow as far back as the 1st century A.C., expressions of joy were also part of the Roman cult of Cybele.[138] Only later, however, perhaps in the Antonine period as Lambrechts suggests, were they institutionalised in a ceremony performed on a particular day, between the moment of mourning and the conclusive one of the sacred bath.

Such manifestations of joy, and the later festival of the *Hilaria*, do not of course express the idea of a "resurrection" of Attis, of which there is no trace in contemporary sources, but rather the certainty of his survival, either in the form of physical incorruptibility or in that, religiously defined, of his constant presence in the cult beside the Great Mother. Moreover, the mythical image of the body of Attis saved from dissolution and able to grow and to move, albeit only in certain features, expresses the idea that his disappearance is neither total nor final.

It is in this sense that we must interpret the statement in Plutarch that "the Phrygians, believing that the god goes to sleep in the winter and awakes in the summer, sing hymns of lamentation in the winter and in the summer sing to wake him, in the manner of the Bacchantes".[139]

We are not told in honour of which *theos* the Phrygians perform a double ritual, both mournful and joyful. It is likely that it is a god connected with the seasonal change, of the type of Attis.[140] This god, at all events, is situated in an alternating rhythm, entailing sleep and reawakening, in a pattern of presence and absence which, in this context, is parallel to the concealment of vegetation in the winter and its reappearance in the summer.

---

at Rome under the Republic?'', *TAPhA* XXXI, 1900, 46-59), even if his figure was confined to the precincts of the sanctuary which contained all the "Phrygian" elements of the cult of Cybele until the Claudian reform. Cf. F. L. Bastet, *BiOr* XXII (1965), 201ff.; M. J. Vermaseren, *Cybele and Attis*, 41ff.

Against Lambrechts' conclusions that Attis only appeared in the Roman World as a deity after the middle of the 2nd century A.D. some fairly obvious considerations can be advanced. On the one hand the Claudian reform cannot be understood unless the Cybele's ritual, in its "Phrygian" form, had in some way passed beyond the bounds of the sanctuary to attract popular attention. On the other hand it is hardly necessary to stress that in that ritual, with the essentially funereal elements which characterise it in this first Roman "phase" (and which can also be directly connected with the "Phrygian" rite), Attis is absolutely central. For the cutting of the pine and the ensuing *penthos* commemorate the vicissitude of a personage who, in so far as he is the object of the cult, is unquestionably of a superhuman, divine rank, also in his specific quality of a god subject to *pathos*.

[138] It is to these that the iconographical types of Attis *hilaris* also refer, for which see M. J. Vermaseren, *The Legend of Attis*, 39-59; Id., *Der Kult der Kybele und des Attis im römischen Germanien*, Stuttgart 1979, Abb. 19-21.

[139] *De Iside* 69.

[140] Elsewhere Plutarch shows that he is acquainted with the myth recounted by the Phrygians concerning Attis as a figure loved by the deity (*Numa* 4 in H. Hepding, *op. cit.*, 26), who came to a doleful end and was killed by a boar (*Sertorius* I, *ibid.*). Cf. *Amatorius* 13.

This would therefore confirm the existence in the Phrygian religious world of an ideology akin to the one expressed in the so-called "fertility cults". The sleep and reawakening of the god of vegetation are ritually encouraged by the song, first sad than gay, accompanied by manifestations of religious enthusiasm. Thus the rite itself guarantees, with the falling asleep and the reawakening of the god, the regular alternation of the seasons.

Even if we cannot claim that the *theos* of Plutarch is Attis,[141] this testimony demonstrates the typically Phrygian characteristics of an annual cult with lamentations followed by manifestations of joy as the expression of the certainty that the god has "reawakened". In the light of this information the Cybele's ritual as it is described by Valerius Flaccus acquires a precise meaning: the joy of the Mother and the *festae taedae* which follow the funeral dirges do not reveal the "resurrection" of Attis but the awareness of his "presence", beyond the doleful moment of death.

Manifestations of joy, moreover, appear in the kindred rituals of Adonis and Osiris where the doleful aspect also prevails, in connection with the departure of, or the agonising quest for, the god. But, as in the case of Adonis, the sadness of the farewell is accompanied by joy, in the certainty of his future ritual return,[142] so the *inventio Osiridis* produces outbursts of joy among the worshippers.[143] Nor should we forget that a typical alternation of

---

[141] This god is identified with Dionysus by E. Rhode, *Psyche*, vol. II², 12 n. 2; U. von Wilamowitz-Moellendorff, *op. cit.*, vol. II, 63; P. Lambrechts, art. cit., *BIBR* XXVII (1952), 160f. n. 5.

[142] See the invocation with which the women of Alexandria greet Adonis, at the same time reminding him that the next day they will accompany him outside the city to the sea shore to send him back to that infernal kingdom in which he, alone of the "demigods", resides merely for a part of the year and then returns to earth (*Idyl.* XV, 130-137): "Grant us your beneficence, dear Adonis, and maintain it for the new year; we have now received you with joy, o Adonis, and when you return we will welcome you fondly" (*ibid.*, 143ff.).

While later Christian sources stress the joyful note on which the ritual practice ends, they talk of a "revival" of Adonis in terms which reflect Christian mentality and language (Origen, *in Ezech.* 8, 14 in Turchi, *Fontes*, 258 n° 298; Jerome, *In Ezech.* 8, 14 ibid., 259 n° 299). Cyril of Alexandria sees in the Adonia a cult commemorating the episode of Aphrodite and Adonis, characterised by manifestations of grief for the death of the youth and of joy when the goddess, "returned from Hades", claims to have found him whom she was seeking (*In Isaiam* 18, 1, 2 ibid., 259 n° 300). Cf. W. Atallah, *op. cit.*, 259-273.

On the relationship between Adonis and Osiris, especially in connection with the cult of Byblos, cf. R. De Vaux, "Sur quelques rapports entre Adonis et Osiris", *RBi* XLII (1933), 31-56; B. Soyez, *Byblos et la fête des Adonies* (EPRO 60), Leiden 1977.

[143] Cf. Seneca in Augustine, *De civ. Dei* 6, 10 in Turchi, *Fontes*, 166 n° 218: "*in sacris Aegyptiis Osirim lugeri perditum, mox autem inventum magno esse gaudio derisit* (sc. Seneca)". Plutarch, illustrating the mournful nocturnal rites celebrated by the Egyptian priests in the month of Atyr, recalls how, at a certain moment, those present utter a cry "as though Osiris had been found" (*De Iside* 39, ibid., 173 n° 224).

It is probably to this ritual cry that Firmicus Maternus refers when he quotes the formula "εὑρήκαμεν, συγχαίρομεν" (*De err. prof. rel.* 2, 9). Moreover he explicitly illustrates the ritual of Osiris, with its typical manifestations of mourning, which also ends with the exultant joy of the *inventio*: "*In adytis habent idolum Osyridis sepultum, hoc annuis luctibus plangunt... Et cum*

anguish and joy characterises the ritual practice of Eleusis when it commemorates the abduction of Kore and her return to her mother.[144]

The later sources which talk of the *Hilaria* do not help us to solve the problem of the prospects offered to the adepts participating in such a festival. Nor do we get any further with the "physical" interpretation of the myth and the rite of Cybele suggested by Macrobius, who establishes a parallelism between Attis and the sun, and sees the grief and joy which accompany the ritual of the Phrygian god as a "symbol" of the alternating phases of the heavenly body.[145]

We cannot, either, apply to the religious reality of the cult of Cybele the Neoplatonic interpretation of Julian, who detects in the myth of Attis the great theme of the relationship between the intelligible world and the sensible world, mediated by the "demiurge", who descends to the lower level of *genesis* and mutability, but soon escapes from it to return to the sphere of the eternal and immutable. He therefore sees in the joy of the *Hilaria* the happiness of the soul "escaped from limitlessness, generation and inner agitation" to return to the gods.[146]

Sallustius' analysis follows the same lines as that of Julian and obviously depends on the Oration "To the Mother of the Gods".[147] Nevertheless he goes deeper into the parallelism between the vicissitude of the soul and the ritual practice, showing in each phase of the spring festivals in honour of Attis a precise correspondence with the decisive moments of that vicissitude. While the cutting of the tree and fasting symbolise being "cut off" from the further progress of *genesis*, he tells that "after this we are fed on milk as though being

---

haec certis diebus fecerint, tunc fingunt se lacerati corporis reliquias ⟨quaerere⟩, et cum invenerint quasi sopitis luctibus gaudent" (*De err. prof. rel.* 3 ed. A. Pastorino, Firenze 1969² 19-21). Cf. also Lactantius, *Div. Inst. Epit.* 18 in Turchi, *Fontes*, 178 n° 288 who concludes in connection with the ritual search for Osiris: *"sic luctuosa sacra laetitia terminantur"*. Macrobius, *Sat.* I, 21, 11: *"...eadem ratio, quae circa Adonin et Attinem vertitur, in Aegyptia quoque religione luctum et laetitiam vicibus annuae administrationis alternat"*.

[144] Cf. Varro in Augustine, *De civ. Dei* 7, 20 in Turchi, *Fontes*, 81 n° 117; Lactantius, *Div. Inst. epit.* 18 ibid., 88 n° 124: *"His (Isidis sacris) etiam Cereris simile mysterium est, in quo facibus accensis per noctem Proserpina inquiritur et ea inventa ritus omnis gratulatione et taedarum iactatione finitur"*.

[145] *Sat.* I, 21, 7-11 in H. Hepding, *op. cit.*, 63: *"...quod ritu eorum catabasi finita simulationeque luctus peracta celebratur laetitiae exordium a.d. octavum Kalendae Aprilis. quem diem Hilaria appellant, quo primum tempore sol diem longiorem nocte protendit"*.

[146] *Oratio* V, 169 d *ibid.*, 55: "οὕπερ γενομένου (i.e. once the necessity of the return from the multiple to the one has been affirmed) πάντως ἔπεσθαι χρὴ τὰ Ἱλάρια· Τί γὰρ εὐθυμότερον, τί δὲ ἱλαρώτερον γένοιτο ἂν ψυχῆς ἀπειρίαν μὲν καὶ γένεσιν καὶ τὸν ἐν αὐτῇ κλύδωνα διαφυγούσης, ἐπὶ δὲ τοὺς θεοὺς αὐτοὺς ἀναχθείσης;". For an analysis of Julian's text cf. G. Mau, *Die Religionsphilosophie Kaiser Julians in seinen Reden auf König Helios und die Göttermutter. Mit einer Uebersetzung der beiden Reden* (Studia Historica 88), Leipzig-Berlin 1908, 90-116.

[147] On the connections between the two authors cf. A. D. Nock, *Sallustius concerning the Gods and the Universe*, Cambridge 1926, L-LV; G. Rochefort, "Le ΠΕΡΙ ΘΕΩΝ ΚΑΙ ΚΟΣΜΟΥ de Saloustios et l'influence de l'Empereur Julien", *REG* LXIX (1956), 50-66.

reborn; that is followed by rejoicings and garlands and as it were a new ascent to the gods".[148]

The process of the transposition of the ritual elements onto a philosophical level of so obviously Neoplatonic an imprint, comes to the fore in Sallustius' disquisitions, where it is stressed, even stylistically, by the continuous resort to the comparative adverb (ὥσπερ, οἷον). This does not entitle us to conclude that the cult of Cybele entailed, in the common consciousness of the worshippers, the idea of a "rebirth" and a "divinisation" of man, based on the vicissitude of the god, for otherwise we would have to admit that the cult included the idea of the divine origin of the soul and its descent into the world of *genesis* seen as a "fall"—an idea which also appears in the texts of Sallust and Julian, thus constituting the premise of all their arguments.

If Julian and Sallustius give us the image of an *Attis platonicus* in the context of a mysteriosophic elaboration of the Phrygian myth and cult as might have been in fashion in the cultivated pagan circles of which the two authors are such eminent representatives, they still cannot be taken as witnesses of the significance which that myth and that cult assumed in the mind of the average worshipper.

We are now left with the late testimony of Damascius who records a dream, the protagonist of which he believes to be Attis, in whose honour the Mother of the Gods celebrates the *Hilaria*: this is regarded as a "salvation from Hades" which has already been obtained.[149]

The manifestations of joy of which Attis is the object appear as the sign of a σωτηρία which concerns both the young paredros of Cybele and man. It is a guarantee against death which, as far as Attis is concerned, is undoubtedly intrinsic to the mythical-ritual structure of which he is the protagonist. "Survival in death", ritually celebrated at the annual festivals by the Mother, is the element which characterises the deity in question. In Damascius' text man receives that form of "salvation from Hades" enjoyed by Attis.

We must not overestimate this testimony in view of the late period from which it comes. Yet it would be wrong to deny it any value. It is, after all, the only explicit attestation of a soteriological prospect in an eschatological sense in the cult of Cybele, at least directly concerning the spring festivals

---

[148] *De diis et mundo*, 4 ed. Nock 8: "εἶτα δένδρου τομαὶ καὶ νηστεία ὥσπερ καὶ ἡμῶν ἀποκοπτομένων τὴν περαιτέρω τῆς γενέσεως πρόοδον· ἐπὶ τούτοις γάλακτος τροφὴ ὥσπερ ἀναγεννωμένων· ἐφ᾽ οἷς ἱλαρεῖαι καὶ στέφανοι καὶ πρὸς τοὺς θεοὺς οἷον ἐπάνοδος".

For these texts cf. G. Sfameni Gasparro, "Interpretazioni gnostiche e misteriosofiche del mito di Attis", M. J. Vermaseren-R. van den Broek (eds.), *Studies in Gnosticism and Hellenistic Religions*, cit., 376-418.

[149] Damascius, *Vita Isidori excerpta a Photio* (*cod.* 242) in H. Hepding, *op. cit.*, 74: "λέγει δ᾽ ὁ συγγραφεὺς ὅτι τότε τῇ Ἱεραπόλει ἐγκαθευδήσας ἐδόκουν ὄναρ ὁ Ἄττης γενέσθαι, καί μοι ἐπιτελεῖσθαι παρὰ τῆς Μητρὸς τῶν θεῶν τὴν τῶν ἱλαρίων καλουμένων ἑορτήν· ὅπερ ἐδήλου τὴν ἐξ ᾅδου γεγονυῖαν ἡμῶν σωτηρίαν". For the interpretation of this report cf. A.-J. Lagrange, art. cit., *RBi*, N.S. XVI (1919), 449f.

celebrating the vicissitude of Attis.[150] So we might assume that, as from a certain period, the participation in the March festival, with its typical alternation of manifestations of grief and joy, established an immediate relationship of familiarity with the gods and offered the worshipper the promise of a benevolent protection by the Great Mother, a guarantee of eschatological prospects based on the "model" of Attis, the object of the goddess' benevolence and rescued by her from the definitive disappearance of death.

In conclusion, the features peculiar to the character of Attis and his cult allow us to define as "mystic" the mythical-ritual complex concerning him, in so far as it is a cult which celebrates a divine vicissitude characterised by a profound pathos, in which the adept participates ritually, establishing a more intense and immediate relationship with the deity. In it there occurs that interaction between the divine, cosmic and human levels in which the destiny of the god and the destiny of man are not identical but enter into a live and deeply felt "sympatheia".

Religious historical comparisons may lead to the discovery of specific analogies and differences between this mythical-ritual complex and other Greek and Near Eastern cults which also include a divine couple connected in various ways with the sphere of animal and vegetal fertility and involved in a similar vicissitude.[151] It would then be possible to identify and circumscribe a typological category, flexible but substantially homogeneous, of "mystic" cults in the sense of the term here suggested, next to that of the "mystery" cults which both contain a divine vicissitude and are characterised by initiatory and esoteric structures.

For the time being suffice it to observe that the themes common to such "mystic" cults, even though characterised in different ways in the various cultural contexts, can be found in the chthonic and vegetal connections of the two deities and in the typical ambivalence of their mutual relationship, according to which the goddess exceeds in power and stability the male paredros who is in turn marked by a doleful destiny as a result of his bond with the goddess.[152] To this we can add the annual recurrence of the rite commemorating the episode and the public context in which the cult is celebrated.

---

[150] On the taurobolium and the evidence provided by the funerary monuments see below.

[151] I refer to the couples Inanna-Dumuzi/Ishtar-Tammuz in Babylon, Isis-Osiris in Egypt, Aphrodite-Adonis in Syria and Greece.

[152] Such is the position of Dumuzi/Tammuz and Inanna/Ishtar who, as Gilgamesh complains, has ordained for "the lover of (her) youth" "wailing year after year" (J. B. Pritchard (ed.), *op. cit.*, 84, v. 46f.; cf. also G. Furlani, *Miti babilonesi e assiri*, Firenze 1958, 200). As for Aphrodite, she "hands over" Adonis to Persephone, who then refuses to give him back. The dispute between the two goddesses is followed by the character's alternating presence and absence in Hades and on earth, a situation which forms the basis of the *Adonia* (cf. Ps. Apollodorus, *Biblioth.* III, 14, 4 in Turchi, *Fontes* 253 n° 291). The case of Osiris is different, since it includes his rivalry with Seth. As far as he is concerned, moreover, Isis appears "stable" in her own prerogatives and functions, while he is subjected to crisis and death.

CHAPTER FOUR

THE PROBLEM OF THE PHRYGIAN MYSTERIES

We have seen that in the Hellenistic period the Phrygian goddess appears as the object of a cult characterised also by esotericism and initiation, in other words with a typically mystery connotation. In this cult, however, the figure of Attis does not intervene. In the Roman Imperial period too there are cases in which the "mysteries" of the Mother of the Gods are mentioned, but in which the goddess' Phrygian paredros seems to be absent.

If this absence cannot be attributed to the reticence or the inadequacy of the sources we would have a double line of development in the Cybele's religion. It starts on the one hand from the Hellenized cult of Cybele, already naturalised in Greece by the end of the archaic era as the figure of the *Meter theon*. This cult, with enthusiastic-orgiastic aspects, undergoes an evolution in the Hellenistic period in a mystery sense which, as far as can be deduced from the relevant sources, would seem to be a purely Greek phenomenon. It is probably part of that process through which, side by side with the persistence of the ancient mysteries of Eleusis and Samothrace, the Hellenistic period sees the flourishing, or anyhow the return to favour, of other cult centres of Demeter and the Cabiri which present an initiatory-esoteric structure,[1] at the same time as the Dionysiac cult moves ever more frequently from its earlier form of the thiasoi to that of the mystery communities.[2]

As far as the cult of Cybele is concerned, the adoption of the mystery form can be interpreted, in the context of the tradition which associates or actually assimilates the Mother of the Gods with Demeter, as the result of a specific influence of the Eleusinian model.

The presence of the figure of Attis beside the Great Mother is attested in Greece at least as early as the 4th century B.C. in the forms which have already been analysed. While the "mystery" nature of the cult practised by the *orgeones* of the Piraeus and that known to Nicander remains largely conjectural, we know of Phrygian "mysteries" which concerned the divine couple formed by Cybele and Attis in the Roman Imperial period both in the East and in the West.

---

[1] Of the centres of the cult of Demeter which present the form of "mysteries" in the Hellenistic period we need only recall Andania. Cf. L. Ziehen, "Der Mysterienkult von Andania", *ARW* XXIV (1926), 29-60; M. Guarducci, "I culti di Andania", *SMSR* X (1934), 174-204. On these cults in general see L. R. Farnell, *The Cults of the Greek States*, vol. III, Oxford 1907, 198-213; M. P. Nilsson, *Geschichte der Griechischen Religion*, vol. I², 477-481; vol. II², 94-99; 345-358.

[2] Cf. M. P. Nilsson, *The Dionysiac Mysteries*, cit., *passim*.

These mysteries coexist, albeit with a frequency and a dissemination which have yet to be specified, with public forms of cult which, in the case of the great March festivals celebrated in Rome and other parts of the Empire, reveal the persistence of those features typical of "fertility cults". So marked are these features that they can actually be said to define the religious historical consistency of the Phrygian mythical-ritual complex.

A basic problem, then, is to establish the sort of relationship that existed between these two forms of cult, esoteric-initiatory on the one hand and public on the other, and to see whether they can both be traced back to that Oriental, Phrygian and, more broadly speaking, Micro-Asiatic world, from which the deities in question originated. In other words we ought to know whether those esoteric-initiatory forms which it sometimes knows in the West, beside its public and official aspects, were already present in the Oriental homeland of the cult of Cybele before it was introduced into Greece and the Hellenized world (7th-6th century B.C.) and into Rome (by way of a direct contact with Pergamum and Pessinus towards the end of the 3rd century B.C.).

To begin with it must be admitted that no solution to this problem can be provided by an interpretation like that of Ramsay who asserts the existence of ancient "mysteries" in Asia Minor on the basis of a heterogeneous body of evidence, concerning disparate phenomena and situations, without any historical links the one with the other.

According to Ramsay[3] these mysteries guaranteed the continuity of the local Anatolian religion, centred on the figure of a great goddess, quite independently from the religious influence of the Phrygian conquerors entailing the prevalence of a male god.

An example of such a religious situation is provided by Antioch of Pisidia, the site of two sanctuaries dedicated to Men.[4] One of these, going back to the

---

[3] W. M. Ramsay, s.v. *Phrygians*, J. Hastings, *ERE* vol. IX, Edinburgh 1917, 900-911. The persistence of the local religious tradition would be due to "the mysteries in which the real character of the religion was displayed to the initiates" (*ibid.*, 901).

[4] Strabo, *Geogr.* XII, 3, 31. He distinguishes between a sanctuary of Men Askaios near Antioch of Pisidia and a second *hieron* to be found in the "region of the Antiochenes". Cf. W. M. Ramsay, "Sketches in the Religious Antiquities of Asia Minor (Plates I-IV)", *ABSA* XVII (1911-12), 37-39. Archaeological excavations have brought to light a sanctuary which can probably be identified with the former one mentioned by Strabo and which does not go beyond the Hellenistic period.

On the archaeological and epigraphic documents see also M. M. Hardie, "The Shrine of Men Askaenos at Pisidian Antioch", *JHS* XXXII (1912), 111-150; J. G. C. Anderson, "Festivals of Men Askaênos in the Roman Colonia at Antioch of Pisidia (Plates XX-XXIII)", *JRS* III (1913), 267-300. The inscriptions of the Roman imperial period mention numerous personages who say they have performed a cultic action expressed by the verb τεχμορεύειν. According to Ramsay we are dealing with a religious association with an initiatory character ("The Tekmoreian Guest-Friends", *JHS* XXXII, 1912, 151-170). But see also the reservations of Hardie (art. cit., 123f.). On the whole documentation and its interpretation see now E. Lane, *Corpus Monumentorum Religionis Dei Menis (CMRDM)*, vol. I, *The Monuments and Inscriptions*, Leiden 1971 (EPRO 19), 100-155; vol. III, *Interpretations and Testimonia*, Leiden 1976, 55-66.

3rd century B.C., came to light yielding a vast quantity of epigraphic and monumental material. While the inscriptions only mention the god Men,[5] a small building within the shrine seems to have been dedicated to a goddess, judging from the presence of numerous statuettes representing a female figure of the type of Cybele or Artemis.[6] This deity would thus have occupied a position inferior to the god whose sanctuary it was. Ramsay maintains, however, that a building located near the shrine was a sort of *telesterion* in which were celebrated mystic rites pertaining not to Men but to the Great Goddess. We would therefore be dealing with the "old Phrygian or Anatolian ritual of a goddess and not the novel ritual of a god".[7]

The archaeological material from the sanctuary at Antioch, however, is not sufficient to justify the hypothesis of such a mystery ritual,[8] reconstructed by Ramsay with appeals to various literary and epigraphic sources of different periods and circles, even if broadly connected with "Anatolian" contexts. He appeals successively to the report of Demosthenes on the mysteries of Sabazius practised in Athens in the 4th century B.C.,[9] to the *symbolon* of the mysteries of Cybele reported by Clement of Alexandria and to certain formulas on the golden laminae relating to the Greek world, whether "Orphic" or "Eleusinian".[10] The rite expressed by the verb ἐμβατεύειν, finally, is interpreted as the second initiatory grade on the basis of a few inscriptions of the Roman Imperial period concerning the "mysteries" celebrated in the sanctuary of Apollo at Claros.[11]

If we come to documents more certainly connected with a Cybele's milieu we see that the earliest mention of "mysteries" of the Great Goddess in her

---

[5] It should be noted, however, that the inscriptions of the late Roman Imperial period (4th century A.D.) referring to the games connected with the cult of Men mention, together with Men, a *thea* with the name of Demeter. Cf. J. G. C. Anderson, art. cit., 287ff., nos. 12-14.

[6] W. M. Ramsay, s.v. *Phrygians*, cit., 901. On the same mountain on which stood the sanctuary of Men two little temples dedicated to female deities have also come to light. Cf. J. G. C. Anderson, art. cit., 272-281 and figs. 52-53 (the goddess is represented according to the type of Demeter); fig. 55 (type of Cybele), 56-57 (type of Artemis-Hecate).

[7] *Phrygians*, cit., 901. For the description of the so-called "hall of initiation" see the same author's article in *ABSA*, cit., 39-44.

[8] The denomination of the so-called Antiochian *telesterion* as ἄντρον as it appears in an inscription discovered there (W. M. Ramsay, art. cit., *ABSA*, 40; cf. *JHS* XXXII, 1912, 163), does not provide sufficient grounds for such an hypothesis (*ibid.*, 37-61). Indeed, even if this term is often used to denote the centre of various cults with mystic connotations or with chthonic references, it does not seem to be methodologically correct to "construct" a mystery ritual on this basis alone.

[9] *De corona* 259 in Turchi, *Fontes*, 11f. n° 14. Cf. W. M. Ramsay, *Phrygians*, cit., 901f.

[10] Thus, for example, the enigmatic expression ("A kid I have fallen into the milk"), sometimes found on the golden laminae, is interpreted by Ramsay as referring to the mystic process of identification of the initiate with the god (Dionysus) and as an indication of the pastoral character of the cultural context in question (*ibid.*, 905).

[11] Cf. Ch. Picard, *Éphèse et Claros*, cit., 303-311.

Anatolian homeland is to be found in the inscription of Sardis I mentioned earlier and published by Robert.[12]

It is not possible to be absolutely sure whether the decree was issued in Greek or Aramaic. In the latter case our document would be a translation, albeit contemporary with the original and consequently ascribable to the 4th century B.C.[13] The text in our possession speaks of μυστήρια of Sabazius, of Agdistis and of Ma as cults which the priests of Zeus, whom we can probably recognise as the Iranian Ahura Mazda,[14] are forbidden to attend.

The existence of rites with an initiatory and esoteric character pertaining to Sabazius in the 4th century B.C. is attested in Athens by the famous passage of the *De Corona*[15] where the ritual cry of the *thiasotai* is mentioned which evokes the person of Attis. Without indulging in a gratuitous confusion between the context of Cybele and that of Sabazius we should nevertheless keep in mind the frequent and varied connections between them. These are demonstrated by Strabo who emphasises Sabazius' pertaining to the Phrygian cycle gravitating round the *Meter* and who would seem to make of him the "son" of the goddess.[16] At the same time the goddess Ma of Cappadocia also has various links with the Phrygian Great Mother, and the spread of her cult in the West is always close to that of Cybele, whose *dea pedisequa* she appears to be.[17]

---

[12] Cf. above ch. III, n. 51. Robert attributes the document to the age of Artaxerxes II Mnemon, placing it in the last years of his reign (368-67 B.C. or 365).

[13] Robert, art. cit., 311.

[14] Lines 9-11: "... μὴ μετέχειν μυστηρίων Σαβα/ζίου τῶν ἔνπυρα βασταζόν/των καὶ Ἀγδίστεως καὶ Μᾶς" (Robert, art. cit., 308).

[15] Demosthenes, *De Corona* 260. Cf. Strabo, *Geogr.* X, 3, 18 who, recalling the ritual of Sabazius evoked by Demosthenes, concludes: "ταῦτα γάρ ἐστι Σαβάζια καὶ Μητρῷα".

[16] *Geogr.* X, 3, 15. The text is corrupt, so it is not clear whether Sabazius is the παιδίον of the *Meter* or the "guardian" of her little son. Cf. the ed. of F. Lasserre (Strabon, *Géographie*, t. VII, Paris 1971, 75) which reads: "καὶ ὁ Σαβάζιος δὲ τῶν Φρυγιακῶν ἐστι καὶ τρόπον τινὰ τῆς Μητρὸς τὸ παιδίον † παραδόντα τοὺς † Διονύσου καὶ αὐτός".

H. L. Jones (*The Geography of Strabo*, vol. V, London-Cambridge 1954, 104), on the other hand, gives the text in the form "... τὸ παιδίον παραδοὺς τὰ τοῦ Διονύσου καὶ αὐτός".

An inscription from Nicopolis (Moesia) closely connects the Great Mother of the Ida with Zeus Sabazius in a context which is not, however, entirely clear owing to the corruption of the text. In the restoration suggested by Domaszewski we get a relationship as between mother and son ([ὑι̯ῷ θεᾶς] Ἰδείας μεγάλης [μητρ]ὸ[ς] Διὶ Ἡλίῳ μεγά[λῳ κυρί]ῳ Σαβαζίῳ ἁγίῳ). Cf. Eisele, s.v. *Sabazios*, Roscher, *Myth. Lex.* IV, 2, 242.

For the relationship between Sabazius and Cybele, already known to Aristophanes (*Birds* v. 875ff.; cf. also *Anth. Pal.* VII, 222), cf. various figurative monuments of the Roman Imperial period, amongst which the famous bronze plaque in Berlin (cf. H. Graillot, *op. cit.*, 186 and Pl. III; Ch. Picard, *Mon. Piot* XLIX, 1957, 59f., fig. 7). For other monuments see Ch. Picard, "Le dieu thraco-phrygien Sabazios-Sabazios à Vichy", *RACentre* I (1962), 10-30; Id., "Sabazios, dieu thraco-phrygien: expansion et aspects nouveaux de son culte", *RA* 1961, II, 129-176.

[17] *CIL* VI, 30851; *ILS*, 3804. Cf. F. Cumont, *Les religions orientales*, 50f.; H. Lehner, "Orientalische Mysterienkulte im römischen Rheinland", *BJ* CXXIX (1924), 44-47; A. García y Bellido, "Estudios sobre religiones orientales. El culto a Ma-Bellona en la España romana", *RUM* V, n. 20 (1956), 471-483; D. Fishwick, "Hastiferi", *JRS* LVII (1967), 142-160.

The inscription of Sardis consequently reflects a real religious situation, referring to local cults which fit into a fairly homogeneous context. To define them as "mysteries", however, raises further questions rather than offering possible solutions to our problem, since it is impossible to establish the religious reality which covers such a denomination. Indeed, while for Ma of Cappadocia this is the only report attesting to the mystery nature of her cult, we cannot tell whether the μυστήρια of Sabazius and Agdistis are religious complexes of an esoteric-initiatory type (something we should be able to deduce from the "technical" meaning of the term defining them), or whether the Persian governor used the term to stress the essential difference between the Mazdaic cult of "Zeus" and the "mystic" rites of the Anatolian deities in which excitement and religious enthusiasm[18] are a decisive feature.

While the denomination of ὄργια[19] or ὀργιασμοί[20] persists, the habit of calling the rites of Cybele "mysteries" becomes quite frequent in the late Hellenistic era and the Roman Imperial period, even though in most cases it is hard to appreciate exactly what this means. It remains uncertain whether the source is referring to the public cult of Cybele, characterised by those enthusiastic and orgiastic manifestations in which the mystic quality of the cult itself is expressed, or whether it indicates more specifically an esoteric form of the cult.

The verses of the *Alexipharmakon* in which Nicander showed the "kernophoros priestess, minister of Rhea" rushing into the street and uttering "the terrible cry of the *Idaia*"[21] give the scholiast the chance to stress the "mystery" aspects of the cult of the Phrygian goddess to whom the Hellenistic author was referring. The epithet of κερνοφόρος given to the character is explained by saying that she is the "priestess who bears the vases", the κέρνοι being special receptacles used in the mystery rites in which lamps are placed.[22] The scholiast then defines the rites of Cybele[23] as μυστήρια.

---

[18] Robert, referring to an observation by G. Dumézil, emphasises the contrast between the notion of orderly divine Law behind the Iranian cult and the passionate emotionalism which appears in the mystery cults (art. cit., 325 n. 68).

[19] Pausanias, *Descr.* VII, 17, 9-12 in H. Hepding, *op. cit.*, 30; Lucian, *De Syr. dea* 15 ibid., 29.

[20] Strabo, *Geogr.* X, 3, 7; cf. *ibid.*, X, 3, 12: the Berecynthians, the Phrygians in general and the Trojans who live near the Ida ὀργιάζουσι in honour of the Mother of the Gods.

[21] Vv. 217-221 in H. Hepding, *op. cit.*, 9.

[22] *Loc. cit.*: "κέρνους φασὶ τοὺς μυστικοὺς κρατῆρας, ἐφ' ὧν λύχνους τιθέασιν".

[23] *Ibid.*, on the ninth day of the month "τὰ μυστήρια αὐτῆς ἐπιτελοῦσιν". In the *Metaphrasis* of the work of Nicander, in connection with the same verses of the *Alexipharmakon*, Eutecnius simply notes the behaviour of the priestess of "Rhea" who, ἐμμανής τε οὖσα καὶ ἔνθεος, utters the terrible ὕλαγμα of the goddess in the streets, striking fear into the hearts of all who hear her (text in U. Cats Bussemaker, *Scholia et Paraphrases in Nicandrum et Oppianum*, Paris 1878, 237). It is obvious that the reference is to the typical orgiastic procedure of the public cult of the Great Mother.

In his treatise "On the rivers" the Pseudo-Plutarch also talks on several occasions about the "mysteries" of the Phrygian goddess, without it being possible to decide on the precise meaning of this terminology.

In an initial passage, on the authority of Agatharchides, the author of Φρυγιακά, he says that whoever sees the stone μάχαιρα "while the mysteries of the goddess are being performed, soon goes mad".[24]

The stone in question is to be found on the sacred mountain Berecynthion, which thus turns out to be the setting where the μυστήρια of the Great Mother are performed. This brings us back to that mountain context which so often characterises the mystic-orgiastic ritual of the Phrygian goddess.

It is to this, too, that the episode of Scamandros, son of Corybas and Demodice refers. Having suddenly seen the goddess while her μυστήρια were being celebrated, he was filled with folly and cast himself into the Xanthus which then changed its name to Scamandros.[25]

It is more difficult to reach a conclusion about the specific consistency of the "mysteries of the Mother of the gods" towards which Sagaris displayed such indifference and contempt as to merit the terrible punishment of the goddess, again in the form of μανία which induced him to take his life by plunging into the waters of the Xerobathes.[26]

Nevertheless the mention of the Galli whom the character insulted leads one to think that the μυστήρια of the Mother here evoked are the public rites characterised by the typical ὀργιασμός expressing the beneficent possession by the goddess of her devotees which turns into destructive madness for the impious.

Finally, there is a reference to "mysteries" in the Pseudo-Plutarch's brief tract, and this is of a more general nature. Alone amongst the passages of the same work examined hitherto, it alludes to a context of seclusion in which the ritual is performed. After describing the vicissitudes of the "kernophoros" Ida who, having generated the Idaean Dactyls from Egestios, was ravished by folly in the *adyton* of Rhea,[27] the author says that on the mountain which was

---

[24] *De fluv.* X, 5 ed. F. Dübner 88: "ὃν ἐὰν εὕρῃ τις τῶν μυστηρίων ἐπιτελουμένων τῆς θεᾶς, ἐμμανὴς γίνεται · καθὼς ἱστορεῖ Ἀγαθαρχίδης ἐν τοῖς Φρυγιακοῖς". On Agatharchides cf. Schwartz in *PWRE* I (1893), 739-741; W. Ruge s.v. *Phrygia, ibid.* XXXIX HB. (1941), 781f.

[25] *Ibid.*, XIII, 1, 90: "Σκάμανδρος, Κορύβαντος καὶ Δημοδίκης παῖς, τῶν τῆς Ῥέας μυστηρίων τελουμένων, αἰφνιδίως θεασάμενος [τὴν θεὸν] ἐμμανὴς ἐγένετο, καὶ μεθ' ὁρμῆς ἐπὶ Ξάνθον τὸν ποταμὸν ἐνεχθείς, ἑαυτὸν εἰς τοῦτον ἔβαλεν, ὃς ἀπ' αὐτοῦ Σκάμανδρος μετωνομάσθη".

[26] *Ibid.*, XII, 1, 89: "Σάγαρις, Μύγδονος καὶ Ἀλεξιρρόης παῖς, τὰ μυστήρια τῆς Μητρὸς ἐξουθενίζων, τοὺς ἱερεῖς (καὶ Γάλλους) αὐτῆς ὕβρισεν. Ἡ δὲ μισοπονήρως ἐνεγκοῦσα τὴν πρᾶξιν τῷ προειρημένῳ μανίαν ἐνέσκηψεν. Ὁ δὲ τῶν φρονίμων λογισμῶν ἐκστάς, ἑαυτὸν ἔβαλεν εἰς ποταμὸν Ξηροβάτην, ὃς ἀπ' αὐτοῦ Σάγαρις μετωνομάσθη".

[27] *Ibid.*, XIII, 3, 90. The term [χερνο]φόρος is the result of a restoration which is almost certainly correct. The function of the *kernophoroi* is fully attested in the cult of Cybele.

to take its name from her there could be found the stone *kryphios* ὃς μόνοις τοῖς μυστηρίοις τῶν θεῶν φαίνεται.[28]

This text does not mention the gods in whose honour the μυστήρια are celebrated during which the "hidden" stone appears. The general meaning of the account, moreover, and the circumstance that the altars of Zeus and of the Μήτηρ θεῶν should be built on the mountain justifies the conclusion that the rites here mentioned concern the Phrygian Great Mother. Their definition as "mysteries" is not sufficient to suppose that they had a specifically initiatory-esoteric character. Nevertheless such a definition, as in the cases discussed above, shows that for the anonymous author of this mythological and erudite composition the orgiastic rites of Cybele fitted into the picture of those cults which Strabo, in his famous theological *excursus* of the tenth book, places among the ἱερουργίαι μυστικαί.[29]

In some cases, then, the authors term "mysteries" that particular form of cult constituted by the gruesome rite of the Galli, implying a very individual type of initiation which should be distinguished from an initiation open to all the worshippers.[30] Sometimes, moreover, this denomination seems to be used in a more specific and technical sense, when we find an esoteric-initiatory aspect of the cult together with the adoption of the sacral qualification of "*mystes*" as a result of participation.

The most significant documents include certain inscriptions from Pessinus, ascribable to the 1st century A.D., which mention an association of "initiates" of the Mother of the gods, whose members take the name of Ἀτταβοχαοί.[31] This epithet has been interpreted as referring, in its first component, to Attis who would consequently have played an important part in the mysteries of the goddess.[32]

---

[28] *Ibid.*, XIII, 4. The source of this information is Heraclitus of Sicyon, the author of a περὶ Λίθων.

[29] *Geogr.*, X, 3, 7; cf. *ibid.*, X, 3, 10.

[30] See below p. 77 and nn. 75-77.

[31] *AM* XXII (1897), 38f., n° 23 in H. Hepding, *op. cit.*, 79 n° 7: "'Ἀτταβοχαοὶ οἱ τῶν τῆ[ς] θεοῦ μυστηρίων μύσται" (cf. *OGIS* 540, 21); *AM* XXV (1900), 437f. n° 63 in H. Hepding, *op. cit.*, 79 n° 8: "'Ἀτταβοχαοὶ οἱ τῶν τῆς θεοῦ μυστηρίων συνμύσται".

[32] Cf. H. Hepding, *op. cit.*, 204. While the first part of the name probably reproduces that of Attis, Hepding wonders if the last part, in which we get the root βο, means "cowherds" (*ibid.*, n. 5). Graillot (*op. cit.*, 400) thinks so too and suggests a comparison with the Dionysiac βουκόλοι.

Ramsay proposes a different division of the term in question and identifies the elements *Attabo* and *kawoi*. The first is interpreted as a Greek transcription of the Phrygian *Attego* or *Attago* which means "goat", while the second indicates the priestly function. We would thus have a reference to "goat-priests". Yet even in this interpretation we still have a reference to Attis, for Ramsay agrees that the Phrygian term (*Attego/Attago*) is "obviously closely related to the name of the god Attes" ("Pisidian wolf-priests, Phrygian goat-priests, and the old Ionian Tribes", *JHS* XL, 1920, 198f.).

A *"mystes* of the Mother *Basileia"*[33] is recorded at Pergamum, and at Sardis an inscription of 200 A.D. talks of a μυστήριον Ἄττει which can probably be identified as a hall for celebrating the mystery rites which had the young paredros of Cybele as their protagonist.[34]

A rock sanctuary formed by various natural caves near Juvadjà housed a θίασος of the *Meter Oreia* whom we can probably see as the Anatolian Great Goddess.[35] It prepared an ἀναδυτήριον, probably a place suitable for the mystery cult inside the caves already used as a sanctuary of the goddess,[36] in honour of the Mother invoked with the attribute of ἐπήκοος. The thiasus had a hierarchical structure, presided over as it was by a ἀρχιθιασείτης (line 6), and an esoteric-initiatory structure, judging from the mention of an ἀρχιμύστης (line 30); the latter makes the dedication to the "Mountain Mother" for the "salvation" of himself and the community over which he presides.[37]

A difficult problem is posed by the identification of the θεά to whom is dedicated a σύνοδος τῶν μυστῶν in Smyrna.[38] We may well wonder whether she should be identified with the Mother of the Gods, the protective deity of the city from which she derives the epithet of *Smyrnaiké*,[39] while, from the nearby Mount Sipylus, she gets the more frequent epithet of *Sipylene*.[40] And indeed, in the same city we have an attestation of a σύνοδος τῶν μυστῶν τῆς μεγάλης θεᾶς

---

[33] M. Fränkel, *Die Inschriften von Pergamon*, Berlin 1890, n° 334: "Σεχοῦνδος μύστης Μη[τ]ρὸς βα[σιλ]ήας ἀνέθηκε". For the cult of Great Mother in Pergamum cf. E. Ohlemutz, *Die Kulte und Heiligtümer der Götter in Pergamon*, Würzburg-Auhmülle 1940, 174-191.

[34] W. H. Buckler-D. M. Robinson, *Sardis*, vol. VII, Leiden 1932, 37-40 n° 17. Cf. A. D. Nock, *Conversion. The Old and the New in Religion from Alexander the Great to Augustine of Hippo*, Oxford 1933, 279 (note on p. 41); G. Wagner, *op. cit.*, 230f. The text of the inscription is also in E. Lane, *CMRDM*, I, 52 n° 79.

[35] G. Moretti, "Le grotte sacre di Juvadià", *ASAA* VI-VII (1923-24), 547-554.

[36] *Ibid.*, 553f.; *SEG* VI (1932), n° 718.

[37] "Μητρὶ Ὀ(ρ)[είᾳ] ὑπὲρ σωτηρίας ἐπηκόῳ εὐχήν" (lines 30-33). For the title ἀρχιμύστης in connection with the organisation of private communities with a mystery character cf. H. Waldmann, "Ein Archimystes in Salagassos", *Hommages Vermaseren*, cit., vol. III, 1309-1315.

[38] *CIG* 3199-3200: in both the inscriptions the σύνοδος τῶν τῆς θεοῦ μυστῶν honours female personages, who receive the title of θεολόγοι, for their εὐσέβεια towards the goddess. We can also recall a μυστῶν ἑορτή.

[39] Μήτηρ θεῶν Σμυρναϊκή: *BCH* III (1879), 328; cf. Μουσαῖον III (1880), 128 n° 166 (165); *CIG* 3137 = *OGIS* 229, lines 47-51. The goddess has a *Metroon* in the town: Strabo, *Geogr.* XIV, 1, 37; Aelius Aristides *Orat.* XVII (=XV), 10-11 (ed. B. Keil, vol. II, Berlin 1958², 4). Cf. H. Graillot, *op. cit.*, 367-369.

[40] *CIG* 3137; 3193; 3260; 3286; 3385-87; 3401; 3411. In Magnesia ad Sipylum the goddess has the same epithet (*BCH* XI, 1887, 300 n° 8; XVIII, 1894, 541 n° 2). The rock sculpture of Sipylus (Strabo, *Geogr.* III, 22, 4; cf. G. Perrot-Ch. Chipiez, *Histoire de l'art dans l'antiquité*, vol. IV, Paris 1887, 754-759, fig. 365; cf. vol. V, Paris 1890, 151 fig. 107; W. H. Ramsay, "Sipylos and Cybele", *JHS* III, 1882, 33-68) with a female figure seated in a niche, dating from the Hittite period, appears to be the image of the Great Goddess worshipped in the whole of Asia Minor under various names (C. J. Cadoux, *Ancient Smyrna. A History of the City from the Earliest Times to 324 A.D.*, Oxford 1938, 25f.).

πρὸ πόλεως θεσμοφόρου Δήμητρος[41] which could be considered the same as the preceding one.

Nevertheless the attribute of μεγάλη θεά, which defines the Demeter *Thesmophoros* whose temple stood outside the city walls,[42] shows that the Greek goddess assumed some aspects peculiar to Cybele, according, moreover, to a well-documented tradition.[43] It is therefore quite likely that the community of the initiates of Smyrna venerated a deity who on the one hand maintained the characteristics of the local Great Goddess but on the other had received the prerogatives of Demeter Thesmophoros[44] as a result of the general process of Hellenisation of the local cults which had reached its maturity by the 2nd century A.D.

The presence of "mysteries" in the cult of this Great Goddess, furthermore, seems to confirm that influence of the Demetrian "model" which seems more than likely in the formation of esoteric-initiatory institutions in the cult of Cybele.

At all events, aside from the problem of the identity of the anonymous θεά of the synod of the *mystai* mentioned earlier and the problem concerning the relationship of the Mother of the Gods with the Demeter Thesmophoros venerated in mystery forms at Smyrna, a special "mystic" connotation of the cult of Cybele in this city would seem to emerge from a frequently reproduced dedicatory epigram.[45]

It is a Greek inscription which accompanied the statue of a certain Hermodorus who dedicated his own image to his "lady" Eucrotion and imposed a fine on anyone removing it.[46] The fine must be paid to Μητρὶ Θεῶν Σμυρ[ναϊκ]ῇ ΤΕΛΕΤΩ.

The obscure term τελετω has been interpreted by Peek as a genitive plural of τελετή, meaning τελετῶν ἕνεκα.[47] The fine was thus intended to contribute to the expenses entailed by the organisation of the ritual celebrations in honour

---

[41] *CIG* 3194; cf. *ibid.* 3211 = *IGRR* IV, 1415 of the 2nd century A.D.

[42] For the meaning of the expression πρὸ πόλεως cf. M. Hasluck, "Dionysos at Smyrna", *ABSA* XIX (1912-13), 89-94.

[43] Cf. G. Sfameni Gasparro, "Connotazioni metroache", cit., 1148-1187, esp. p. 1181 for the inscriptions of Smyrna.

[44] A substantial identity between the *Meter* of Smyrna and the Demeter *Thesmophoros* to whom the *synodos* of the *mystai* is dedicated is claimed by Cadoux, who regards the simultaneous presence in the city of two such important goddesses, both the objects of mysteries and the possessors of sanctuaries outside the walls, as most unlikely (*op. cit.*, 215-218).

[45] *BCH* III (1879), 328; Μουσαῖον III (1880), 128 n° 166 (165); L. Robert, "Epigramme de Smyrne", *Hellenica* II (1946), 109-113; Id., *Hellenica* XI-XII (1960), 558-560; G. Petzl "Hasenjäger Epigramn (Taf. XI b)", *ZPE* XVIII (1975), 315f.; W. Peek, "Zum Hasenjäger-Epigramme aus Smyrna", *ZPE* XXI (1976), 146.

[46] According to Robert it is the temple of the *Meter theon* herself.

[47] The final nasal consonant seems to have been pronounced as a γ and consequently is not indicated in the written text. The text does not, therefore, need to be restored in its present form since it reflects the linguistic usage of the author of the inscription.

of the goddess. Their definition as τελεταί might then represent a festival context with mystery aspects.

We are probably not entitled, however, to attribute to the Great Mother's followers an inscription of *Kyme* which mentions *"mystai"* and *"mysteries"*.[48] Indeed, despite the appearance of a Μέ]νανδρος ἀρχιγάλλος, the religious community to which it refers seems to be placed under the patronage of a male deity, a Καίων Μάνδρος, not otherwise known.[49]

Finally the relationship with the cult of Cybele of the μύσται of Cyzicus, recorded in some inscriptions which also mention the μυστάρχαι,[50] is highly conjectural.

All the reports quoted hitherto refer to localities in Asia Minor where, ever since the beginning of the Imperial period, the cult of Cybele takes the form of mysteries; we know nothing, however, about their ritual and ideological content.[51]

As far as Greece is concerned we have an interesting report by Pausanias who describes the principal monuments of Corinth and recalls a bronze statue of Hermes, represented seated, with a ram next to him. He adds: "The story told in the τελετή of the Mother about Hermes and the ram is one that I know but which I shall not repeat".[52]

Pausanias' reservations about the λόγος referring to Hermes reveals clearly that the *teleté* of the Mother to which he refers is a cult of a mystery type.

The presence of Hermes next to the goddess can be documented, as we know, in numerous figurative monuments which show the character, often accompanied by a torch-bearing girl, in the function of *propolos* of the Great Mother.[53] In these cases he seems to substitute the Phrygian paredros, em-

---

[48] J. Keil, "Mysterieninschriften aus dem äolischen Kyme", *JÖAI* XIV (1911), Beibl., 133-140.

[49] *Ibid.*, line 5f. The inscription can be dated in the Roman Imperial period, perhaps in the 1st century A.D. On the name Μάνδρος cf. W. H. Buckler-D. M. Robinson, "Greek Inscriptions from Sardes", *AJA* XVIII (1914), 58-61.

[50] *CIG* 3662; 3663 A-B; 3664 and 3666. On the cult of Cybele at Cyzicus cf. H. Graillot, *op. cit.*, 374-377, who seems to refer to it the inscriptions in question. Von Fritze has deduced from the type of coins current in the city certain indications about the procedure of the cult of Attis practised there: it appears to have included *lampedophoriae* and a στρῶσις τῆς κλίνης as amongst the *orgeones* of the Piraeus ("Der Attiskult in Kyzikos", *Nomisma* IV, 1909, 33-42 and Pl. III). On the coins of Cyzicus with the figure of Attis cf. also C. Bosch, "Die kleinasiatischen Münzen der römischen Kaiserzeit", *JdI, AA* XLVI (1931), 443f., Abb. 10.

[51] We should keep in mind that Dionysius of Halicarnassus talks of ὄργια and τελεταί which were founded by the mythical *Idaios* in honour of the Mother of the Gods and persisted in his own day "in the whole of Phrygia" (*Ant. Rom.* I, 61, 4).

[52] *Descr.* II, 3, 4: "τὸν δὲ ἐν τελετῇ Μητρὸς ἐπὶ Ἑρμῇ λεγόμενον καὶ τῷ κριῷ λόγον ἐπιστάμενος οὐ λέγω".

[53] See the monuments cited in G. Sfameni Gasparro, *I culti orientali in Sicilia*, cit., 137-141. Cf. also M. J. Vermaseren, "Kybele und Merkur", S. Şahin-E. Schwertheim-J. Wagner (eds.), *Studien zur Religion und Kultur Kleinasiens*, cit., vol. II, 956-966, Taf. CCXXIII.

phasising the Hellenisation of the Oriental deity who had become, in Greece, the solemn *Meter theon*. Nevertheless there is no lack of monuments of the Roman Imperial period representing Hermes together with Attis next to Cybele.[54]

In any case, Pausanias' report attributes to Hermes a rôle in the mystic rites of the *Meter* about whose specific nature we can say nothing. There is also, of course, the testimony of Julian who confirms the presence of Hermes in the mysteries of Attis and records the title of Ἐπαφρόδιτος by which the initiates address the god "who claims to light the torches for the wise Attis".[55]

In the Latin West the titles of *sacrati*[56] and *consecranei*[57] reveal the presence of initiates in some centres of the cult of Cybele, while that of *religiosus* seems to refer to a special category of worshippers, entirely devoted to the Great Mother.[58] A list of μύσται is contained in an inscription from Sofia which seems to attest a particular initiatory grade with the mention of a μεμυίασα στολίδος.[59]

Finally, we should keep in mind that, according to the interpretation of certain monumental remains proposed by Picard,[60] the city of Vienne in France appears to have been the site of a sanctuary of Cybele with a theatre for the celebration of "mysteries".

We cannot, however, assert the existence of genuine mysteries solely on the basis of architectural traces whose identification has anyhow met with serious

---

[54] G. Sfameni Gasparro, *op. cit.*, 135ff.

[55] *Oratio* V, 179 b-c: "Προσήκει δὲ σὺν τούτοις ὑπομνῆσαι καὶ τὸν Ἐπαφρόδιτον Ἑρμήν· καλεῖται γὰρ οὕτως ὑπὸ τῶν μυστῶν ὁ θεὸς οὗτος, ὃς τὰς λαμπάδας φησὶν ἀνάπτειν Ἄττιδι τῷ σοφῷ" (ed. G. Rochefort, *L'Empereur Julien, Oeuvres complètes*, t. II, 1, Paris 1963, 129). Rather than reading ὃς τὰς λαμπάδας...., as in Rochefort, we could read ὅσοι λαμπάδας, in which case it is the *mystai* who declare that Hermes lights the torches for Attis. Cf. ed. W. Cave Wright, *The Works of the Emperor Julian*, vol. I, London-Cambridge 1962⁴, 500.

[56] Mactaris: *CIL* VIII, 23400-23401 from which it emerges that *sacrati utriusque sexus* took part together with the dendrophoroi in a taurobolium. Cf. R. Duthoy, *The Taurobolium. Its Evolution and Terminology*, Leiden 1969 (EPRO 10), 31f. nos. 60-61. A third previously unpublished inscription from the same city, containing the same formula, has been published by G. Picard ("Inscriptions relatives au culte de Cybèle à Mactar", *BCTH*, N.S. IV 1968, 220f.). The presence of *sacrati* at a taurobolium is also attested in Utica (J. Le Gall, "Inscription criobolique découverte à Utique", *Karthago* IX, 1959, 121-127 = Duthoy, *op. cit.*, 34 n° 68).

[57] *CIL* XIII, 7865 from Pier (*Germania inferior*). Cf. E. Schwertheim, *Die Denkmäler orientalischer Gottheiten im römischen Deutschland* (EPRO 40), Leiden 1974, 31f. n° 34, Taf. 73.

[58] *CIL* VIII, 9401 = *ILS* 4167; VI, 2262 = *ILS* 4168; VI, 2263 = *ILS* 4169; IX, 734 = *ILS* 4170. Cf. H. Graillot, *op. cit.*, 283; F. Cumont, "A propos de Cybèle", *RA* VI (1917), 422.

[59] Cf. B. Filow, "Sodalicia vernaculorum", *Klio* IX (1909), 253-259; O. Walter, *AM* XXXV (1910), 144f. In this inscription the term δοῦμος recurs which seems to indicate a cultic community with a special relationship with Cybele. See K. Buresch, *Aus Lydien. Epigraphisch-geographische Reisefrüchte*, Leipzig 1898, 58-72; L. Deubner, "Dumopireti", *JdI* XLIV (1929), 131-136. Cf. also G. Petzl, "Vier Inschriften aus Lydien (Taf. CLXXVII-CLXXXI, Abb. 1-10)", S. Şahin-E. Schwertheim-J. Wagner (eds.), *Studien zur Religion und Kultur Kleinasiens*, cit., 746-755.

[60] Ch. Picard, "Le théâtre des mystères de Cybèle-Attis à Vienne (Isère) et les théâtres pour représentations sacrées à travers le monde méditerranéen", *CRAI* (1955), 229-247; "Vestiges d'un décor sculptural au théâtre des mystères de Cybèle et Attis à Vienne (Isère)", *RA* XLV

objections.[61] The presence of "sacred representations" suggested by the existence of a theatre in the precincts of the sanctuary or attested by literary sources such as the scholiast to Nicander's *Alexipharmakon*[62] or Hippolytus who refers to the "sacred hymns" recited in the theatres by the citharists,[63] does not necessarily imply a mystery context, with individual initiation and esotericism. On the contrary: we know that even the *Megalesia*, the great patrician festivals in honour of the Mother of the Gods in Rome, included the performance of *ludi scaenici* which, at a late period, also contained mimed representations of the Phrygian myth.[64]

A typical ritual object in use in the mystery cults, the *cista mystica* in which were kept the *hierà* and which recurs in certain Cybele's monuments, probably constitutes an allusion to the esoteric aspects of the Phrygian cult.

Apart from the great cist of the Archigallus of Ostia *Modius*,[65] this ritual object appears amongst the various cultic symbols present in the bas-relief of the Gallus at the Capitoline Museum[66] and in the funeral monument of *L. Valerius Firmus*, priest of Isis and Cybele at Ostia.[67]

A cist surrounded by a serpent stands close to the feet of the Archigallus lying on the lid of the sarcophagus found at the *Portus Romae*[68] and a specimen

---

(1955), 59-62; "Quelques aspects nouveaux d'Attis et de son culte", *Atti dell'VIII Congresso Internazionale di Storia delle religioni, Roma 17-23 aprile 1955*, Firenze 1956, 346-348.

The theory of Picard is accepted by A. Audin ("Les martyrs de 177", *Cahiers d'Histoire* XI, 4, 1966, 361) and A. Pelletier who has provided information about various archaeological discoveries in what, according to him, is the "Cybele's" area of the town ("Nouveautés sur l'histoire de Vienne: les fouilles du 'Temple de Cybèle' " *CH* XI, 1966, 9-16; "Les fouilles du 'Temple de Cybèle' à Vienne (Isère). Rapport provisoire", *RA* (1966), I, 113-150; "Le culte métroaque chez les Allobroges", *Hommages Vermaseren*, vol. II, 922-930. See now, by the same author, *Le sanctuaire métroaque de Vienne (France)* (EPRO 83), Leiden 1980.

[61] R. Turcan, *Les religions de l'Asie dans la vallée du Rhône* (EPRO 30), Leiden 1972, 68-74. Turcan denies that the monumental remains come from a sanctuary dedicated to the cult of Cybele.

[62] See above.

[63] *Philos.* V, 9 in H. Hepding, *op. cit.*, 34f. Cf. Tertullian, *Apol.* XV, 2 and 5; *Ad Nat.* I, 44-47 (A. Schneider, *Le premier livre Ad Nationes de Tertullien*, Roma 1968, 90f.; 236-238); Minucius Felix, *Octavius* XXII, 4 and XXXVII 12; Arnobius, *Adv. Nat.* IV, 35; V, 42 and VII, 33; Augustine, *De Civ. Dei* II, 4. For the connection between the cult of Cybele and theatrical performances see J. M. Pailler, "A propos d'un nouvel oscillum de Bolsena", *MEFR* LXXXI (1969), 627-658.

[64] It is probably to these that the attestations of the Christian authors cited above refer. Cf. H. Graillot, *op. cit.*, 84-87; J. A. Hanson, *Roman Theater-Temples*, Princeton 1959, 13-16; Ch. Picard, "Le rôle religieux des théâtres antiques", *JS* III (1961), 51f.

[65] R. Calza, "Sculture rinvenute nel santuario", *MemPontAcc* VI (1942), 215f. n° 7; M. J. Vermaseren, *CCCA* III, 123f. n° 395, Pl. CCXLV.

[66] F. Cumont, *Les religions orientales*, cit., Pl. II, 1; M. J. Vermaseren, *CCCA* III, 152f. n° 466, Pls. CCXCVI-CCXCVII.

[67] H. Graillot, *op. cit.*, Pl. VI; M. J. Vermaseren, *CCCA* III, 133f. n° 422, Pl. CCLXVI.

[68] G. Calza, "Ostia. Isola sacra. La necropoli del 'Portus Romae' (tavv. XIV-XVI)", *NSc* (1931), 511-517, figs. 1-4; Id., "Una figura-ritratto di Archigallo scoperta nella necropoli del Portus Romae", *Historia* VI (1932), 221-237; *La necropoli del porto di Roma nell'Isola sacra*,

of considerable proportions appears on the seat of Cybele carried by the Galli in procession as it is represented on an altar in London.[69]

If we turn to the literary sources, whether they be Christian or pagan, in the hope of finding elements useful for characterising the "Phrygian" mysteries, the insufficiency of these sources becomes all too obvious, especially in relation to the problem with which we are most directly concerned, that of the "soteriological" prospects offered to the participants in this esoteric form of cult.

Minucius Felix says that in the mysteries which are particularly esteemed and appreciated even by the cultivated pagans, all that is celebrated is *exitus tristes, fata et funera et luctus atque planctus miserorum deorum.*[70] Further on he talks of the Phrygian myth and the ritual connected with it, showing that he believes them to be part of the category of mystery cults, even if he is in fact referring to Cybele's love for Attis and the practice of the Galli.[71]

According to Hippolytus, who reports the doctrines of the Naassene Gnostics, the Naassenes took part "in the so-called mysteries of the Great Mother",[72] and Arnobius, as we saw, says, in his exposition of the Phrygian version of the myth of Attis, that he is basing himself on the authority of the theologian Timotheus who derived his information *ex intimis mysteriis*, in other words from the secret doctrines of the mysteries (*adv. Nat.* V, 5).

As for Julian, he distinguishes the ceremonies performed "according to mystic and secret laws" (διὰ τοὺς μυστικοὺς καὶ κρυφίους δεσμούς) from the rites known to everybody (*Oratio* V, 169A). These are the March festivals whose performance he knows about according to the order illustrated by the Philocalian Calendar. This has led some scholars to assume that the mysteries were celebrated in the same period and that the esoteric rites thus coincided with the public ceremonies.[73] It has also been assumed that the "mystic and hidden" ceremonies mentioned by Julian were in actual fact the gruesome

---

Roma 1940, 205-210, figs. 108-111; F. De Ruyt, "La nécropole romaine de l'Isola sacra et l'archigalle de Cybèle", *EC* V (1936), 29-34; M. Floriani Squarciapino, *op. cit.*, 13ff.; M. J. Vermaseren, *CCCA* III, 140f. n° 446, Pls. CCLXXXII-CCLXXXIII.

[69] E. M. W. Tillyard, "A Cybele Altar in London", *JRS* VII (1917), 283-288, Pl. VIII; F. Cumont, *Les religions orientales*, cit., 53 fig. 3; M. J. Vermaseren, *CCCA* VII, 11ff. n° 39, Pls. XXVI-XXIX. A small cist surrounded by pine-cones is represented on a terracotta disk from Volubilis which, according to Thouvenot, is a *signum* of a comunity of Cybele's worshippers ("Disque sacré du cult de Cybèle", *PSAM* VIII, 1948, 145-162, Pl. XI). For a survey of sources relating to the *cista mystica* in the mystery cults cf. O. Jahn, "Die cista mystica", *Hermes* III (1869), 317-334.

[70] *Octavius* 22, 1 in H. Hepding, *op. cit.*, 30f.

[71] *Ibid.*, 22, 4.

[72] *Philos.* V, 9, 9 in H. Hepding, *op. cit.*, 35.

[73] Cf. H. Hepding, *op. cit.*, 182-199. So too M. J. Vermaseren, *Cybele and Attis*, 116-119.

rites of mutilation performed on the *dies sanguinis* by those worshippers who thus became part of the group of Galli.[74]

Indeed, as we saw earlier, certain sources call the practice of the Galli "mysteries".[75] There is, for example, a fragmentary text contained in a recently discovered papyrus in which a Gallus is mentioned in words which have a clearly mystery intonation.[76] Even if the general character of the work in question seems decidedly satirical, the mention of ἀπόρρητα pronounced by the Gallus, of a μυστικὸς λόγος and of a συμμύστης as a character to whom he turns[77] is significant.

This would confirm the fairly frequent use of a terminology of a mystery type applied to that particular sphere of the Cybele's religion occupied by the category of the sacred eunuchs. Only through very individual channels and by retaining a significance all of its own can this gruesome practice be fitted into the context of initiatory typology.

At all events, although the time of year at which the esoteric ceremonies of the cult of Cybele were celebrated remains uncertain, their existence is confirmed by the documents cited. Difficult though they are to interpret, we find interesting indications of their ritual content in a passage of Clement of Alexandria who mentions the *symbolon* of the Phrygian mysteries, the mystic formula pronounced in the course of the esoteric ceremonies.

In his lively anti-pagan polemic Clement talks of the "mysteries of Deo". In this connection he evokes a complex myth whose protagonists are Zeus and Demeter, understood both as "mother" and wife of the god.[78] These "mysteries", he says, "commemorate the amorous union of Zeus with his mother Demeter and the wrath of (I hardly know whom to say: his mother or his wife?), let us say Deo, who, it would appear, was called Brimo because of this, the supplications of Zeus, the cup of bile and the tearing out of the heart, and the infamous deed".

---

[74] So, for example, M. P. Nilsson, *Geschichte*, vol. II², 647. On the "initiation" of the Galli cf. *ibid.*, 645ff. where we read that as well as including a special treatment of the *vires*, distinctive marks were made on the body of the Gallus with burning needles. Nilsson uses the interpretation of a passage of the *Peristephanon* suggested by F. J. Dölger, "Die religiöse Brandmarkung in den Kybele-Attis-Mysterien nach einem Texte des christlichen Dichters Prudentius", *Antike und Christentum*, Bd. I, Münster i W. 1929, 66-72.

[75] *Schol. in Aves* v. 877 where we read that "the effeminate take part in the mysteries of Rhea"; Paulinus of Nola, *Carmen* XIX, 186f.: *abscisa colant miserumque pudorem/erroris foedi Matris mysteria dicant* in H. Hepding, *op. cit.*, 71; *Carmen* XXXII, 88: *nunc quoque semiuiri mysteria turpia plangunt, ibid.*

[76] P. Parson, "A Greek Satyricon?", *BICS* XVIII (1971), 53-68, Pl. VII. It is *Pap. Oxyr.* XLII, 3010.

[77] *Ibid.*, line 1f.; line 5; line 15; 35f.: "ὑπὸ τοῦ μυστικοῦ διδάσκεται".

[78] *Protr.* II, 15, 1 (ed. C. Mondésert [SC 2] Paris 1949², 71f.); cf. H. Hepding, *op. cit.*, 31f.

He then tells us that "the same things are performed by the Phrygians in honour of Attis, Cybele and the Corybantes".[79] He adds that the rest of the episode is well-known: Zeus mutilated a ram and offered the animal's genitals to the enfuriated goddess almost as though he had mutilated himself as a punishment for the violence done to her.[80]

"Is it necessary," Clement continues, "to list the symbols of this initiation (τὰ σύμβολα τῆς μυήσεως ταύτης)? I know full well that they would make you laugh even if you had no desire to do so from these attestations: 'I have eaten from the tympanum; I have drunk from the cymbal; I have borne the *kernos*; I have entered into the *pastos*' ".[81]

This passage is difficult to interpret because of the author's simultaneous reference to two mythical-ritual complexes which are different but also, as he emphasises, profoundly analogous: on the one hand we have what he calls the "mysteries of Deo" and on the other the cult of Cybele and Attis.

The relevance of the initiatory *symbola* to the Phrygian mysteries rather than to those of Deo (Demeter) emerges from a comparison with the text of Firmicus Maternus, to which we shall return later. For the time being we should enquire about these "mysteries of Deo" which, according to Clement, are essentially analogous to the secret rites celebrated by the Phrygians in honour of Cybele and Attis.

The mythical vicissitude underlying them does not reveal any connection with the Eleusinian milieu[82] but reminds us, rather, of those Orphic circles which speculated variously about the true identity of the female deity with a maternal character with whom the male principle of the universe, Zeus, is in some way connected: she is called Rhea in as far as she is the mother of the

---

[79] *Ibid.*: "ταῦτα οἱ Φρύγες τελίσχουσιν Ἄττιδι καὶ Κυβέλῃ καὶ Κορύβασι".
See also Arnobius, *Adv. Nat.* V, 20-21, who, before recounting the myth of the double marriage of *Iuppiter* with *Ceres*, presented as his mother, and with his daughter Proserpine, states that the myth is connected with *mysteria, quibus Phrygia initiatur atque omnis gens illa*. At the end of his account, however, the Christian polemicist connects the mythical episode in question with the *sacra atque ritus initiationis ipsius, quibus Sebadiis nomen est* (*ibid.* V, 27). These, therefore, were the mysteries of Sabazius which, in their turn, display close connections with Orphic-Dionysiac circles. We need only recall that in the Orphic text contained in the Gurob papyrus of the 3rd century B.C. (cf. below n. 83) we have a mention not only of Διόνυσος and σύμβολα, but of a θεὸς διὰ κόλπου who evokes the formula of the mysteries of Sabazius known to Clement of Alexandria (*Protr.* II, 16, 2: Σαβαζίων γοῦν μυστηρίων σύμβολον τοῖς μυουμένοις ὁ διὰ κόλπου θεός), the expression of a rite also familiar to Arnobius (*ibid.* V, 21; cf. Firmicus Maternus, *de err. prof. rel.* 10). This is how we can account for the reference in Arnobius' text to the Phrygians as the recipients of the mystery rites in question, while the motives which induced Clement to identify the Phrygian mysteries of Cybele with the Orphic mythical-ritual complex are also further elucidated.
[80] *Ibid.*, II, 15, 2.
[81] *Ibid.*, II, 15, 3: "Ἐκ τυμπάνου ἔφαγον· ἐκ κυμβάλου ἔπιον· ἐκερνοφόρησα· ὑπὸ τὸν παστὸν ὑπέδυν".
[82] For a criticism of the theory which attributes Clement's report to the Eleusinian mysteries of Demeter cf. G. Mylonas, *op. cit.*, 289-291.

god, Demeter in so far as she is his wife.[83] These speculations, at the same time, are connected with the myth of the birth of Dionysus and of his murder by the Titans.[84] It is to this that Clement is alluding when he mentions the "tearing out of the heart" and the "infamous deed", although no other source seems to contain the mythical detail about Zeus simulating a mutilation to placate the resentment of Demeter-Rhea, forced to undergo an undesired wedding.

The elements which led the Christian polemicist to identify the Orphic myth to which, in some cases, a mystery practice is linked,[85] with the Phrygian rites and the relevant mythical traditions are, at least in part, fairly obvious. For on the one hand Cybele was commonly identified with Rhea and on the other a certain religious tradition was acquainted with the assimilation of Cybele and Demeter, so that a polemical observer of pagan myths could jump to the conclusion that there was a substantial identity between the Phrygian goddess and the Rhea-Demeter of the Orphic tradition. To this we can add that the theme of mutilation was very much present in the mythical-ritual context of Cybele and Attis.

The mystic formula cited by Clement in his complex disquisition on the subject can be referred to the Phrygian mysteries rather than to the Orphic ones thanks to the parallel attestation of Firmicus Maternus, who writes: "*In quodam templo, ut in interioribus partibus homo moriturus possit admitti, dicit: 'de tympano manducavi, de cymbalo bibi et religionis secreta perdidici', quod graeco sermone dicitur* ἐκ τυμπάνου βέβρωκα, ἐκ κυμβάλου πέπωκα, γέγονα μύστης ᾿Αττεως".[86]

If we pass on to the examination of the two testimonies we see at once that while the first part of the formula is identical in Clement and in the two versions reported by Firmicus Maternus, the conclusion is different in all three cases.[87] The first ritual acts which the initiate claims to have accomplished do

---

[83] See the Orphic text contained in a papyrus of the 4th century B.C., published by Kapsomenos ("Ho orphikos papyros tes Tessalonikes", *AD* XIX, 1964, 24, col. XVIII, 7-10), besides the one in the Gurob papyrus (Kern, *Orph. Frag.*, F 31, 101-104) which would seem to be illustrating a ritual practice with a mystery character. Cf. M. Tierney, "A New Ritual of the Orphic Mysteries", *CR* XVI (1922), 77-87; A. J. Festugière, *Les mystères de Dionysos*, 40ff.; M.-J. Lagrange, *L'orphisme*, 113-117. The mention of τελετή in the Gurob papyrus does not seem to Nilsson a sufficient reason for attributing a liturgical character to the text contained in it (*The Dionysiac Mysteries*, 12). For the Orphic speculations on Demeter-Rhea see also Proclus, *in Plat. Cratyl.* 403e, 401c; *Theol. Plat.* V, 11 in Kern, *Orph. Frag.*, F 145, 188f.

[84] Of the various sources related to this myth, cf. Athenagoras, *Suppl. pro Christianis* 20 and 32, from which it emerges that there were Orphic circles which elaborated a complex myth relating to the successive marriages of Zeus with Demeter (who, identified with Rhea, also turned out to be the god's "mother") and with Persephone, from whom Dionysus was born.

[85] Cf. above n. 83.

[86] *De err. prof. rel.* 18, 1-2 in H. Hepding, *op. cit.*, 49. Cf. also *Schol. in Gorgiam* 497c.

[87] On the basis of the attestations of Clement and Firmicus Usener believed it was possible to reconstruct an original formula of the Phrygian mysteries including the following statements: "ἐκ

not give rise to any particular difficulty: they consist in eating and drinking from the sacred instruments which we know to be typical of the cult of Cybele. These acts can be seen as constituting a mystic meal by way of which a special bond of familiarity is laid between man and the goddess.[88] It fits into a well-known typology, attested as it is in various mystery cults, from Eleusis to Mithraism.[89]

As for the content of the meal, it is not easy to reach any conclusion; it has been suggested that bread and wine were consumed, although this has not been confirmed in any source, or fish.[90] Rather than advance gratuitous theories, we should look at the attestation of Sallustius who, as we saw, talks of milk drunk by the worshippers. He does not explain, however, whether the drinking of the milk takes place on the occasion of the public rites or at the esoteric ceremonies, even if the general context of his arguments would point to the former rather than the latter.[91]

τυμπάνου βέβρωκα, ἐκ κυμβάλου πέπωκα, κεκερνηφόρηκα, ὑπὸ παστὸν ὑποδέδυκα, γένονα μύστης "Ἀττεως" (*Altgriechischer Versbau*, Bonn 1887, 89).

A. Dieterich has reservations about such a "contamination" of the *symbola* mentioned by the two authors and sees in them the *signa* of two different mystery communities (*Eine Mithrasliturgie*, Leipzig-Berlin 1923³, 216f.). Cf. also H. Hepding, *op. cit.*, 185. For an examination of the various interpretations of this formula see U. Fracassini, *op. cit.*, 137-142. A critical survey of the studies on the mysteries of Attis is provided by G. Wagner, *op. cit.*, 229-244.

[88] On the significance of the sacred meal as a "first initiation" cf. H. Hepding *op. cit.*, 185-188. Boyancé attributes a metaphorical significance to the act of eating and drinking from the sacred instruments; it would be a reference to the sound produced by them and consequently to the atmosphere of excitement created by the music in the ritual of Cybele ("Sur les mystères phrygiens 'J'ai mangé dans le tympanon, j'ai bu dans la cymbale", *REA* XXXVII, 1935, 161-164 repr. in *Études sur la religion romaine*, cit., 201-204).

[89] Cf. G. Sfameni Gasparro, "Il mitraismo nell'ambito della fenomenologia misterica", cit., 331f.

[90] Thus Hepding (*op. cit.*, 188f.) who refers to the funeral inscription of Aberkios which he believes, with Dieterich (*Die Grabschrift des Aberkios*, Leipzig 1896), to be connected with the cult of Attis (text *ibid.*, 84f. n° 19). But see the criticism of this attribution by F. J. Dölger, IX-ΘΥΣ. *Das Fischsymbol in Frühchristlicher Zeit*, Bd. I, Roma 1910, 133-138.

[91] The drink of milk mentioned by Sallustius is attributed to the "mysteries" of Attis by K. Wyss, who sees in it a "symbol of immortality" (*Die Milch im Kultus der Griechen und Römer* (RGVV XV, 2), Giessen 1914, 54). Cf. also D. M. Cosi, "Aspetti mistici e misterici del culto di Attis", U. Bianchi-M. J. Vermaseren (eds.), *La soteriologia dei culti orientali*, cit., 485-502 who supposed that honey was mixed with milk in that drink. As far as the use of milk for ritual purposes in the cult of Cybele is concerned we have only to think of the festival called Γαλάξια, celebrated in Athens with the participation of the Ephebes (*IG* II², 1011, 13. Cf. A. Dumond, *Essai sur l'éphébie attique*, vol. I, 1875, 132 and 267f.; vol. II, 1876, Inscr. VII, 166; L. Deubner, *Attische Feste*, Berlin 1956², 216; Vermaseren, *CCCA* II, 16 n° 29). Hesychius' Lexicon explains that it is a ceremony in which a pap of barley is cooked in milk (s.v. Γαλάξια; cf. Bekker, *Anecd.* 1, 229, 25).

An altar from Thessalonica, which Robert, with good arguments, attributes to the Cybele's milieu, mentions a γαλακτηφόρος ("Sur deux inscriptions grecques II. Inscription de Thessalonique", *AIPhO* t. II (*Mélanges Bidez*), Bruxelles 1934, 795-812. The pertinence of the monument to the cult of the Great Mother had been recognised by A. Reinach ("Bulletin d'épigraphie grecque", *RevEp* II, 1914, 109 n° 7). Ch. Avezou and Ch. Picard, who were the first to report on the monument—which they however attributed to a Mithraic community—had assumed, owing

While the formula reported by Firmicus Maternus in the Latin version concludes with a somewhat vague expression, with the initiate's claiming to have taken part in the secrets of the mysteries, in the Greek version it contains an explicit reference to the acquired quality of "*mystes* of Attis".

Of the two other ritual acts mentioned in the *symbolon* known to Clement of Alexandria, the first consists in carrying the *kernos*. Even if the *kernophoria* is a ceremony variously connected with the cult of Cybele[92] we know nothing of the content of the vase carried by the would-be initiate into the mystery rite. According to the scholium to the *Alexipharmakon*, the *kernos* in the Phrygian cult contained lamps.[93] This remains the only positive testimony on the subject, apart from the many inferences suggested.

The next ritual act is expressed with the formula ὑπὸ τὸν παστὸν ὑπέδυν which has given rise to very different interpretations. For some scholars this expression refers to the initiate's entry into a sacred building in order to celebrate a rite implying the performance of a mystic wedding with the goddess, in imitation of Attis.[94] Others exclude a nuptial symbology in the Phrygian mysteries[95] and believe, rather, that they imply the admission of the worshipper in an inner and more secret room of the temple to receive the highest initiation, owing to the double meaning of the term παστός, "nuptial chamber" or "cell" of a temple.[96]

The second interpretation seems to me the most acceptable in view of the fact that the mythical tradition, with the exception of the euhemeristic version reported by Diodorus and the heavily ironical allusions of the Christian polemicists and pagan satirical writers, does not include a marriage between Cybele and Attis.

---

to the presence of the *pedum* and the caduceus in the decoration, that this community venerated also the couple Cybele-Attis together with Hermes ("Inscriptions de Macédonie et de Thrace", *BCH* XXXVI, 1913, 97-100).

[92] Cf. *Alexipharmakon* vv. 217-221 in H. Hepding, *op. cit.*, 9. *Kernophorai* are frequently mentioned in inscriptions connected with the cult of Cybele and a rite of the *kernos* takes place in the context of the taurobolium (see below).

[93] Cf. above n. 22.

[94] A. Dieterich, *Eine Mithrasliturgie*, 126f.; H. Graillot, *op. cit.*, 182f.; Ch. Guignebert, *RH* CXIX-CXX (1915), 162f.; R. Pettazzoni, *I misteri*, 117f.; J. Leipoldt, *Von den Mysterien zur Kirche. Gesammelte Aufsätze*, Hamburg-Bergstedt 1962, 38f. Hepding is far less certain. He emphasises the complete silence of our sources about a nuptial symbology in the mysteries of Cybele (*op. cit.*, 193f.).

[95] K. Prümm, s.v. *Mystères* in *Dictionnaire de la Bible*, Suppl. VI, 1, Paris 1957, 102ff.; G. Wagner, *op. cit.*, 228f., 239-244.

[96] Cf. M. P. Nilsson, *Geschichte*, vol. II², 648f.; J. Schmid, s.v. *Brautschaft heilige*, *RAC* II (1954), 538. See also the interpretation of A.-J. Festugière who compares the formula of the phrygian mysteries to an analogous expression on the gold "Orphic" laminae and emphasises the symbology of "descent" into the subterranean area sacred to the goddess as the equivalent to "being initiated" ("Note sur la formule Δεσποίνας ὑπὸ κόλπου ἔδυν", *RBi* XLIV, 1935, 382-396 repr. in *Études*, 48-62).

It also finds some confirmation in the words with which Firmicus Maternus introduces the mystery formula: it has to be pronounced so that the candidate can be admitted *in interioribus partibus*, i.e. into the recesses of the sanctuary. The *symbolon*, in the form adopted by Clement, would sum up the entire initiatory *iter*, including the access to the inner part of the temple to which Firmicus Maternus alludes with the expression quoted.[97]

Our sources do not contain any explicit statement about the prospects open to the *mystai* of Cybele and Attis. It is probable that the worshippers expected some benefits from their participation in the rites of mysteries. A more intimate familiarity with the Great Mother, the divine principle of natural fertility, could surely offer some guarantee of prosperity and well-being.

Yet there is little basis in the documents in our possession for the idea, so frequently advanced, that the *mystes* of Attis was submitted to a ritual containing a symbology of death and resurrection to a new life. To support this theory reference is normally made to Firmicus Maternus who calls the man who accedes to the Phrygian mysteries *moriturus*, and to the words of Sallustius, according to whom the act of drinking milk after fasting is performed by the worshippers "as by men born anew".

We have already discussed the significance of Sallustius' report. It refers anyhow to the public ritual of the March festivals and not to the "mysteries". As for the attribute *moriturus* in the work of the Christian polemicist, it reflects the condemnation of the pagan cults which he believes to contain spiritual death for man, and should not be seen as an allusion to a rite entailing the "mystic death" of the would-be initiate. Indeed, Firmicus refers to the ritual acts of drinking and eating mentioned in the *symbolon* of the mysteries of Attis and says that whoever performs them has drunk a deadly poison: *cibum istum mors sequitur semper, et poena.*[98]

Once the theory of a spiritual "rebirth" achieved in the esoteric ritual practice by way of identification with an Attis "resurrected" in his turn has been rejected, the problem of possible soteriological prospects in an eschatological sense in the cult of Cybele still remains open. For a deeper investigation of this problem it will be necessary to consult different evidence, since those testimonies explicitly referring to the mystic and mystery cult of Cybele and Attis have proved inadequate.

Ever since its earliest manifestations the "mystic" quality of the mythical-ritual complex of Cybele appears certain, and the attestation of an esoteric in-

---

[97] H. Hepding, *op. cit.*, 194f.

[98] *De err. prof. rel.* 18, 2; cf. *ibid.* 8, 5; 18, 8; 28, 4, 9, 13 and *passim*. On the specific procedure of the anti-pagan polemic of Firmicus Maternus cf. J. Opelt, "Schimpfwörter in der Apologie De errore profanarum religionum des Firmicus Maternus", *Glotta* LII (1974), 114-126.

This is the conclusion of M. P. Nilsson, *op. cit.*, 649ff. See also F. J. Dölger, "Mysterienwesen und Urchristentum", *ThRev*, 15 Jahrg., Nr. 17/18 (1916), 389f.; J. Dey, ΠΑΛΙΓΓΕΝΕΣΙΑ, Münster 1937, 79-86.

itiatory practice entitles us to speak of "mysteries" in the Phrygian cult in the situations and forms so far examined. As we have seen, however, with the exception of Damascius' late report, the relevant sources tell us nothing about benefits, for the present and future life, promised to the initiates. Nor is it permissible to attribute to the sphere of the "mysteries" those indications or explicit attestations of soteriological or specifically eschatological prospects which can also be detected in the cult of Cybele, if this relationship does not emerge from the documents themselves. I shall not posit a necessary connection between mysteries and eschatology; I shall however try to detect in the cult of Cybele all the possible traces of concepts both of the future destiny of man and of positive prospects in this life.

CHAPTER FIVE

SOTERIOLOGICAL PROSPECTS IN THE CULT OF CYBELE

The analysis conducted hitherto has yielded little concerning the problem of the advantages offered to the worshipper by the celebration of the cult of the Great Mother Cybele. If the earliest "mystic" forms of this cult in Classical Greece appeared to confer on man that state of bliss achieved in the practice of an enthusiastic-orgiastic ritual, in a direct relationship with the deity, we have no indication as to the particular prospects from which the members of those of Cybele's communities with an esoteric-initiatory practice in the Hellenistic era thought they would benefit.

The spring festival cycle in honour of Cybele and Attis, of Phrygian origin and institutionalised in the Roman world after the 1st century A.D. in the March ceremonies, has revealed its quality as a mystic cult, re-evoking a divine vicissitude in which the god is subject to crisis, disappearance and death but also to "survival" in his capacity as guarantor of vegetal fertility and his effective presence in the practice of the rite. Our sources do not bother to tell us what reflections this cultic celebration had on the condition of the worshippers, even though they give a rich, detailed and lively illustration of the emotional intensity with which the adepts participated.

The abundance of blessings on an earthly and collective level can be considered the main benefit sought by the celebration of such a cult, bound so closely, in its original forms, to the idea of the promotion of fertility.[1]

The character of the goddess as guarantor of natural fertility, expressed in her epithet *Meter* and in the original mountainous and rustic setting peculiar to her, progressively adopted a series of "Demetrian" aspects in the sense of a connection with the agrarian rhythms and with the crops themselves.

This emerges from the late iconography of the goddess and from the attributes of *Cereria* and *Agraria* which designate Cybele in certain parts of the Empire.[2] Nevertheless, notwithstanding this insistence on her faculty as

---

[1] For the persistence of this notion in the March festivals during the Empire cf. the words of Joannes Lydus according to whom on 15 March, the day of the *canna intrat*, there also occurred the sacrifice of a six-year-old bull "for the fields on the mountains". This rite was presided over by the high priest and the cannophoroi of the Mother (*De men.* IV, 49 in H. Hepding, *op. cit.*, 75). Cf. F. Cumont, *Les religions orientales*, 52; D. Fishwick, art. cit., *TAPhA* XCVII (1966), 197ff.; M. J. Vermaseren, *Cybele and Attis*, 114.

[2] *CIL* V, 796: *Cereria* = M. J. Vermaseren, *CCCA* IV, 92 n° 220; G. Tomassetti, "Notizie epigrafiche", *BCAR* XX (1892), 358 n° 7: Μητρὶ Θεῶν ἀγραρίᾳ. Cf. H. Graillot, *op. cit.*, 93; 118f.; 200f.

Of the various representations of the Great Mother with agrarian symbols (ears of corn, fruit, cornucopia) see, for example, the large marble statue probably of Roman origin in M. J. Vermaseren, *CCCA* III, 84f. n° 311, Pl. CLXXVII. Cf. also the taurobolium altar of Villa Albani

dispenser of fruits of the earth, we cannot deny that, as the result of the general religious development in the Hellenistic-Roman period, participation in the March ritual acquired a different and more personal meaning in the eyes of the individual worshipper who re-evoked the divine vicissitude. In view of the lack of positive attestations, a methodological caution advises us to withold from defining the specific content of the "hopes" which could arise from participating in the "interaction" between the divine and human level achieved in that cult. The testimony of Damascius, late though it is, can, as we said, be considered an indication of this development of the religious concepts connected with the cult of Cybele and of the soteriological prospects which it could offer to the adept in the public form of the March festivals.

The sources relating to the "Phrygian mysteries" of the Roman period do not allow us to reach any conclusion on the problem in question. It is not to the cult of Cybele that we can attribute the mystery formula reported by Firmicus Maternus in which the "*mystai* of the rescued god" are told to rejoice in the hope of themselves obtaining ἐκ πόνων σωτηρία[3].

On the other hand it is difficult to decide on the meaning of the formula ὑπὲρ σωτηρίας which ends the long dedication made to the *Meter Oreia* by the

---

(*ibid.*, 101f. n° 357, Pls. CCVIII-CCIX) in which the goddess carries some ears of corn in her right hand and the painting from Pompeii with the image of Cybele on a throne with the modius and the cornucopia (M. J. Vermaseren, *CCCA* IV, 13 n° 28).

To confirm the goddess' connection with fertility we also have Pliny's report (*Nat. hist.* XVIII, 16) where we read *quo verum anno Mater deum advecta Romam est, maiorem ea aestate messem quam antecedentibus annis decem facta esse tradunt*. This character of the goddess survived until a late period, if Gregory of Tours could recall the procession in honour of the *Berecynthia* at *Augustodunum*, her image transported *in carpento pro salvatione agrorum ac vinearum* (*De glor. confess.* 7, *P.L.* 71, 884A-C). Cf. G. Wissowa, *op. cit.*, 270. To this we can add the report of Joannes Lydus who mentions, amongst the various Roman festivals in the months of November and December, an interesting cultic practice of the πολιτικοί. They "τὰς ἀπαρχὰς τῶν συγκλεισθέντων καρπῶν, οἷον καὶ ἔλαιον, σῖτον καὶ μέλι καὶ πάντα τὰ ἀπὸ δένδρων ὅσα διαμένουσι καὶ σώζονται, ἐποίουν ἄρτους ἄνευ ὕδατος καὶ ταῦτα προσῆγον τοῖς ἱερεῦσι τῆς Μητρός".

The author emphasises the persistence, until his own day, of this ritual practice and observes how the offering of the foods in question to the priests of the *Meter* takes place throughout the period preceding the new production ("φυλάττεται δὲ ἡ τοιαύτη συνήθεια ἔτι καὶ νῦν καὶ κατὰ τὸν Νοέμβριον καὶ Δεκέμβριον ἄχρι τῶν αὐξιφωτίων προσφέρουσι", (*De mens.* IV, 158 ed. R. Wuensch, Stuttgart 1898, 174). We should remember that Artemidorus (*Onir.* II, 39, 24) defines the Mother of the Gods γεωργοῖς .... ἀγαθή.

[3] *De err. prof. rel.* 22, 1, 3 in H. Hepding, *op. cit.*, 50 who interprets the passage as referring to the mysteries of Attis (*ibid.*, 166f.; 196f.). So also G. van der Leeuw, "The ΣΥΜΒΟΛΑ in Firmicus Maternus", *Egyptian Religion* I (1933), 61-71. This view, which is shared by various authors (cf. G. Wagner, *op. cit.*, 227 n. 137), has given rise to some valid objections, since the general context of Firmicus' arguments refers rather to the mystery cult of Osiris. See, for example, A. Loisy, *Les mystères païens et le mystère chrétien*, cit., 104; M.-J. Lagrange, *Attis et le christianisme*, cit., 447f.; M. P. Nilsson, *Geschichte*, vol. II[2], 613; G. Wagner, *op. cit.*, 96ff. More recently D. M. Cosi has attributed the formula quoted by Firmicus Maternus to the cult of Attis ("Salvatore e salvezza nei misteri di Attis", *Aevum* L, 1976, 67), although he does not believe that the ritual to which the formula itself refers can be defined as "mysteries" ("Firmico Materno e i misteri di Attis", *AFLPad* II, 1977, 72f., 76-79).

religious association based in the sacred caves of Juvadjà.[4] It is part of the language common to religious epigraphy and it is impossible to decide whether the dedicators expected from their divine protector only a guarantee of earthly and material order or also salvation of a spiritual and eschatological nature.

We should consequently turn to another type of document which illuminates other aspects of Cybele's personality and can contribute to defining the picture of the benefits bestowed by her to a man both in the present life and in an eschatological perspective.

Invoked by Pindar in the 3rd Pythian Ode for the health of Hieron of Syracuse,[5] the Great Mother appears frequently as a healing deity. From Diogenes Tragicus who defines her ὑμνοδὸς ἰατρός[6] to the euhemeristic version of Diodorus who shows Cybele capable of healing children's diseases with her καθαρμοί[7] and the inscriptions of the Piraeus in which the worshippers turn to her as εὐάντητος ἰατρίνη,[8] a whole series of attestations underline these medical

---

[4] Cf. above p. 71 and the relevant notes.

[5] *III Pyth.*, v. 77f.; after having formulated augural wishes for the health of the Tyrant of Syracuse the poet exclaims: "ἀλλ᾽ ἐπεύξασθαι μὲν ἐγὼν ἐθέλω/Ματρί....". And the scholiast glosses: "φησὶν οὖν ὅτι κατεύξομαι τὴν 'Ρέαν, παρόσον δοκεῖ τῶν νόσων αὐξητικὴ καὶ μειωτικὴ εἶναι· κατεύξομαι οὖν αὐτὴν, φησίν, εὐμενῆ εἶναι τῷ 'Ιέρωνι" (*Schol. III Pyth. 137 a* ed. A. B. Drachmann, vol. II, 80).

[6] *Semele fr.* in Nauck[2], 776f.

[7] *Bibl. Hist.* III, 58. The special protection accorded by Cybele to children could account for the particular iconography of two statuettes (one in terracotta, the other larger one in marble) of the goddess found at Argos, where she bears on her knees a child who, at least in the case of the terracotta, can probably be identified as Attis (S. Charitonides, "Recherches dans le quartier est d'Argos", *BCH* LXXVIII, 1954, 412; 414f. and fig. 1; 425; Vermaseren, *CCCA* II, 147 n° 471, Pl. CXLII). There is also a relief from the Agora of Athens with a similar image of Cybele with a child in her lap (cf. M. J. Vermaseren, *The Legend of Attis*, 10) and a marble statuette, which I believe to be unpublished, in the Museo delle Terme in Rome (inv. n° 8683). To these can be added the pieces in the Museum of Istanbul published by Lambrechts in which, however, the child has a tall pointed cap which allows us to identify him as Attis (cf. above p. 31, n. 19f.).

On the typology of the *kourotrophos*, in which Cybele participates in the cases mentioned, see Th. Hadzisteliou Price, *Kourotrophos. Cults and Representations of the Greek Nursing Deities*, Leiden 1978 (Cybele *kourotrophos*: *ibid.* 64f. n° 679, fig. 50; nos. 680-681).

The metrical epigram inscribed on the pediment of the Metroon of Phaestos (3rd-2nd century B.C.) guarantees the favour of the goddess to all those who care for their own children. Cf. D. Comparetti, "Su alcune epigrafi metriche cretesi", *WS* XXIV (1902), 265-275; G. De Sanctis, "L'epigramma festio di Rea", *RFIC* LX (= N.S. 10) (1932), 222-226. A different interpretation of the monument has been given, on the other hand, by A. Dieterich (*Mutter Erde*, Leipzig 1925[3], 112-115) and O. Kern ("Orphiker auf Kreta", *Hermes* LI, 1916, 554-567). Cf. Vermaseren, *CCCA* II, 211f. n° 661.

[8] *IG* II[2], 4714 (1st century A.D.); 4759 (2nd century A.D.); 4760 (1st/2nd century A.D.). Cf. Vermaseren, *CCCA* II, 84f. nos. 273, 275-276. The goddess is also invoked as ἰατρίνη εὐάντητος in an inscription from Kula (J. Keil, "Die Kulte Lydiens", W. H. Buckler-W. M. Calder, eds., *Anatolian Studies presented to Sir W. M. Ramsay*, Manchester 1923, 257).

On the medical aspects of Cybele cf. H. Graillot, *op. cit.*, Index s.v. *médicine (déesse de la)*. It is probably to these aspects that the association of the goddess with Aesculapius refers in a fragmentary inscription from Carthage (J. Ferron-Ch. Saumagne, "Adon-Baal, Esculape, Cybèle à Carthage", *Africa* II, 1967-68, 83. Cf. *ibid.*, 81-86: dedication to Aesculapius by a

capacities which extend to the flocks⁹ and which give rise, in the Latin West, to frequent identifications of the *Magna Mater* with local deities connected with thermal springs.[10]

Above all the goddess is the "purifier" of that *mania* which she herself is capable of inspiring, both as the beneficial possession produced by her cult and as the terrible and destructive expression of her wrath.[11]

---

sacerdos of the *Magna Mater Idaea* and Attis). For the goddess' healing faculties, finally, see Joannes Lydus, *De mens.* IV, 106: "Χρησμὸς ἐδόθη Ῥωμαίοις πρὸς τῆς Μητρός, μηδ' ὅλως ἀφροδισίοις χρῆσθαι ἀνὰ πάντα τὸν Ἰούλιον μῆνα, εἴπερ αὐτοῖς ὑγιαίνειν τὰ σώματα μέλλοι" (ed. R. Wuensch 144).

⁹ Diodorus, *loc. cit.*; Dio Chrysostomus, *Orat.* I, 54 ed. J. von Arnim, Berlin 1912², vol. I, 10: "ἔχειν δὲ μαντικὴν ἐκ μητρὸς θεῶν δεδομένην, χρῆσθαι δὲ αὐτῇ τούς τε νομέας πάντας τοὺς πλησίον καὶ τοὺς γεωργοὺς ὑπὲρ καρπῶν καὶ βοσκημάτων γενέσεως καὶ σωτηρίας".

It is probably with a Cybele's milieu that we can connect the γραῦς ἀγύρτρια who pronounces answers ὑπὲρ προβατίων καὶ τῶν τοιούτων according to Philostratus, *Vita Apollon.* III, 43.

To the literary sources we can add a direct testimony of popular devotion, a votive dedication of the late Imperial period made by the shepherd Alypos to the *Meter Malene* for the health of his masters, the cattle and the dogs (ὑπὲρ δεσποτῶν καὶ τῶν θρεμάτων καὶ τῶν κυνῶν). The goddess, represented on the stele as seated in a throne in the act of receiving the homage of her devotee, was identified by Robert as the Anatolian Great Mother, here characterised by one of her many epithets with a local reference ("Dédicaces et reliefs votifs. 7. Dédicace d'un berger", *Hellenica* X, 1955, 28-33 and Pl. VII). An inscription from Seyit Gazi invokes the Μήτηρ Κυβήλη περὶ βοῶν (*MAMA* V, 102 n° 213, Pl. 49).

It is to this context of popular religiosity, in which Cybele is venerated as the guarantor of the fertility of the fields and the flocks, that we can probably attribute an interesting Phrygian monument published by Lambrechts. It is a marble block with a dedication to the god *Hosios kai Dikaios* represented in a quadriga. The presence of the goddess on the pediment of the monument indicates her connection with the agrarian and pastoral world in which the cult of the "holy and just" god, so popular in Phrygia and in Lydia, was very widespread. Cf. P. Lambrechts, "Documents inédits de Cybèle au Musée d'Eskişekir", *Hommages à Marie Delcourt* (Coll. Latomus 114), Bruxelles 1970, 215-218, Pl. III, figs. 8-9. Finally there is a figurative monument from Macedonia which shows a shepherd with the *pedum* in the act of handing a gift to the Mother of the Gods (*SEG* I, n° 268), a further confirmation of the special relationship between the goddess and the pastoral environment.

[10] Cf. H. Graillot, "Mater deum salutaris. Cybèle protectrice des eaux thermales", *Mélanges Capart*, Paris 1912, 213-228; F. Di Capua, "Un'epigrafe stabiese e il culto della 'Deum Mater' presso le sorgenti di acque minerali", *RAAN* XXI (1941), 75-83; E. Thévenot, "Le culte des déesses-mères à la station gallo-romaine de Bolard (Nuits-Saint-Georges, Côte-d'Or)", *RAE* II (1951), 7-26; S. J. de Laet, "Le fanum de Hofstade-lez-Alost (Flandre Orientale) et le culte de la déesse gauloise de la fécondité", *Latomus* XI (1952), 45-56. The epithet of Θερμηνή conferred on the *Meter* in an inscription from the region of *Dorylaeum* (Eskişehir) in Phrygia shows that the goddess' medical capacities in connection with the thermal waters were well-known also in her Anatolian homeland. Cf. L. Robert, "Dedicaces et reliefs votifs. 14. Meter Therméné", *Hellenica* X (1955), 78-82, Pl. XXI, 2. The same city of *Dorylaeum*, moreover, the site of thermal waters celebrated in Antiquity, has yielded some dedications to a Μήτηρ whose qualifying attribute (ἀπὸ Κρανοσμεγάλου) can probably be connected with the very spring of which she was regarded as the protectress (*MAMA* V, XIV and 4f. nos. 8-9, Pl. 15). Such an interpretation of the divine epithet has been opposed by Robert, art. cit., 82; cf. *ibid.*, 111 n. 5.

[11] Cf. the texts cited above on the *kybebos* (ch. I, p. 15f. and nn. 35 and 38). For the goddess' cathartic faculties see *Schol. III Pyth. 139b*: "καθάρτιά ἐστι τῆς μανίας ἡ θεός"; Pseudo-Apollodorus, *Bibl.* III, 5, 1f.

It is to this healing faculty that the epithet σώτειρα refers which is sometimes attributed to the Mother of the Gods.[12] She can therefore be situated in the category of the "saviour" gods, beneficent healers and guarantors of the well-being of their worshippers, so numerous in the Hellenistic-Roman period amongst the traditional deities of Graeco-Roman paganism and amongst the Oriental divinities.[13]

Yet the documents which attest that epithet of Cybele do not allow us to attribute to it that more extensive significance in a spiritual or eschatological

---

[12] SEG XXIII (1968), n° 678; Vermaseren, CCCA II, 220f. n° 689: inscription from Cyprus of the 2nd century B.C. with the dedication Μητρὶ θεῶν Σωτείραι/ὑπὲρ Μεννέου ἡγεμόνος; CIG 4695: a dedication made by a husband and wife for themselves and their children to the goddess invoked with the titles of Μήτηρ θεῶν σώτειρα ἐπήκοος. Cf. the inscription CIG 3993 from Iconium, already cited, which invokes Agdistis amongst the "saviour gods". An altar from Doghalar, a village in Phrygia, bears an inscription with a dedication "to the Mother of the Gods Ζινγοτηνή", made "for the safety" of the dedicator, his household and the κώμη (W. M. Ramsay, art. cit., JHS V, 1884, 260f. n° 13). The mention of the "village" as the beneficiary of the σωτηρία bestowed by the goddess shows that this safety is a guarantee of well-being in an entirely earthly perspective. We should also note that the specific epithet here borne by the Mother of the Gods is a toponym derived from the name of the locality (Ζίνγοτος) of which she consequently appears as the protective deity. Cf. also the inscription from Tomi (SIG³ 731, 36-38) where annual sacrifices to the Mother of the Gods and the Dioscuri are recorded ὑπὲρ τῆ[ς] τοῦ δήμου σωτηρία[ς].

The epithet of "saviour" seems to assume a public character in the case of the bronzes of Faustina which bear the title Mater deum salutaris in relation to a temple erected to the goddess with this epithet (H. Cohen, Description historique des monnaies frappées sous l'Empire Romain communément appellées Médailles Impériales, vol. II, Paris 1880, 431, nos. 229-230). Cf. H. Graillot, op. cit., 151f., 335; M. Bieber, "The Images of Cybele in Roman Coins and Sculpture" J. Bibauw (ed.), Hommages à Marcel Renard, Bruxelles 1969, vol. III, 33f. n. 3. According to Beaujeu it is, rather, a title which illustrates the salvific qualities of the goddess in a mystic and eschatological perspective (op. cit., 313).

The same title recurs in the Contorniates of Faustina which are amongst the first issues (between 356 and 359) of these pseudo-coins regarded by Alföldi as an instrument of anti-Christian religious propaganda used by the Roman aristocracy (Die Kontorniaten, Budapest-Leipzig 1943, 15; 107 n° 39, Taf. VIII, 12 and XXIII, 1). Similar pieces bear the image of Agrippina (ibid., Taf. XXIII, 2), of Alexander (Taf. IV, 9) and of Trajan (Taf. LV, 10).

In the Orphic hymn XXVII, 12 the goddess is termed Φρυγίης σώτειρα. According to Graillot (op. cit., 107 n. 3) Lucretius was already alluding to the Great Mother's faculty of bestowing salus in his description of the sacred pompé of the goddess (De rer. nat. II, v. 625: munificat tacita mortales muta salute). On the significance of the tacita salus in the context of the exegesis of the Phrygian cult proposed by Lucretius see now D. J. Stewart, "The Silence of Magna Mater", HSPh LXXIV (1970), 75-84.

[13] For the notion of σωτηρία in late Antiquity cf. P. Wendland, Σωτήρ, ZNTW V (1904), 335-353. See also E. B. Allo, "Les dieux sauveurs du paganisme gréco-romain", RSPh XV (1926), 5-34; F. Dornseiffs, s.v. Σωτήρ, PWRE, Z. Rh., V (1927), 1211-1221; O. Höfer, s.v. Σωτήρ, Roscher, Myth. Lex., IV (1909-15), 1247-1272; M. P. Nilsson, Geschichte, vol. I², 414ff.; vol. II², 154-185 with extensive references to the cult of the sovereigns in the Hellenistic era, also called θεοὶ σωτήρες.

The σωτηρία procured by the god or by the sovereign is to be viewed in a completely earthly perspective as the preservation from dangers or recovery from illnesses. According to Nilsson "es ist die grosse und geniale Tat des Paulus, daß er, alle andere Beziehungen abstreifend, die Erlösung in die Welt der Religion erhoben hat" (ibid., vol. II², 391).

sense which it nevertheless started to acquire in late Antiquity.[14] It is with the risks of navigation and war, for example, that we can identify the "great dangers" from which a certain Marcus, σύμβίος of the Gallus Soterides who had invoked for him the assistance of his divine patron, was saved, thanks to the benevolent protection of the goddess.[15]

We should now enquire into whether the notion of protection and well-being bestowed by the goddess in connection with the physical health of the worshippers, and, in a wider sense, with their earthly condition,[16] is accompanied—in other aspects of her cult—by the notion of a guarantee for a future life.

The function of Cybele as protectress of tombs, as it emerges from the ancient Phrygian rock monuments according to the interpretation proposed by Ramsay,[17] has often been emphasised. Yet such monuments, as we have said, seem rather to be the sites of a cult without a precise funerary reference.[18] At

---

[14] Cf. R. Reitzenstein, *Die hellenistischen Mysterienreligionen*, 25f.; 30; 39-41; F. Dornseiffs, art. cit., 1216f.

[15] Inscription from Cyzicus of 46 A.D. (*CIG* 3668 = *SIG*³ 763): "... καὶ τῆς θεᾶς εἰπάσης μοι κατ'[ἐνύπνιον ὅ]τι ἠχμαλώτισται Μάρχος, ἀλ[λὰ σωθήσεται ἐκ τῶν] με[γάλω]ν [κι]νδύνων ἐπικα[λεσάμενος αὐτήν]", lines 9ff. Cf. E. Schwertheim, art. cit., 810f. n° 3.

See also the episode of the Amazon Myrina who, meeting a storm at sea, invokes the Mother of the Gods ὑπὲρ σωτηρίας. After landing safely in the island of Samothrace she dedicates it to the goddess who helped her to "safety" (Diodorus Siculus, *Bibl.* III, 55, 8). This report fits into the tradition which connects Cybele with the cult of Samothrace; for this association cf. R. Pettazzoni, "Le origini dei Kabiri nelle isole del Mar Tracio", *MemAccLinc*, Cl.Sc.mor.stor.e fil., S.Va, vol. XII (1906), 663-667; 696-701; H. Graillot, *op. cit.*, 498-501; O. Kern, s.v. *Kabeiros und Kabeiroi*, *PWRE* X, 2, 1429; F. Chapouthier, *op. cit.*, 153-183, 237-248; B. Hemberg, *op. cit.*, 82-85.

As we know the mysteries of the Island included the figure of a Great Goddess whose name and whose deeds were subject, like those of the other divinities of the Cabirian group, to the initiatory secret (cf. Strabo, *Geogr.* X, 3, 19: "τὰς δὲ πράξεις αὐτῶν μυστικὰς εἶναι"; *ibid.* X, 3, 21: "τὰ δ'ὀνόματα αὐτῶν ἐστι μυστικά"). Of the various identifications proposed by the early sources (cf. B. Hemberg, *op. cit.*, 82-92; 306f.), the one which sees the Phrygian Great Mother as the object of the mysteries of Samothrace reveals the existence of typological analogies between Cybele and the goddess of the Cabirian group and their respective cults, besides probably also being an indication of historical connections between the island and the Anatolian world. It poses complex interpretative problems for the correct formulation and solution of which we would need to examine specifically the question of Samothrace, which is outside the confines of the present work. All we can say is that this identification confirms the mystic connotations of the Phrygian goddess. Like Demeter or Hecate (who often alternate with Cybele as the objects of the cult of Samothrace) she could appear as the exoteric equivalent of the Great Goddess of the mysteries in her prerogatives and attributes.

[16] The helpful and benign nature of the goddess also emerges from the epithet of ἐπήκοος by which she is sometimes invoked. Cf. H. Graillot, *op. cit.*, 206; O. Weinreich, "ΘΕΟΙ ΕΠΗΚΟΟΙ", *AM* XXXVII (1912), 5 n° 1; 15 n° 63; 16 nos. 68-70. To these documents we can add an ex-voto from Philadelphia to the *Meter Phileis* ἐπήκοος (J. Keil-A. v. Premerstein, "Bericht über eine Reise in Lydien und der südlichen Aiolis, ausgeführt 1906 im Auftrage der Kaiserlichen Akademie der Wissenschaften", *Denkschr. d. Kais. Akad. d. Wiss. in Wien*, Philol.-hist. Kl., Bd. 53, Wien 1910, 25 n° 34 Abb. 15).

[17] Cf. H. Graillot, *op. cit.*, 16.

[18] See above, Introduction, p. 3.

the same time, however, it is certain that in the Roman Imperial period the Great Mother and Attis appear frequently among the divinities invoked as guarantors of the inviolability of graves in many localities in Asia Minor.

Numerous inscriptions from Smyrna prescribe the payment of a tribute to the *Mater theon Sipylene* on the part of whoever violated the dispositions established by the proprietor of the monument with regard to the grave itself.[19] The Mother of the Gods is also indicated as the recipient of the fine in the grave inscriptions of two Archigalli of Termessus.[20]

Countless inscriptions in the Neo-Phrygian language contain deprecatory formulas against the violators of tombs, the interpretation of which remains largely uncertain. But we frequently come across the name of Attis in a context which indicate quite clearly his quality as protector of the tomb.[21] The same function is attributed to the goddess and expressed both in the form of the dedication to her of the συνγενικόν, in other words of the grave itself,[22] and in the symbolism of the representation. The image of the lion, for example, recurs frequently on the tombstone,[23] as does that of the goddess herself accompanied by the animal.[24]

The fairly widespread custom of placing the grave under the protection of a deity is in keeping with the need to guard the earthly "dwelling" of the deceased from violations. It does not necessarily entail the idea that the protective action of the divinity also acts on the destiny of the soul in the life to come.

At all events, the documents cited attest a fairly frequent connection of Cybele and Attis with the sphere of death and burial in their Anatolian homeland. Also in the East, though not in Asia Minor, we have, on the slopes

---

[19] *CIG* 3260; 3286; 3385-3387; 3401; 3411. Μουσεῖον III (1880), 129 n° 168 (169); V (1885), 29 n° 255; 32 n° 262; 84 n° 273. Cf. G. Hirschfeld, "Ueber die griechische Grabinschriften welche Geldstrafen anordnen", *Königsberg. Studien* I (1887), 115. Two other pieces from Smyrna which mention the Σιπυλήνη as the beneficiary of the tribute have been published respectively by A. Plassart-Ch. Picard ("Inscriptions d'Éolide et d'Ionie", *BCH* XXXVII, 1913, 243ff. n° 50) and by W. H. Buckler ("Lydian Records", *JHS* XXXVII, 1917, 112f. n° 25). On the payment of fines to the town treasure or the coffers of the sanctuaries by the violators of tombs in Asia Minor cf. B. Keil, "Ueber kleinasiatische Grabinschriften", *Hermes* XLIII (1908), 522-577; W. Arkwright, "Penalties in Lycian Epitaphs of Hellenistic and Roman Times", *JHS* XXXI (1911), 269-275.

[20] R. Heberdey (ed.), *Tituli Asiae Minoris*, Vindobonae 1941, vol. III, 1 n° 267 and n° 740.

[21] W. M. Calder, "Corpus Inscriptionum Neo-phrygiarum", *JHS* XXXI (1911), 161-215. The Neo-Phrygian formula τετιχμενος ATTIC ΑΔΕΙΤΟΥ appears to be the equivalent of the Greek χατηραμένος Ἄττι ἔστω. Cf. Id., *MAMA* VII, XXXII-XXXVI, nos. 10, 136-137, 215, 317, 436, 454, 487, 492.

[22] *MAMA* VII, n° 515: συνγενιχὸν Μητρὶ Ζιμμηνῇ (*sic*). The author refers to *MAMA* VI, nos. 24 and 48 for the term συνγενικόν and emphasises that it is a protective formula in use in Northern Phrygia.

[23] *MAMA* VII, nos. 14a, 18, 55, 132 and 335; cf. *MAMA* I, nos. 32, 93, 116, 259 and 296.

[24] *Ibid.*, nos. 113 and 475.

of Mount Stavrin overlooking Antioch, in the area of a necropolis, a rock sculpture of the Roman Imperial era representing two characters, a bust and a complete figure interpreted respectively as Cybele and Attis. The monument seems to have a funerary character and would confirm the quality of the two deities as "custodians of the tomb".[25]

This same quality also persists in the West where it is expressed in the presence of images of the two gods in funerary ornaments. As we know, terracotta statuettes of Attis have come to light in large quantities in the necropolises of Amphipolis in Macedonia[26] and of Myrina.[27] The presence of the Phrygian headdress has led Robinson to identify, albeit with reservations, the seated boy represented in a terracotta deposited in a tomb at Olynthus with Attis.[28] In Abydos, on the Hellespont, a statuette of Cybele has been discovered in a tomb,[29] while from the necropolis of Phanagoria (northern coast of the Black Sea) comes a terracotta image of the boy Attis, with bird and dog.[30]

The necropolises of Southern Italy have yielded other examples of Attis[31] and from the Carthaginian necropolis of St. Monica we have a clay statuette in which we can probably recognise the image of Cybele rather than that of Astarte, as Ferron will have it.[32] If this identification is correct the little

---

[25] P. Perdrizet-Ch. Fossey, "Voyage dans la Syrie du Nord", *BCH* XXI (1897), 79-85 Pl. II. Cf. H. Graillot, *op. cit.*, 387f.

[26] P. Perdrizet, "Terres cuites d'Amphipolis", *BCH* XXI (1897), 514-528, Pl. VIII; H. Sitte, "Antiken aus Amphipolis", *JÖAI* XI (1908), 97-99, figs. 65-66; Ch. Avezou-Ch. Picard, "La nécropole de Thessalonique", *MEFR* XXXII (1912), 341-343 nos. 3-5, figs. 2a, 3b and 4a.

[27] E. Pottier-S. Reinach, *La Nécropole de Myrina*, Paris 1887, Cat. 195 bis and ter; 413 bis (Cybele); 210; 215 and Pl. XXXI, 279 bis-281. Cf. *ibid.*, 405-408. H. Graillot, *op. cit.*, 370 n. 1. On these types see the classificatory scheme suggested by D. M. Robinson (*Excavations at Olynthus*, Part XIV, Baltimore-London-Oxford 1952, 13-16 nos. 20-33 and 121-125, Pl. 42) and the iconographical analysis of M. J. Vermaseren, *The Legend of Attis*, 13-21 and *passim*.

[28] "The Third Campaign in Olynthus", *AJA* XXXIX (1935), 239 fig. 40; *Excavations at Olynthus*, Part XIV, cit., 215f. n° 275, Pl. 92. We should note, however, that the type of the child seated or lying down, with various attributes, is widespread in the terracottas of this city, where so many pieces have come to light both in the tombs and in the houses (cf. D. M. Robinson, *op. cit.*, nos. 273-273A Pl. 91; n° 274 Pl. 92; nos. 276-277 Pl. 93; nos. 278-82 Pl. 94; Id., *Excavations at Olynthus*, Pars VII, Baltimore-London-Oxford 1933, nos. 280-287 Pl. 36; nos. 397-399 Pl. 56).

[29] E. Meyer, *Geschichte von Troas*, Leipzig 1877, 25. Cf. H. Graillot, *op. cit.*, 374 n° 3.

[30] M. Kobylina, *Divinités orientales sur le litoral nord de la Mer Noire* (EPRO 52), Leiden 1976, 6f.; 23f. Mon. I, 19 and Pl. XIII.

[31] A lamp with the figure of Attis has been found at Cumae in the tomb of a child (V. Tran Tam Tinh, *Le culte des divinités orientales en Campanie en dehors de Pompéi, de Stabie et d'Herculanum* [EPRO 27], Leiden 1972, 108 C 11, fig. 49); at Curti, near S. Maria Capua Vetere, a terracotta image of Attis recumbent was also discovered in a tomb (*ibid.*, 117 C 12). Cf. M. J. Vermaseren, *CCCA* IV, 4 n° 3, Pl. I; 34f. n° 92, fig. 7. The Roman necropolis in Contrada Scozzo at Tindari has yielded a bust of Attis or a Phrygian priest (G. Sfameni Gasparro, *op. cit.*, 280 n° 339 bis, fig. 151; M. J. Vermaseren *CCCA* IV, 67 n° 169, Pl. LXVI).

[32] "Les statuettes au tympanon des hypogées puniques", *AntAfr* III (1969), 11 and 28, fig. 9. The goddess is represented seated on a chair with a high back; her left hand supports a large tympanum and in her right she holds a patera. It is therefore a very different type to all those of the

Carthaginian monument enriches still further the documentation which illustrates the function of the goddess as protectress of the deceased.

This function probably accounts for the presence of Cybele in the extreme right hand side of a funerary slab found in Tuscany (at Pietrasanta) in which is represented the banquet of the heroicised deceased.[33] The identification of the Phrygian goddess with the majestic female figure seated on a throne with a high back is probably correct owing to the presence, above the *parapetasma* which forms the background of the entire scene, of three figures with a helmet and a broad shield, in whom we can recognise the Corybantes, according to the scheme of the κουρητική τρίας which recurs with a certain frequency in the monuments of the Cybele's cult.[34] Owing to its stylistic characteristics the relief has been dated in the Hellenistic era (2nd century B.C.); of Greek workmanship, it was probably imported into Italy in the Roman period.[35]

That series of funerary monuments so numerous in Gaul[36] and in Germany[37] but also present in Italy[38] and other regions of the empire,[39] which

---

series examined by Ferron (standing figures, clutching a tympanum to their breast or holding it near their shoulder in their left hand, while they strike it with their right hands). The iconographical scheme of the statuette in question, on the other hand, is typical of Cybele, although the lion is missing.

[33] S. Ferri, "Pietrasanta (Luni). Rinvenimento di un rilievo greco", *NSc* S. VIII, vol. I (1947), 46-48 and fig. 1; M. J. Vermaseren, *CCCA* IV, 84 n° 204, Pl. LXXVII.

[34] Cf. O. Walter, art. cit., *JÖAI* XXXI (1939), 53-80. It should also be added that the group of three warriors with helmet and shield, sometimes accompanied by horses, recurs in various funerary reliefs, with banqueting scenes similar to ours and without any reference to Cybele (cf. O. Walter, art. cit., 72-76 and Abb. 27-30).

[35] S. Ferri, art. cit., 47. The author thinks that the monument probably comes "from the islands or the Thessalonian-Macedonian-Thracian-Anatolian coastal area, most likely the latter".

[36] É. Espérandieu, *Recueil général des bas-reliefs de la Gaule romaine*, vol. I, Paris 1907, 353; 356-357: Vienne; 622-625; 627-629; 704, 707, 710, 746, 761, 789: Narbonne. Cf. H. Graillot, *op. cit.*, 446-451. We can add the pieces published by M. Renard, "Attis funéraires de Toulouse", *Latomus* XI (1952), 59-62.

[37] *CIL* XIII, 7684; 7514; 7627; 6808; 8056. Cf. H. Graillot, *op. cit.*, 466-469. É. Espérandieu, *Recueil général des bas-reliefs, statues et bustes de la Germanie romaine*, Paris-Bruxelles 1931, 381f. n° 605 (= *CIL* XIII, 6372); 382 n° 606 (= *CIL* XIII, 6368). G. Ristow, "Denkmäler hellenistischer Mysterienkulte in Kölner Museumbesitz—Kult der Göttermutter und des Attis", *KJB* XIII (1972-73), 118 nos. 12-16, Taf. 52, 1-3; 53, 3; 54, 4.

[38] *CIL* V, 1148 and other examples in Graillot, *op. cit.*, 440 n° 4. See now the complete inventory of Italian monuments of the Cybele's cult drawn up by Vermaseren in the *CCCA* III-IV (cf. also *CCCA* VII) from which it appears that there are numerous types of Attis *tristis*. Amongst the dedications made to deities in memory of the deceased in the region of Aquileia one is to the *Mater Deum Magna* (*CIL* V, 520, from Trieste). Cf. M. J. Vermaseren, *CCCA* IV, 98 n° 244, Pl. XCIX.

[39] For Britain cf. E.-J. Harris, *The Oriental Cults in Roman Britain*, Leiden 1965 (EPRO 6), 103f., Pl. XX, 2. For Spain, H. Graillot, *op. cit.*, 474f.; A. García y Bellido, *Les religions orientales dans l'Espagne romaine*, Leiden 1967 (EPRO 5), 56-59; Moesia: *CIL* III, 14544; Graillot, *op. cit.*, 481f.; Dacia: *CIL* III, 1243; 1336; 1496; 1552; Graillot, *ibid.*, 484; G. Florescu, "I monumenti funerari romani della 'Dacia superior' ", *EphD* IV (1930), 72-148; Pannonia: *CIL* III, 11076; 4278; 4391; Graillot, *ibid.*, 486f.; Noricum: *CIL* III, 5680; 5655; Graillot, *ibid.*, 487f.; Dalmatia: *CIL* III 14219, 17; Graillot, *ibid.*, 491-493.

bears the image of a character in Phrygian dress usually identified as Attis,[40] seems to have the same value. It is the type of the so-called *Attis tristis*[41] which, rather than a prospect of happiness in the afterlife, stresses the moment of grief and mourning. The situation of the deceased is thus apparently connected with that aspect of suffering and of death which characterises to a large extent the vicissitude of the young Phrygian shepherd.[42]

An analogous significance seems to be assumed by the representation of Attis as winter in some sarcophagi decorated with the symbols of the four seasons.[43] The salient characteristic of the figure is the moment of disappearance and concealment, connected with the "sleep" of the vegetation in the winter season.

The image of Attis in the usual attitudes of grief is accompanied, in a figurative stele from Cologne, by that of Dionysus. It expresses the component of mourning and death in a context centred on the theme of the disappearance and seasonal return of vegetation and fertility.[44]

---

[40] On the iconographical problem of the funerary "Attis", to whom B. Schröder attributed an exclusively decorative character (*BJ* CVIII, 1903, 75; against: S. A. Strong, *JRS* I, 1911, 17 and n. 1; H. Lehner, "Orientalische Mysterienkulte im römischen Rheinland", *BJ* CXXIX, 1924, 58ff.; F. Cumont, *Les religions orientales*, 226 n. 49), see now E. Will, *Le relief cultuel gréco-romain*, Paris 1955, 198-204.

[41] Cf. M. J. Vermaseren, *The Legend of Attis*, 39-59, where he also examines the type of the young dancer, often winged, to whom the epithet of *hilaris* is given. For the iconography of Attis see not only J. D. Leipoldt's brief notes (*Die Religionen in der Umwelt des Urchristentums*, Leipzig-Erlangen 1962 (Bilderatlas zur Religionsgeschichte 9-11), XVI-XX), but also S. Karwiese's unpublished dissertation (*Attis in der antiken Kunst*, Wien 1967). Karwiese has partially published the results of his research in two successive articles on the theme of Attis "chained" ("Der gefesselte Attis", *Festschrift für Fritz Eichler zum achtzigsten Geburtstag dargebracht vom Oesterreichischen Archäologischen Institut*, Wien 1967, 82-95) and Attis "dead" ("Der tote Attis", *JÖAI* L, 1968-1971, 50-62).

[42] According to Boyancé ("Funus acerbus", *REA* LIV, 1952, 275-289, repr. in *Études sur la religion romaine*, cit., 73-89), the iconographical motif of Attis *tristis* in funerary monuments has a religious and not a purely decorative character. Rather than a specific connection with the religion of Cybele, however, it expresses the theme of the ἄωρος, the destiny of the prematurely deceased. It is in this sense that Boyancé interprets the presence of four images of Attis *tristis* in the central hall of the Basilica of Porta Maggiore where the abduction of Ganymedes is depicted (Vermaseren *CCCA* III, 97f. n° 344, Pls. CCII-CCV, where a bibliography is given).

For a different interpretation of this complex representation in relation to Attis, also identified with the winged figure with *anaxirides* who carries Ganymedes to heaven, cf. M. J. Vermaseren, *Cybele and Attis*, cit., 55-57. F. L. Bastet, art. cit., 202 had also expressed himself along these lines. According to Turcan, on the other hand, the figure repeated in the four corners of the vault is Ganymedes himself, whose abduction is evoked in the centre of the scene ("Masques corniers d'orientaux: Attis, Ganymède ou Arimaspes?", *Mélanges de Philosophie, de Littérature et d'Histoire ancienne offerts à Pierre Boyancé*, Roma 1974, 722f.).

[43] Cf. G. M. Hanfmann, *The Season Sarcophagus in Dumbarton Oaks*, vols. I-II, Cambridge 1951; M. J. Vermaseren, *The Legend of Attis*, 39 n. 9, Pl. XXIV; *CCCA* III, 86f. n° 315, Pl. CLXXII.

[44] G. Ristow, "Zur Eschatologie auf Denkmälern synkretistisch-orientalischer Mysterienkulte in Köln", *KJb* IX (1967-68), 107f.

Needless to say this aspect does not exhaust the significance of his personality and cult. Attis, as we saw earlier, is subject, in his quality of "mystic god", to a vicissitude characterised by the convergence and the typical alternation of the moment of grief and the moment of joy, of disappearance and "presence". This explains why, in the figurative documents, the image of Attis *tristis* alternates with that of Attis *hilaris* and the "winter" symbology of the Phrygian god with the spring one.

In this context I should mention, together with Vermaseren, a representation of Attis as spring on a Roman sarcophagus.[45]

All I wish to do is to stress, in connection with the funerary theme, that the moment of mourning in the vicissitude of Attis constantly takes precedence over the joyful moment of the "return". There is little room, however, for the hypothesis of a specific link of that same theme with ultimate positive eschatological prospects.

This interpretation of the iconographical theme of the funerary Attis[46] would seem to be confirmed by a Roman metrical inscription pertaining to the Phrygian Hector who appears as an adept of Cybele and Attis. While this document emphasises the basically sad tone of the cult,[47] it also recalls the past joys of earthly life which are contrasted with the vision of the *cineres* as an object of lamentation. There is no prospect of happiness in the hereafter, however.

Van Doren believes that the character mentioned in this inscription is a Gallus and he consequently defines him as an "initiate" of the highest grade.[48] The absence of any reference to a life of bliss in the hereafter, on the other hand, leads him to conclude, in contradiction with his definition of the character, that the Phrygian cult of the 1st century A.D. had not yet assumed the form of the "mysteries". For he believes that these consisted essentially in the promise of eschatological happiness.

Without repeating what has already been said about the special position of the category of the Galli in the cult of Cybele we should simply note that, while the character's quality of sacred eunuch cannot be deduced from the inscription in question,[49] it does evoke a cult with clearly funereal and doleful

---

[45] *The Legend of Attis, loc. cit.*

[46] Along the same lines see also A. D. Nock, "Cremation and Burial in the Roman Empire, 6. The Mystery Religions and the Afterlife", *HThR* XXV (1932), 344-357 repr. in *Essays*, vol. I, 296-305.

[47] *CIL* VI, 10098 = H. Hepding, *op. cit.*, 91 n° 43: "*Qui colitis Cybelen et qui Phryga plangitis Attin,/ dum vacat et tacita Dinduma nocte silent,/ flete meos cineres: non est alienus in illis/ Hector, et hoc tumulo Mygdonis umbra tegor,/ ille ego qui magni parvus cognominis heres,/ corpore in exiguo res numerosa fui,/ flectere doctus equos, nitida certare palaestra,/ ferre iocos, astu fallere, nosse fidem./ At tibi dent superi, quantum, Domitilla, mereris/ quae facis, exigua ne iaceamus humo*".

[48] M. van Doren, "L'évolution des mystères phrygiens à Rome", *AC* XXII (1953), 79-88.

[49] Cf. Ch. Picard, "Le phrygien Hector était-il Galle de Cybèle?", *RA* XLIII (1954), 80-82.

features, in which Attis is the object of a ritual "dirge". The worshipper who has participated in this cult does not seem to expect anything after death other than the compassionate memory of those who were his companions in the celebration of the rite. No consolatory prospect illuminates his condition in the "shadow" of the grave which covers him.

A similar situation seems to emerge from another funerary inscription (3rd century A.D.), made for a child termed ἱερεύς of various deities, amongst whom, in addition to the *Bona Dea*, Dionysus and *Hermes Hegemonios*, appears the Μήτηρ θεῶν.[50] The child has piously performed the sacred "mysteries" of all these deities.[51] But, apart from this, there is not a word of hope to compensate for the premature death of the child who has abandoned "the sweet light of the sun"; all we have is the painful certainty that "nobody can loosen the thread of the Moirae".[52]

Nor is there any allusion to prospects in the hereafter in two funeral odes in the Anthologia Palatina, both written in memory of women, devotees of Cybele. The first, composed by Philodemus, a contemporary of Cicero,[53] recalls the courtesan Thryphera, assiduous in the orgiastic cult of the Mother of the Gods;[54] the second, by Thyillos, evokes the enthusiastic atmosphere of that cult by describing Aristiones in the act of dancing to the sound of the crotala and the flute, by the light of the torches.[55] Now that the furies (μανίαι) of the *orgia* and of the nightly vigils (παννυχίδες) are over, there remains the bitter reality of the tomb, beyond which the funeral epitaph holds out no eschatological hope.

If silence can be eloquent, it certainly is in the case of the documents cited. They all refer to adepts of Cybele and are all equally oblivious to special benefits in the future life guaranteed by such a religious status.

In documenting the existence of positive eschatological prospects in the Phrygian cult Cumont has provided another funerary inscription, of which he quotes a line which would seem to connect the practice of the cult with the

---

[50] *CIG* 6206 = Kaibel, *Epigr. graec.*, 238f. n° 588.

[51] *Ibid.*, line 4: "τούτοις ἐκτελέσας μυστήρια πάντοτε σεμνῶς".

[52] *Ibid.*, line 8: "οὐδεὶς γὰρ δύναται μοιρ[ῶν] μίτον ἐξαναλῦσαι". We know, however, that in this late period participation in the Dionysiac mysteries guaranteed certain eschatological prospects and, in particular, that the precocious initiation of children tended to ensure for them a better lot in the hereafter in the event of their dying premature. Cf. Plutarch, *Cons. ad uxor.* 10, 611 D. F. Cumont, *Lux Perpetua*, 250-258.

[53] *Anth. Pal.* VII, 222 ed. P. Waltz, Paris 1960², 152. Cf. P. Foucart, *Des associations religieuses*, cit., 158f.

[54] *Ibid.*, line 3f.: "ἣ καλύβη καὶ δοῦπος ἐνέπρεπεν, ἣ φιλοπαίγμων/στωμυλίη, Μήτηρ ἢν ἐφίλησε θεῶν".

[55] *Anth. Pal.* VII, 223 ed. P. Waltz 152f.: "Ἡ κροτάλοις ὀρχηστρὶς Ἀρίστιον, ἡ περὶ πεύκαις/καὶ Κυβέλῃ πλοκάμους ῥῖψαι ἐπισταμένη, ἡ λωτῷ κερόεντι φορουμένη" (lines 1-3).

certainty of a happy destiny in the hereafter: *"sacra cymbala concrepui, securus morte quiesco"*.[56]

Nevertheless a direct examination of the epigraph brings to light various difficulties which advise a greater caution in drawing conclusions. The expression cited by Cumont, for one thing, is not to be found in the text in the form which he adopts but is the result of a "fusion" of elements which are actually separated in the text.

The deceased tells the passer-by to pause and describes to him his principal occupations during his lifetime: he was an expert singer and horn player, and he was particularly proficient in making the "sacred cymbals" resound.[57] There follow some very incomplete lines in which seem to contain exhortations and invocations to the living, and the inscription concludes with the hope that the character will be received by *Dis Pater* in the infernal regions.[58]

We are therefore dealing with the usual prospect of a dark and subterranean afterlife, without there being any indication of a special destiny reserved for the deceased in virtue of his earthly activities and in particular of his skill in the use of the *sacra cymbala* which could show him to be a devotee of the *Mater*.[59]

After having established the uselessness of grieving over death, the common lot of mankind, the character concludes his address with a statement of resignation and serenity: *"nihil doleo nec deest, (s)ecur(us) morte quiesco"*.[60] The "rest" and certainty which the deceased enjoys are thus presented not so much in relation to a special condition of bliss connected with the practice of a "salvific" cult, but as the absence of the needs and troubles typical of earthly life. He has now crossed the threshold which awaits every man and beyond which, as so many funerary epigraphs testify, there lies an eternal *quies*.[61]

---

[56] *Lux Perpetua*, 264 n. 5. The epigraph is quoted to support the claim that the eschatology of the Magi of Asia Minor modified the eschatological doctrines of the mysteries of Cybele. The author concludes: "C'est au ciel, enseignèrent désormais ceux-ci, dans l'éther lumineux, au milieu des astres que montent les âmes pieuses, et le monde souterrain n'est plus que le séjour des réprouvés". Now, it is precisely in the infernal region that the character in our inscription thinks he is going to be received by *Dis Pater*.

[57] F. Bücheler, *Carmina latina epigraphica*, Leipzig 1895, vol. I, 245f. n° 513, vv. 5-7: "*Dum vixi, [multi]s (lud)is cantavi ceraules/ Iam doctus no[t]us et noctib(us) pervigilavi./ Ut miro ingenio sacr(a) cymbal(a) concrepui*".

[58] "*Sit precor ut mo[llis]...dico vale.../Parcite...ri...miseri/Ad man[es]...r...no...in terr[a].../ Ut me infern(as) Stygias Dis pater accipia[t]...*" (vv. 8-11).

[59] This hypothesis, moreover, cannot be considered as the only valid one for the obvious reason that those musical instruments were also used in other cults, like the Dionysiac one.

[60] *Ibid.*, v. 14; cf. v. 12f.: "*Lamenta quid prosunt?.../ Iam prid[em]... et vos veniet(is) ibidem*".

[61] Cf., for example, F. Bücheler, *Carm. lat. epigr.*, 246 n° 514 in which the deceased, after having said that he is now deprived of light, clearly defines the sense of "quiet" which he enjoys in death: "*Regna infra caeli fraudatus luce quiesco,/ Iam secura quies, nullum iam vitae periculum*".

In spite of the interpretative efforts of various scholars[62] the identification of the *sanctissima mater* in a Roman inscription whom the deceased asks to "relieve" him *a finibus Tartariis*[63] remains uncertain. We do not have sufficient elements on which to base the hypothesis that the *mater* here invoked is, as has been claimed,[64] the Phrygian Great Mother, who would thus have the faculty of removing man from the gloom of Hades and of offering him a positive, soteriological prospect.

I also regard the *cognomina* of certain devotees of Cybele in Gaul as too fragile an indication of "eschatological hopes",[65] although we have such words as *Anthus*,[66] *Quietus*,[67] *Carpus*[68] and *Hilarius*[69] which do indeed display a far from negligeable religious significance.

Other sources, too, provide indications which suggest an eschatological possibility in the expectations of the worshippers of Cybele and Attis, even if it is not possible to establish a precise relationship between them and one or other of the two forms of the cult of Cybele.

The Elysium described by Propertius as a blessed place where "the sonorous harp makes music, and the turbaned choirs dance to the Lydian lyre and to the cymbals of Cybele"[70] can appear as an essentially poetic image.

---

[62] Cf. R. Egger, "Sanctissima Mater", *Studi in onore di Aristide Calderini e Roberto Paribeni*, Milano 1956, 239-250 where he gives a full bibliography. The inscription concerns a man and wife who died prematurely and is written in the form of a dialogue.

[63] The editor has dated the epigraph in the mid-1st century A.D. (G. Bendinelli, "Roma, Via Labicana, Titoli sepolcrali di colombario dai pressi della 'Marranella' ", *NSc*, S.V, XX, 1923, 357-359 with plates). The expression cited is in line 5f.: *"si quicquam pietatis habes, sanctissima mater,/ subleva me abiectum a finibus Tartariis!"* According to the interpretation of L. Wickert, "Ein neues lateinische Grabgedicht", *Hermes* LXI (1926), 448-458, the deceased is here addressing his own mother.

[64] Cf. M. Lechantin De Gubernatis, "Il titolo sepolcrale metrico di Via Labicana", *BFC* XXXII (1925), 38-43. Although A. Annaratone attributes the inscription to a devotee of Cybele too, he sees the *sanctissima mater* not as the goddess herself but as the priestess of the community to which the deceased belonged ("Sulla nuova iscrizione metrica di Via Labicana", *Athenaeum*, n.s. IV, 1926, 103-111).

[65] This is also the conclusion reached by A. Audin and Y. Burnand in a study on the funerary epigraphs of Lyons ("Alla ricerca delle tracce di cristianesimo sulle tombe di Lione prima della pace delle Chiesa", *RivArch* XXXV, 1959, 51-70, esp. 53-55).

[66] *CIL* XIII, 1754 = R. Duthoy, *op. cit.*, 51f. n° 129. It is a priest participating in a taurobolium.

[67] *CIL* XIII, 2300. The *cognomen* in question alludes to the spiritual "peace", enjoyed by a member of a Cybele's confraternity (A. Audin-Y. Burnand, art. cit., 54).

[68] *CIL* XIII, 1751: the author is an *L. Aemilius Carpus*, dendrophorus and *sevir augustalis*. A *Messorius Florus* also belongs to a Cybele's community whose funerary epitaph is adorned with a palm, interpreted by scholars as the symbol of salvation in the hereafter (*ibid.*, 55 and 58).

[69] On the connection of this *cognomen* with the *Hilaria* cf. J. Hatt, *La tombe gallo-romaine. Recherches sur les inscriptions et les monuments funéraires gallo-romains des trois premiers siècles de notre ère*, Paris 1951, 43-62 where other *cognomina* connected with the Phrygian cult are also examined.

[70] *Eleg.* IV, 7, 59-62: *"Ecce coronato pars altera lapsa phaselo,/ mulcet ubi Elysias aura beata rosas,/ qua numerosa fides quaque aera rotunda Cybelles/ mitratisque sonant Lydia plectra choris"* (tr. by G. Lipparini, Bologna 1958, 235). Cf. F. Cumont, *Recherches sur le symbolisme funéraire des Romains*, Paris 1942, 507 (Add. 284 and 291).

What does reveal eschatological hopes connected with the practice of the cult of Cybele, on the other hand, is the representation of the myth of Alcestis and Admetus which, together with the symbols typical of that cult, adorns the sarcophagus of *C. Iunius Euhodus* and *Metilia Acte*, the latter a priestess of the Great Mother of the gods of the Colony of Ostia in the Antonine period.[71]

According to Cumont[72] the *vates frugeae matris* whose funerary inscription, which links him with his wife, proclaims the idea of the celestial immortality of the soul,[73] is a priest of the Phrygian goddess. We know, however, that this idea was widespread in late Antiquity. It arose as the result of the conjunction of Pythagorean speculations and astrological beliefs, and found acceptance in numerous religious circles.[74] If Cumont's interpretation is correct, therefore, we can only conclude that a devotee of the Great Mother accepted the notion of the celestial origin of the soul and of its return to the upper spheres from which it had descended,[75] without this implying a specific pertinence of this concept to the religious milieu of Cybele as such.

It is along these lines, moreover, that we should interpret the statement in the epigraph of a funerary cippus adorned with the image of Attis *tristis*: *"corpus habent cineres, animam sacer abstulit aer"*.[76]

On the other hand the possible connection of Attis with the idea of a celestial immortality of the soul could legitimately be situated in the process of

---

[71] C. Robert, *Die Antiken Sarkophag-Reliefs*, vol. III, 1, Berlin 1897, 31-34 n° 26, Pl. VII, 26. Two heads of a boy with Phrygian cap (Attis) are carved on the corners of the lid showing cymbals, flutes, the *pedum* and the tympanum, as well as two large lighted torches. Cf. T. Brennecke, *Kopf und Maske. Untersuchungen zu den Akroteren an Sarkophagdeckeln*, Inaugural Dissertation d.Philosoph.-Fakultät d. Freien Universität, Berlin 1970, 21-24; R. Turcan, *Les sarcophages romains à représentations dionysiaques*, cit., 44, 201f.; M. J. Vermaseren, *CCCA* III, 134f. n° 423, Pl. CCLXVII. For the eschatological symbolism of the myth of Alcestis and Admetus represented there see F. Cumont, *Symbolisme*, 30 n. 4. According to Turcan this is the only case in which the youthful masks with Phrygian cap which often adorn the corners of the lids of Roman sarcophagi can definitely be identified as images of Attis. In numerous other monuments, for which such an identification has been suggested, the general iconographical context points to different interpretations ("Masques corniers d'orientaux", cit., 724ff. and fig. 1).

[72] Art. cit., *RA* VI (1917), 421 n. 2; Id., *Symbolisme*, 88-90. The image of the Dioscuri decorating the sarcophagus together with the figure of a serpent would confirm the belief in a blissful immortality of a celestial nature expressed in the inscription. Cf. also F. Altheim, *Römische Religionsgeschichte. II. Von der Gründung des kapitolinischen Tempels bis zum Aufkommen der Alleinherrschaft*, Berlin-Leipzig 1932, 147.

[73] *CIL* VI, 13528. Mommsen already identified the character as a priest of the Great Mother. Against: F. Bücheler, *Carm. lat. epigr.*, 752f. n° 1559.

[74] Cf. F. Cumont, *Lux Perpetua*, 142-188. For the introduction of the idea of celestial immortality in the cult of Cybele cf. *ibid.*, 264.

[75] Cf. lines 1-3: *"Bassa vatis, quae Laberi coniuga hoc alto sinu/ Frugeae matris quiescit, moribus priscis nurus;/ animus sanctus cum marito, si anima caelo reddita est"*. There follow various considerations on the eternal celebration of the wedding between the couple and then we read: *"Hic corpus vatis Laberi. Nam spiritus ivit/ illuc, unde ortus; quaeritur fontem animae./ Quod fueram, non sum; sed rursus ero, quod modo non sum;/ ortus et occasus, vitaque morsque itid(em) est"* (lines 13-16).

[76] *CIL* III, 6384 = H. Hepding, *op. cit.*, 86 n° 25.

profound transformation experienced by Cybele's young paredros who, from a figure with chthonic and vegetal traits in the 3rd-4th century A.D., assumed, like the Great Mother herself,[77] the features of a cosmic power with clearly marked astral connotations. One such feature, expressed figuratively in the famous image of the *Attideion* of Ostia which shows the Phrygian god with a half-moon and radiate crown,[78] is amply elaborated in the mysteriosophic interpretations of a Julian and a Sallustius, as well as in the "solar" one of Macrobius. The epithet of *Menotyrannos*, which seems to imply an identification with the lunar deity Men, and the qualification of *invictus* which sometimes accompanies it,[79] also stresses the transformation in an astral and cosmic sense of the deity in question.[80]

Cumont, analysing the theme of the celestial sojourn of the soul and above all the notion of the moon as the dwelling place of the deceased, noted that in some sepulchral monuments of Gaul the crescent moon is often surmounted by a pine cone;[81] in some cases it is this latter object which substitutes the astral symbol.[82]

---

[77] Cf. H. Graillot, *op. cit.*, 194-208; F. Chapouthier, "Cybèle et le tympanon étoilé", *Mélanges Syriens offerts à M. Dussaud*, t. II, Paris 1939, 723-728.

[78] Cf. J. Leipoldt, "Eine römische Attis figur", ΑΓΓΕΛΟΣ II (1926), 51f. and fig.; R. Calza, *Sculture rinvenute nel santuario*, cit., 216f. n° 8, fig. 17; F. Cumont, *Les religions orientales*, Pl. IV, 1; M. Floriani Squarciapino, *I culti orientali ad Ostia*, 10; M. J. Vermaseren, *Cybele and Attis*, fig. 44; Id., *CCCA* III, 123 n° 394, Pl. CCXLIV. The sculpture is usually dated in the time of Hadrian. This would imply a greater antiquity for the "cosmic" interpretation of the Phrygian god.

[79] *IGSI* 913 = H. Hepding, *op. cit.*, 82 n° 14; *CIL* VI, 499-500 = *ibid.*, 86f. nos. 28-29; *CIL* VI, 508 = *ibid.*, 89 n° 36; *CIL* VI, 511-512 = *ibid.*, 89f. nos. 38-39. Cf. H. Graillot, *op. cit.*, 208-222.

[80] The lunar aspect of Attis is also evoked in a cippus from the Isola sacra, which bears a relief of a Phrygian cap surmounted by the half moon and star between two torches. Cf. F. Cumont, *Symbolisme*, 207f. and fig. 38; M. Floriani Squarciapino, *op. cit.*, 10 n. 2 and Pl. IV, 6. On the celestial and astral symbolism of the pileus of Attis, elaborated in the works of Julian and Sallust, cf. R. Turcan, "L'aigle du pileus", *Hommages Vermaseren*, vol. III, 1281-1292, Pls. CCLIII-CCLVIII.

For the raising of Attis to the rank of highest cosmic power see the Roman taurobolic altar (370 A.D.) which invokes him as ὕψιστος καὶ συνέχων τὸ πᾶν (*IGSI* 1018 = *CIL* VI, 509 in H. Hepding, *op. cit.*, 82f. n° 15). The quadriga of the Mother of the Gods with Attis is represented in a vast cosmic setting in the famous patera of Parabiago (cf. A. Levi, *La patera d'argento di Parabiago*, Roma 1935; C. Albizzati, "La lanx di Parabiago e i testi orfici", *Athenaeum*, N.S. XV, 1937, 187-198, and most recently M. J. Vermaseren, *CCCA* IV, 107ff. n° 268, Pl. CVII with bibliography). A similar representation is in some contorniates of the 4th-5th century A.D. (cf. A. Alföldi, *op. cit.*, 107 nos. 36-37, Taf. VII, 11; IX, 3 and XV, 7). For the strongly Hellenized character of this representation and of other Cybele's monuments see C. Schneider, "Die griechischen Grundlagen der hellenistischen Religionsgeschichte", *ARW* XXXVI (1939), 306-308. Finally, we should recall the definition of Attis as ποιμὴν λευκῶν ἄστρων in the hymn known to the Naassenes (Hippolytus, *Philos.*, V, 9 in H. Hepding, *op. cit.*, 35), on which see T. Wolbergs, *op. cit.*, 76-82.

[81] *Symbolisme*, 219 n° 14, Pl. XVII, 4.

[82] *Ibid.*, nos. 11, 13, 16, 29a, 28; Pl. XVII, 2.

He went on to attribute the same meaning to the two symbols and recognised that the pine cone recurs in funeral art as the symbol of immortality. Attis' association with the pine-tree led him to establish a specific relationship between that symbolism and the religion of Cybele, and to conclude that it is probably to this religion that we can attribute the transformation of the indigenous beliefs of Gaul concerning the relationship of the soul of the deceased with the moon. This, too, would have determined the spread of the motif of the pine cone in the sepulchral monuments in Gaul.[83]

Cumont's arguments were accepted by Boyancé[84] and by Picard[85] who, in the light of the symbolism in question, analyses numerous new documents from the Balkans and from Gaul itself in which, besides the theme of the pine-tree, we get that of the cone.

If, in these monuments, the relationship with Attis and more generally with the cult of Cybele is unquestionable, however, we cannot say with any certainty that the symbolism of the pine cone can always be traced back to that cult, especially when there is no explicit evidence. We know, of course, that the pine cone also recurs in the figurative monuments relating to Sabazius[86] and to Men,[87] as well as in the Dionysiac ones.[88]

Besides, as Robert emphasises in connection with an Anatolian funerary monument containing a deprecatory formula of clearly Jewish origin,[89] there is no necessary connection between the pine cone and the cult of Attis, since it is such a widespread symbol in funerary art.[90]

A precise reference to the idea of a blessed immortality, guaranteed by Cybele to Attis and also promised to all the worshippers, has been detected in the iconographical motif of the bough, sometimes in the hand of the Great Mother and sometimes carried by the members of her priesthood.[91]

---

[83] *Ibid.*, 220f.

[84] Note to F. Delage, "Ovoïdes gallo-romains", *Gallia* XI (1953), 25-37, *ibid.*, 37-39.

[85] "Sur quelques monuments nouveaux," cit., 1-23. Cf. also M. Renard, "Attis-pilier de Clavier-Vervoz et d'ailleurs", *BAB* 5e S., t. LXI (1975), 14-29, Pls. I-XI, who insists on the eschatological value of the symbolism of the pine cone, an image of the "promise of immortality" bestowed on the devotees of Attis.

[86] See, for example, the plaques of Berlin and Ampurias and other documents published by Ch. Picard, *Sabazios, dieu thraco-phrygien*, cit., *passim*.

[87] Cf. Lane, *CMRDM* vol. I, n° 64 Pl. XXVI; n° 102 Pl. XLV; n° 104 Pl. XLVI; n° 112 Pl. XLIX; n° 123 Pl. LVIII; nos. 137-138 Pls. LXII-LXIII etc.

[88] See, for example, a Hellenistic relief in M. P. Nilsson, *The Dionysiac Mysteries*, 31 and fig. 5; an amphora in Florence, *ibid.*, fig. 14, where we get the pine-tree with many cones, and the famous sarcophagus of Villa Medici (*ibid.*, fig. 20b).

[89] L. Robert, "Inscriptions mal classées. 4. Autel funéraire à Thyatire", *Hellenica* X (1955), 247-256, Pls. XXXII-XXXIV.

[90] For the presence of pine cones in tombs see also D. Wortmann, "Ein Pinienzapfen aus einem Bleisarg von Lommersum-Bodenheim, Kreis Euskirchen", *BJ* CLXX (1970), 252-266, who connects this symbolism with the cult of the Great Mother.

[91] H. Seyring, "Le rameau mystique", *AJA* XLVIII (1944), 20-25. On the eschatological symbolism of the bough brought by the mystai to Eleusis and in other mystic cults see, by the same author, "Quatre cultes de Thasos", *BCH* LI (1927), 202-207.

Amongst the monuments in which this symbol recurs, accompanied in some cases by the poppy or the pomegranate, or substituted by them,[92] we have a clay lamp from Rome, in which the goddess hands a leafy bough to Attis,[93] an altar in London which shows the goddess with a basket full of fruit and a large branch,[94] the large fresco of Via dell'Abbondanza in Pompeii[95] and various Roman coins with the figure of Cybele.[96]

The bough appears, together with the pomegranate, in the portrait of the Archigallus from Ostia[97] and in that of the Gallus of the Capitoline Museum.[98] It is also carried by the priestesses standing by the effigy of the goddess in the procession represented in the painting from Pompeii mentioned above.[99] Finally, a Roman sarcophagus shows a small Attis standing next to Cybele who is watching the contest between Apollo and Marsyas and holds in her right hand a large pine branch.[100]

---

[92] Cf. H. Graillot, *op. cit.*, 202 and Pl. III. The author quotes the bronze diptych of Berlin which shows on one face Cybele between Hermes and Attis; the latter and the goddess hold a flower in their hand (cf. M. J. Vermaseren, *CCCA* III, 82 n° 304, Pls. CLXVIII-CLXIX). There is also a terracotta lamp from Rome with a similar representation (*CCCA* III, 187f. n° 316, Pl. CLXXXIII).

[93] H. Seyring, art. cit., 23f. and fig. 2; M. J. Vermaseren, *The Legend of Attis*, 44f., Pl. XXV, 1; *CCCA* III, 90 n° 324, Pl. CXC.

[94] Cf. above p. 76 n. 69.

[95] V. Spinazzola, *op. cit.*, vol. I, 223-242, figs. 250-251, Pl. XIV; M. J. Vermaseren, *CCCA* IV, 17ff. n° 42, Pls. XI-XVII. Cf. also Tran Tam Tinh, "Les problèmes du culte de Cybèle et d'Attis à Pompei", B. Andreae-H. Kyrieleis (eds.), *Neue Forschungen in Pompeji und den anderen von Vesuvausbruch 79 n.Chr. verschütteten Städten*, Recklinghausen 1975, 279-283, figs. 245-257.

[96] Cf. the coins of Julia Domna, Caracalla and Julia Soaemias in H. Cohen, *Description historique des monnaies frappées sous l'Empire Romain, communément appellées Médailles Impériales*, vol. IV, Paris 1884², 114f., nos. 116-120; 115f. nos. 122-129; 117 n° 141; 153 n° 98 (where the goddess is identified as *Caelestis*); 388 nos. 4-5. Also in the fine piece of Faustina *senior* Cybele, accompanied by Attis, is represented with a large flowery bough on her left arm (*ibid.*, II, 439 n° 306; F. Gnecchi, *I medaglioni romani*, Milano 1912, vol. II, 25 n° 8, Pl. 57, 4). Cf. M. J. Vermaseren, *The Legend of Attis*, cit., 25 and Pl. XIV, 1; Id., *Cybele and Attis*, 75 and fig. 28. The type recurs in the coins of Faustina *iunior* (H. Cohen, *op. cit.*, vol. III, 164 n° 295; F. Gnecchi, *op. cit.*, 41 n° 21, Pl. 68, 7) and of Lucilla (H. Cohen, *op. cit.*, vol. III, 223 n° 101; F. Gnecchi, *op. cit.*, 50 n° 8, Pl. 76, 5). For the presence of Cybele in Roman coins see M. Bieber, art. cit., 29-40. Cf. now R. Turcan, *Numismatique romaine du culte métroaque* (EPRO 97), Leiden 1983.

[97] Cf. above p. 75, n. 68; F. Cumont, *Symbolisme*, 388-391 who sees in the pine branch an "emblem of immortality" and establishes a parallelism with Plutarch's report about the god who falls asleep in the winter and awakens in the summer (*De Iside* 69). He concludes that "the devotee, like Attis, goes to sleep to reawaken to a new life; his death is a transitory sleep which must be followed by a glorious reawakening. The burial of the recumbent priest corresponds to this eschatological concept". It seems to me, however, that the theme of the deceased lying on the sarcophagus is too common an iconographical motif to permit conclusions of this type.

[98] F. Cumont, *Les religions orientales*, Pl. II, 1; Vermaseren, *CCCA* III, 152f. n° 466, Pls. CCXCVI-CCXCVII.

[99] V. Spinazzola, *op. cit., loc. cit.*, figs. 264-265.

[100] C. Robert, *op. cit.*, vol. III, 2, Berlin 1904, 259f. n° 207, Pl. LXVII; Vermaseren, *CCCA* III, 95 n° 338, Pl. CXCVIII.

A comparison with the celebrated episode in Virgil of Aeneas' *descensus* into the infernal regions with the aid of the Sibyl's "golden bough" which also guarantees the hero's return to earth[101] and with the symbology of the bough in the Eleusinian mysteries, as illustrated by Servius,[102] has led scholars to attribute an analogous "mystic" significance to the flowery branch which appears in the monuments of Cybele's cult.[103] A pledge of the salvation from Hades procured by the goddess for Attis, it is also an image of the guarantees bestowed on the worshippers for their future life.

A further indication of eschatological prospects in the cult of Cybele could be provided by the title of *collegium salutare* adopted by the association of dendrophoroi in an inscription from *Bovillae* of the time of Antoninus Pius.[104] Carcopino believes that the attribute *salutare* expresses the idea of salvation in the life to come guaranteed by the Mother of the Gods, with whose cult the college of the dendrophoroi was closely connected.[105]

As the same scholar observes, however, the denomination of *collegium salutare* was commonly used to designate the most varied religious communities, besides being typical of funerary associations. It is therefore difficult to decide whether the title in question has assumed, in the context of Cybele's religion, the specific eschatological significance which Carcopino attributes to it or whether, according to its more commonly accepted meaning, it expresses, rather, that guarantee of well-being and security in the present life which the membership of a community with both a professional and a religious character could offer to its members.

We should also mention, moreover, the dedication made by *C. Antonius Eutyches archidendroph(orus)* to Attis *pro salute sua.*[106] Here too it is impossible to know the specific meaning of the *salus* which the character expected from his divine protector.

From the observations made hitherto it emerges clearly that the promise of blessed immortality, so frequently indicated as one of the fundamental elements of the cult of Cybele, does not seem to have had that importance or

---

[101] *Aeneid* VI, 136-636.

[102] Servius, *Ad Aen.* VI, 136. For the custom of the Eleusinian *mystai* of carrying a bough we can also quote, with Seyring, the famous ex-voto of Niinnion (cf. G. E. Mylonas, *op. cit.*, 213-221 and fig. 88). See also M. P. Nilsson, *Geschichte*, vol. I², 126 who records the use of boughs in the mysteries, and above all in those of the Dionysiac cult, as we see from a scholium to Aristophanes (*Schol. in Equites* v. 408) where a fragment of Xenophanes is quoted (fr. 17 Diels⁸). Cf. Suidas, *Lex.* s.v. βάκχος; Hesychius, *Lex.* s.v. βάκχος ... κλάδος ὁ ἐν ταῖς τελεταῖς and *Etym. Magnum* 185, 13f.

[103] Seyring, art. cit., 23f.

[104] R. Paribeni, "Marino. Rinvenimenti nell'area dell'antica Bovillae", *NSc*, Ser. VI, II (1926), 206-209 and fig. 1.

[105] J. Carcopino, "Note sur une inscription métroaque récemment découverte", *RendPontAcc* S. III, IV (1925-26), 231-246.

[106] *CIL* III, 763 = Dessau, *ILS* 4116: from Tomis.

that central position usually attributed to it without sufficient evidence. In fact we are faced with a series of documents whose significance is ambiguous to say the least, since it is always possible to have reservations about the specifically eschatological character of the symbolism of the funerary monuments or even, in some cases, about their pertinence to the Mother's milieu. In this sense the epigraph discussed above is emblematic—the deceased rests "securely" in death and recalls having made the sacred cymbals resound, a statement which seems to evoke the better known manifestations of the mystic-orgiastic cult of Cybele, although we cannot make any definite claims for a specific relationship between the practice of such a cult and the "quiet" enjoyed by man in death.

Equally useless for our purpose is the reference to the chthonic quality of the Great Goddess, seen as the Mother Earth from whom every life issues only to return to her in the end. This notion, which has frequently been called upon to confirm the presence of eschatological hopes in the cult of Cybele[107] and which, in the ancient sources, finds its clearest exemplification in the *Precatio Terrae*,[108] actually expresses an essentially immanent and cyclical vision in which there is no place for that beatific survival supposed to constitute the benefit offered by participation in the cult of the Great Mother. Needless to say, a notion such as that of Mother Earth or of a maternal divinity bestowing life is, in itself, far too vague. By referring to generic, or even to psychological classificatory schemes, moreover, it removes from the religious context in question that specificity expressed in its complex history, its myths and the procedure of its cult which characterises it as an object of historical research.

Having said this, however, we must not go to the opposite extreme and deny the existence of an eschatological component in the cult of Cybele, the outlines of which should, rather, be specified in relation to the various aspects of the cult and in the broader picture of the "soteriology" expressed in it,

---

[107] Cf., for example, H. Graillot, *op. cit.*, 16; 200-208; F. Cumont, *Lux Perpetua*, 263-264.

[108] A. Riese, *Anthologia Latina*, Leipzig 1894, vol. I², 27f., vv. 10-16: "*Itemque, cum vis, hilarem promittis diem;/ alimenta vitae tribuis perpetua fide/ et, cum recesserit anima, in te refugimus./ Ita, quidquid tribuis, in te cuncta recidunt./ Merito vocaris Magna tu Mater deum,/ Pietate quia vicisti divum numina*".

In this context we can recall the "physical" interpretations of the deities and their myths as they are given by Varro who, inkeeping with his own *theologia naturalis*, identifies the *Magna Mater* with *Tellus* (in Augustine, *De civ. Dei* VII, 24). Cf. also Arnobius, *adv. Nat.* III, 32 (ed. C. Marchesi, Torino 1953, 189): "*Terram quidam e vobis, quod cunctis sufficiat animantibus victum, Matrem esse dixerunt Magnam*"; Servius, *in Verg. Aen.* III, 113 (*rec.* G. Thilo, vol. I, Leipzig 1878, 363): "*ideo autem mater deum curru vehi dicitur, quia ipsa est terra, quae pendet in aëre*"; *Schol. in Apollonium Rhodium vet., Argon.* A 1148b (ed. C. Wendel 103): "καὶ τοῖς φυσικοῖς γὰρ δοκεῖ ἡ αὐτὴ εἶναι τῇ γῇ"; Joannes Lydus, *De mens.* IV, 63 (ed. R. Wuensch 114): "λέγεται δὲ καὶ Κυβέλη ἀπὸ τοῦ κυβικοῦ σχήματος κατὰ γεωμετρίαν ἡ γῆ, διὰ τὸ βάσιμόν τε καὶ στάσιμον"; Macrobius, *Sat.* I, 21, 7ff.: "*quis enim ambigat Matrem Deum terram haberi?*" (ed. J. Willis, Leipzig 1963, 117; cf. *ibid.* I, 23, 20, p. 127).

understood as a flexible complex of guarantees provided by participation in this cult. We should also note that a direct connection between "mysteries" and eschatological prospects cannot be demonstrated but only supposed by analogy with the Eleusinian context. Such an analogy would repose on a historical basis if, as seems likely,[109] the formation of an initiatory-esoteric structure first in the Hellenized cult of the Mother of the Gods and then in the more directly Phrygian cult of Cybele in the Roman world, had taken place under the influence of the Eleusinian "model".

Nevertheless, while at Eleusis the ἀγαθὴ ἐλπίς for the future destiny of man was the salient feature of the entire religious complex ever since the earliest manifestations known to us, it does not appear that the eschatological moment ever had a central importance in the mysteries of Cybele, judging, at least, from the documents in our possession which are curiously silent on the subject. In other words, even if the promise of a better lot in the hereafter was offered to the *mystai* of Cybele and Attis, it does not appear to have been the primary and specific objective of the esoteric cult.

Nor are these conclusions contradicted by the wish, formulated with sincere fervour by Julian at the end of the oration *To the Mother of the Gods*, that the end of his life might be "painless and glorious, sustained by the hope of journeying" to the goddess herself.[110]

As Cumont[111] has demonstrated, the mention of "hope" which recurs on other occasions in the works of Julian,[112] displays a clear reminiscence of the Eleusinian formula familiar to him who had been initiated in the mysteries. On the other hand, in the author's cosmosophic vision inspired by Neoplatonic premises, the return of the soul to the superior divine spheres from which it had descended into the body is the end and the final goal of the whole vicissitude. The Great Mother, the figure of the supreme principle of All, can then rightly be regarded as the object of the eschatological expectations of the man who participates in this vision of the world.

At the same time a guarantee after death seems to be connected with the public forms of the cult or rather with the category of the Galli, whose "initiation" was of a very particular kind and very different from that of the normal devotee who, after the ritual *iter*, acknowledged himself a μύστης Ἄττεως. Indeed, the testimony of Damascius, late though it is, speaks of a "salvation" from Hades in connection with the celebration of the *Hilaria* and

---

[109] See my observations on the subject in ' Il mitraismo nell'ambito della fenomenologia misterica'', cit.

[110] *Orat.* V, 180c: "καὶ τὸ τοῦ βίου πέρας ἄλυπόν τε καὶ εὐδόκιμον μετὰ τῆς ἀγαθῆς ἐλπίδος τῆς ἐπὶ τῇ παρ᾽ ὑμᾶς πορείᾳ".

[111] *Lux Perpetua*, 402.

[112] *Orat.* X (*Caes.*) 336c on the subject of Mithras, who will guide him towards the upper world; *Orat.* VII, 233d; *Epist.* 89, 452c and 298d.

the mysteriosophic interpretations of Julian and Sallust appeal to the March festivals.

Although these authors do not mention a specific eschatological prospect for those who participate in such ceremonies, they nevertheless draw from them and from the myth on which they are based an argument for that grandiose cosmological vision which illustrates Platonically the destiny of the divine entity with faculties demiurgic and "medial" and, at the same time, the destiny of the soul, its descent into matter and generation and its return to the divine level. It is the mythical-ritual scheme of the great festivals of Cybele which provides the elements for this "Sophic" elaboration, and not the esoteric rites which—if they were indeed exclusively connected with the idea of a blissful destiny in the hereafter or if they did have a specifically "soteriological" value—would have appeared better suited to such an interpretation.

Augustine, finally, mentions the typical context of religious exaltation and orgiasm inherent in the public cult of the *Magna Mater* in order to ask, polemically, how all this could give rise to a promise of eternal life.[113] If, as Lagrange maintains, this passage attests the existence of such a prospect in the cult of Cybele,[114] we must admit that it concerned the public component of the cult at least as much as the esoteric one.

In Augustine's text the emphasis is primarily on the figure and behaviour of the Galli who, in the pagan authors and the Christian polemicists,[115] are the favourite target of a bitting criticism directed at the crude and barbarous aspects of religious enthusiasm in the exotic cults.

For the Galli in particular there would indeed appear to have been a prospect of future bliss according to another passage in Augustine, where the dissolution of the present life of the sacred eunuchs is contrasted with the happiness *post mortem* at which their "consecration" would be aimed.[116]

---

[113] *De Civ. Dei* VII, 24, 2: "...*tympanum, turres, Galli, iactatio insana membrorum, crepitus cymbalorum, confictio leonum, vitam cuiquam pollicentur aeternam?*".

[114] "Attis et le christianisme", 476. We see, however, that both the passages of Augustine form part of the discussion about the "naturalistic" interpretation of the pagan religious traditions suggested by Varro, and the allusions to "life eternal" are probably due to the implicit comparison, by opposition, between the ritual of Cybele and the Christian religion. On this topic cf. J. Pépin, "Réactions du christianisme latin à la sotériologie métroaque. Firmicus Maternus, Ambrosiaster, Saint Augustin", U. Bianchi-M. J. Vermaseren (eds.), *La soteriologia dei culti orientali*, cit., 256-272.

[115] Besides the extensive discussion of the sources provided by Graillot and the observations of Carcopino (cf. above ch. 3, n. 2) see also L. Richard, "Juvénal et les galles de Cybèle", *RHR* CLXIX (1966), 51-67. A detailed analysis of the multiple references to the figure of the Gallus of Cybele in the works of Tertullian is undertaken by G. Sanders, "Les Galles et le Gallat devant l'opinion chrétienne", *Hommages Vermaseren*, vol. III, 1062-1091.

[116] *De Civ. Dei* VII, 26: "*Hisne diis selectis quisquam consecrandus est, ut post mortem vivat beate, quibus consecratus ante mortem honeste non potest vivere, tam foedis superstitionibus subditus et immundis daemonibus obligatus?*"

Prudentius, moreover, mentions the *vulnerum crudelitas* of the *fanaticus* of Cybele as something which is thought to "deserve heaven".[117]

Lagrange, who cites these passages, believes that the notion of a happy lot in the hereafter reserved for the Galli should be connected with the "expiatory" character of the practice of eunuchism.[118] Quite apart from the significance of this practice, which this is no place to discuss, we have seen that its connection with a positive eschatological prospect is only suggested by Augustine and Prudentius, authors who, in the context of the anti-pagan polemic, can be suspected of having accentuated the contrast between the "soteriological" claims of the Phrygian cult and its specific procedure. This consists in typical manifestations of orgiasm, frequently associated with the figure of the Galli, whose immoral behaviour was also stressed as a distinctive element.

These, furthermore, are late sources. They reflect an extreme point in the evolution of the cult of Cybele which, before declining for ever, seems to have gathered around itself the last manifestations of pagan religiosity in a lucid and lively effort to resist the ever more powerful advances of Christianity.[119] The rite of the taurobolium was a major expression of this rôle assumed by the Phrygian cult which was now so perfectly assimilated by the Western world as to appear as the emblematic form of the traditional religion of the Empire, and it is to the taurobolium that I shall now turn in order to illustrate a last aspect of the varied and composite picture provided by the cult of Cybele.

---

[117] *Peristeph.* X, 1061-1065: "*cultrum in lacertos exerit fanaticus/ sectisque Matrem bracchiis placat deam,/ furere ac rotari ius putatur mysticum;/ parca ad secandum dextra fertur inpia,/ caelum meretur vulnerum crudelitas*" (in H. Hepding, *op. cit.*, 66).

[118] Art. cit., 476f.

[119] Of the vast bibliography on the problem I should mention D. N. Robinson, "An Analysis of the Pagan Revival of the Late Fourth Century, with Especial Reference to Symmachus", *TAPhA* XLVI (1915), 87-101; P. De Labriolle, *La réaction païenne. Étude sur la polémique antichrétienne du Ier au VIe siècle*, Paris 1934 (9th ed. 1948), esp. 348-354; H. Bloch, "A New Document of the Last Pagan Revival in the West", *HThR* XXXVIII (1945), 199-244; Id., "The Pagan Revival in the West at the End of the Fourth Century", A. Momigliano (ed.), *The Conflict between Paganism and Christianity in the Fourth Century*, Oxford 1963, 193-218; B. Kötting, *Christentum und heidnische Opposition in Rom am Ende des 4.Jahrhunderts*, Münster i.W. 1961; J. F. Matthews, "Symmachus and the Oriental Cults", *JRS* LXIII (1973), 175-195; J. Wytzes, *Der letzte Kampf des Heidentums in Rom*, Leiden 1977 (EPRO 56).

CHAPTER SIX

MYSTIC AND SOTERIOLOGICAL ASPECTS OF THE TAUROBOLIUM

We are all familiar with the complex problems of the origins and the history of the taurobolium which appears, together with the criobolium usually connected with it, as an important component of the cult of the Great Mother of the Gods in the Roman world after the mid-2nd century A.D.

Duthoy's recent analysis[1] has focussed the question by providing a brief but exhaustive synthesis of the various interpretations proposed, which it would be absurd to sum up at this point. Even if some scholars thought that there was an original connection between the taurobolium and the cult of Cybele,[2] while others maintained that the rite had been borrowed from a different religious sphere,[3] everybody was acquainted with those epigraphic documents which, already in the 2nd century B.C. in Asia Minor[4] and in the first half of the 2nd century A.D. at Pozzuoli,[5] attest the practice of taurobolia and criobolia outside the Cybele's cult. It is only after 160 A.D., with the inscription of Lyons which mentions a taurobolium "of the Great Mother of the Gods *Idaea*", celebrated *ex imperio* by the goddess herself[6] that the rite appears to be connected with Cybele. From then on it becomes a phenomenon

---

[1] R. Duthoy, *The Taurobolium. Its Evolution and Terminology*, Leiden 1969 (EPRO 10). See also the clear exposition of the principal theories provided by G. Wagner, *op. cit.*, 244-254.

[2] Thus, for example, C. H. Moore, "On the Origin of the Taurobolium", *HSPh* XVII (1906), 43-48; H. Graillot, *op. cit.*, 153-158.

[3] Cumont particularly, in various studies, has sought the origins of the rite in the cult of Anahita identified by the Greeks with Artemis Tauropolos ("Le taurobole et le culte de Anahita", *RA* XII, 1888, 132-136; cf. *RPhLH* XVII, 1893, 194-197) and in that of Ma-Bellona ("Le taurobole et le culte de Bellone", *RHLR* VI, 1901, 97-110).

[4] Inscriptions from Pergamum one of which can be dated in 135 B.C. and the others around 10 A.D. The earliest of these mentions τὰ κριοβόλια in connection with the games of the ephebes (*IGRR* IV, 294 = Duthoy 6 n° 2) and the others the taurobolium (*IGRR* IV, 494, 499 and 500 = Duthoy 6f. n° 3). We also have an inscription from Troy where we see that ταυροβόλια were celebrated in connection with the *Panathenaia* (J. L. Caskey, "New Inscriptions from Troy", *AJA* XXXIX, 1935, 589-591 = Duthoy 5f. n° 1: 1st century B.C.) and another from Pinara, of the same period (J. A. O. Larsen, "Tituli Asiae Minoris II 508", *CPh* XXXVIII, 1943, 177-190; 246-255 = Duthoy 7ff. n° 4). The Micro-Asiatic origin of these documents confirms that the rites in question belong to the Anatolian religious traditions, even if it is difficult to establish which deity they were originally referring to.

[5] *CIL* X, 1596 = Duthoy 29 n° 50: the repetition of a rite indicated in the form *ecitium taurobolium...et Panteliu(m?)* in honour of *Venus Caelestis* in the year 134 A.D. We cannot accept the view of Beaujeu, according to whom this denomination really designates Cybele, while the taurobolia celebrated in Pergamum in 105 are "undoubtedly" connected with her cult (*op. cit.*, 102-104).

[6] *CIL* XIII, 1751 = Duthoy 50 n° 126.

pertaining exclusively to her, though Attis is also sometimes mentioned next to her.[7]

Nor did anyone fail to notice the distinction between the various forms of the rite, at least as far as its destination was concerned. One was of a "public" character, the taurobolium being celebrated "for the health" of the emperor, and often for other members of the imperial house, as well, in some cases, for the welfare of the entire civic community. The other was of a "private" character; we only get the name of the dedicator (or dedicators), without there being any mention of the beneficiary of the rite, who was probably the dedicator himself.[8] At other times it is explicitly stated that a person has "received" the taurobolium (accipere, percipere taurobolium) or, according to a later verbal formula, that he has been "tauroboliated" (tauroboliatus). As for the details of the rite, apart from some indications provided by the formula of the inscriptions placed to record its celebration, what was usually used by scholars was the vast and colourful description of the Peristephanon which, as we know, presents it as a sort of "baptism" of the devotee with the blood of the animal.[9]

Duthoy's study, based on former research and significant evidence of this type[10] has shown that the distinction between the "public" and "private" taurobolia is insufficient if we overlook the historical perspective which includes a "development" of the rite in question, with deep transformations of both the form and the purpose. In other words, emphasising the considerable differences in the formula used in the taurobolium dedications of various epochs, he detects an earlier type of taurobolium which appears as a sort of "sacrifice" in honour of the Mother of the Gods in favour of the Emperor, the community or the individual, and a more recent type to which Prudentius' description and the allusions in other literary sources of the 4th century[11] must refer. And so the problem of the meaning of the rite in the general context of the cult of Cybele is well on the way to being solved.

---

[7] A particular problem is raised by certain inscriptions of Benevento which recall the celebration of taurobolia and criobolia performed in honour of a *Minerva Berecinthia* (or *Paracentia*), as well as of Attis and, in one case, of the Mother of the Gods. See on this subject R. Duthoy, "La Minerva Berecyntia des inscriptions tauroboliques de Bénévent (*CIL* IX, 1538-1542)", *AC* XXXV (1966), 548-561.

[8] We can note with Duthoy that in the "private" taurobolia we never come across the formula *pro salute sua* or *pro se* which would correspond to the customary *pro salute* accompanying the taurobolia performed for the benefit of the Emperor.

[9] Prudentius, *Peristeph.* X, 1006-1050 in Duthoy, *op. cit.*, 55f. n° 4.

[10] Cf. M.-J. Lagrange, "Attis et le christianisme", cit., 450-470; J. Dey, *op. cit.*, 65-81. The research of B. Rutter, equally sensitive to the transformations undergone by the rite in its historical development ("The Three Phases of the Taurobolium", *Phoenix* XXII, 1968, 226-249), leads to similar conclusions to those of Duthoy.

[11] Firmicus Maternus, *De err. prof. rel.* 27, 8; *Carmen contra paganos* vv. 57-62 ed. E. Baehrens, *Poetae Latini Minores*, III, Leipzig 1881, 286-292; Aelius Lampridius, *Vita Heliogabali* VII, 1. The texts are assembled in Duthoy, *op. cit.*, 54f.

This is no place in which to repeat Duthoy's arguments or to discuss the viability of all his observations on the subject of that "intermediary" phase which would mark the passage from one type of taurobolium to the other. As he himself admits, his "reconstruction" of that moment is largely based on hypotheses in view of the scarcity of documentary evidence.[12] We should simply note that in the 2nd and, up to a point, in the 3rd century A.D. the taurobolium seems to have been a sacrificial rite with a specific character, evident from its exclusive pertinence to the cult of Cybele, its name and perhaps certain ceremonial aspects connected with its original relationship with hunting and animal trapping. Substantially, however, it was akin to the common rite of sacrificing a victim to the deity so as to derive protection and well-being for the social community, by way of the Emperor, its highest representative, or for the individual.[13] Indeed, in this period "public" and "private" taurobolia coexist without there being any perceptible difference in the celebration of one or the other and above all without there being any indication of the presence in the ritual of that sprinkling with the animal's blood so characteristic of the rite described by Prudentius.

We should also note, however, that a particular treatment is reserved for the animal's *vires*. In the inscription from Lyons they are transferred "from the Vatican", either the Roman hill on which the *Phrygianum* stood or a place of the same name in the French city,[14] in order, it would appear, to be buried under the altar commemorating the rite. Two inscriptions from *Lactora*, undated but probably ascribable to the first "phase" of the taurobolium, record the "consecration" of the *vires tauri*.[15]

---

[12] *Op. cit.*, 95-101; 118f.

[13] Nock sees in the taurobolium the expression of the idea, typical of the religiosity of late Antiquity, of absolute divine power, since it is a rite through which man participates in this power. This participation was desired not only for the individual but also for the Emperor, from whose well-being that of the citizens themselves depended. He regards this as the reason for which the taurobolium, an effective means of obtaining such a participation in divine power, was performed for the health of the emperor and the prosperity of the state ("Studies in the Graeco-Roman Beliefs of the Empire", *JHS* XLV, 1925, 87-93, repr. in *Essays*, vol. I, 34-40).

[14] On this problem cf. now R. Turcan, *Les religions de l'Asie*, cit., 83-88. Apart from this specific question it should be pointed out that Turcan is particularly critical of Duthoy's theory and believes that the taurobolium consisted, ever since its first manifestations, in a "bath" of blood as described by Prudentius. The rite of the *vires* would be a substitute for the practice of mutilation and would confer priestly "consecration". T. D. Barnes also has considerable reservations about Duthoy's conclusions (*Gnomon* XLIII, 1971, 523f.).

[15] *CIL* XIII, 522 = Duthoy 48 n° 120: "*Severus/ Iulli fil(ius)/ vires tauri/ quo propri[e]/ per tauropo/lium pub(lice) fac/tum fecerat/ consacravit*". *CIL* XIII, 525 = Duthoy 49 n° 123. In these inscriptions the formula *taurobolium facere* recurs which could express the sacrificial character of the rite, since *facere*, together with *movere*, is the verb used for the performance of the *sacrum*.

What is uncertain is the meaning of the formula *viribus aeterni taurobolio* which appears in two inscriptions from Turin (*CIL* V, 6961-6962 = Duthoy 13 nos. 8-9, and of the dedication *Natalici virib(us)* from Bordeaux (*CIL* XIII, 573 = Duthoy 49 n° 124).

A great deal has been said about the significance of this ritual treatment and discussions continue without either of the interpretations being acceptable with absolute certainty.[16] At all events it confirms the specificity of the taurobolium "sacrifice" as a rite pertaining to a religious context in which the practice of eunuchism and its mythical roots in the traditions concerning Attis confer a particular importance on this aspect of the cultic practice.

As for the objectives of the taurobolium in this first phase, they seem to consist in a guarantee of well-being in the present life, as expressed in the formula *pro salute, salus* indicating not only physical health but all the values (success, good fortune, protection from danger) which confer security on the life of the individual and the community.

It is along these lines that we can explain the celebration of the rite in favour of the Emperor and on the special orders of the highest official representative of the cult of Cybele, the Archigallus.[17] It thus became a manifestation of loyalty on the part of the individual or the civic community towards that civic power which, on the one hand, protected and regulated the cult and, on the other, enjoyed the effective benefits resulting from its practice.

In the course of the 3rd century, however, while "public" taurobolia for the health of the Emperor were still being celebrated, a new type of "private" taurobolium gradually asserted itself. And, in the 4th century, it was to become the only form in which the rite was performed, both because of the prevalence of the individualistic tendencies of that period and because of precise historical circumstances, the state now being ruled by Christian emperors, with the exception of the reign of Julian.

The process by which this second and individual form of taurobolium was formed can only be reconstructed hypothetically, since there are no concrete historical elements on which to rest. Nevertheless, in the definitive form which it appears to have adopted by the beginning of the 4th century,[18] it can be

---

[16] Cf. B. Rutter, art. cit., 235-238.

[17] We should recall the passage in the *Fragments of the Vatican* (§ 148) in which economic benefits are guaranteed for him who *in Portu pro salute imperatoris sacrum facit ex vaticinatione archigalli*, where the *sacrum*, as Cumont has rightly observed (s.v. *Dendrophori, PWRE* Hb IX, 1903, 219) is the taurobolium.

Cf. J. Carcopino, *Aspects mystiques de la Rome païenne*, 70-74. For the problems connected with the institution of the office of Archigallus *ibid.*, 76-171; cf. the observations of A. Momigliano, *Archigallus, RFIC* LX (N.S. 10) (1932), 226-229. The institution of the office of Archigallus and of the taurobolium, rather than being the work of Claudius as Carcopino would have it, should be attributed to Antoninus Pius in the context of his further "reform" of the cult of Cybele (P. Lambrechts, "Les fêtes "phrygiennes" de Cybele et d'Attis", 155-159; J. Beaujeu, *op. cit.*, 313-317).

[18] According to the reconstruction suggested by Duthoy the intermediate period, in which the rite implies a *tradere* by the officiant and an *accipere* by him who performs the rite in person, can be placed between 228 and 319. After this date the formula commonly used is *percipere taurobolium* or *tauroboliatus*, which would refer to the "bath" of blood as described by Prudentius. There remains the difficulty of fitting into this scheme certain Roman inscriptions of the 3rd

identified with the rite described by Prudentius and mentioned in the few contemporary literary texts.

This rite raises the problem of its mystic and soteriological significance, both in order that we may gain an exact understanding of the religious values connected with the cult of Cybele and in the broader perspective of the "soteriology" of the mystic cults of late Antiquity. For it is the ritual act which, in the last years of paganism, seemed to constitute the highest sanction of the religious status of those representatives of the Roman aristocracy who assumed the traditional priestly functions and performed various initiations with the object of contraposing the sacredness of the religious traditions of their own forebears to the new religious message which was spreading ever further.

In order to understand this significance the ironical question which the anonymous author of the *Carmen contra paganos*[19] put to his pagan interlocutor, a distinguished figure in the public life of Rome at the end of the 4th century, is decisive. If the brief reference to the details of the rite, with the descent "below the earth", *pollutus sanguine tauri*, conforms fully to the description of Prudentius, that question tackles the theme of the efficacy attributed to the shedding of the bull's blood: "*Vivere cum speras viginti mundus in annos?*".[20]

The *tauroboliatus* thus thinks that he has achieved purification. This purification, however, is circumscribed in time to those "twenty years" which

---

and 4th century which use the verb *facere* for the celebration of the rite and thus reflect a terminology which Duthoy believes to be relevant only to the first, exclusively sacrificial "phase" of the rite (*CIL* VI, 505-507 = Duthoy 16f. nos. 18-20). Moreover, numerous other inscriptions which present one or other of the formulas have no date and consequently their attribution to one of the two "phases" of the history of the taurobolium is determined by Duthoy's own classificatory presuppositions. Despite all these reservations, however, an evolution of the procedure of the rite and of its significance would seem to be perceptible, very broadly speaking, in the period running from the 2nd to the 4th century.

[19] The *Carmen* is directed against a member of Roman senatorial aristocracy. On the identity of this character and the period of composition of the text, see C. Manganaro, "La reazione pagana a Roma nel 408-409 d.C. e il poemetto anonimo 'Contra paganos' ", *GIF* XIII (1960), 210-224; Id., "Il poemetto anonimo Contra paganos", *ND* XI (1961), 23-45. The conclusions of Manganaro, who rejects the traditional attribution of the work to 394 and the identification of the Roman senator with Nicomachus Flavianus, are criticised by Bloch ("A New Document of the Last Pagan Revival", 217). See also J. F. Matthews, "The Historical setting of the 'carmen contra paganos' (Cod. Par. Lat. 8084)", *Historia* XIX (1970), 464-479; J. Wytzes, *op. cit.*, 348f.; S. Mazzarino, "Il *Carmen* 'contro i pagani' e il problema dell''Era costantiniana' ", *Antico, tardoantico ed èra costantiniana*, vol. I, Roma 1974, 398-465; L. Cracco Ruggini, "Il paganesimo romano tra religione e politica (384-394 d.C.): per una reinterpretazione del *Carmen contra paganos*", *MemAccLinc* S. VIII, XXIII (1979), 3-141.

[20] Vv. 57-62 in Duthoy, *op. cit.*, 54: "*Quis tibi taurobolus vestem mutare suasit,/ inflatus dives, subito mendicus ut esses?/ Obsitus et pannis, modica stipe factus epaeta/ sub terram missus, pollutus sanguine tauri,/ sordidus, infestus, vestes servare cruentas,/ vivere cum speras viginti mundus in annos?*"

seem to indicate a "cycle" of life, after which it is necessary to perform the rite again.[21]

This is confirmed by those inscriptions which commemorate the "repetition" of a taurobolium, even if they do not indicate the period which elapsed between the first and the second celebration;[22] in one case, however, it turns out to have been twenty years.[23] The Roman inscription of the Lateran recording a period of twenty-eight years as a parenthesis of darkness which has been ended by the taurobolium,[24] can probably be interpreted in relation to the years in which the Constantinian basilica of St Peter's was being built. Placed in the immediate vicinity of the *Phrygianum*, the movement of men and objects necessary for its construction would have prevented the celebration of the rites of Cybele.[25]

If the repetition of the rite after a fairly extensive, albeit defined, period of years is in keeping with the essentially cathartic character of the taurobolium blood "bath", a new element is introduced in the words of a *tauroboliatus* who proclaims himself *in aeternum renatus*.[26]

Together with Moore[27] and Nilsson[28] most scholars agree in recognising this declaration not so much as the sign of a doctrine which attributed

---

[21] Cf. C. H. Moore, "The Duration of the Efficacy of the Taurobolium", *CPh* XIX (1924), 363-365; M. P. Nilsson, *Geschichte*, vol. II², 653. J. Beaujeu assumes a connection between the twenty-year duration of the efficacy of the taurobolium and the *Vicennalia* celebrated for the first time with this name under Antoninus Pius (*op. cit.*, 314f.).

[22] *CIL* VI, 502 = Duthoy 15 n° 15: "...*taurobolio/ crioboliooque repetito*"; cf. *CIL* VI, 504 = Duthoy 15f. n° 17 where the dedicator expresses the wish *ut mactet repetens aurata/ fronte bicornes*.

[23] *CIL* VI, 512 = Duthoy 19f. n° 25: "*iterato viginti annis exp[le]/tis taurobolii sui aram constitu[it]/ et consecravit*". Inscription of 23 May 390.

[24] O. Marucchi, "Cippo marmoreo con iscrizione greca e rilievi riferibili al culto frigio della Magna Mater", *NSc*, Ser. V, XIX (1922), 81-87 (= Duthoy 22ff. n° 33). This interesting document has given rise to contrasting interpretations, especially in connection with the παλίνορσον referred by some to Attis, in his capacity of "risen god", and by others to the repetition of the taurobolium ("again"). See P. Fabre, "Un autel du culte phrygien au Musée du Latran", *MEFR* XL (1923), 3-18; H. J. Rose, "A Greek Taurobolic Inscription from Rome", *JHS* XLIII (1923), 194-196; Id., "A Taurobolic Inscription from Rome: ΔΕΥΤΕΡΑΙ ΦΡΟΝΤΙΔΕΣ", *ibid.*, XLV (1925), 180-182; A. Vogliano, "Una nuova epigrafe storica", *RendAccLinc* VI (1925), 3-9; P. Fabre, "Encore l'autel phrygien du Latran-Réponse à M. A. Vogliano, *ibid.*, 858-865; M.-J. Lagrange, "Attis ressuscité?", *RBi* XXXVI (1927), 561-566.

[25] Cf. *CRAI* 1950, 434-435; M. Guarducci, *Cristo e San Pietro in un documento precostantiniano della necropoli vaticana*, Roma 1953, 65-69; J. Carcopino, *Études d'histoire chrétienne*, Paris 1953, 129-130. See also a new interpretation suggested by M. Guarducci in a paper at the Colloquium on "The Soteriology of the Oriental cults in the Roman Empire", Rome 24-28 September 1979 ("L'interruzione dei culti nel *Phrygianum* del Vaticano durante il IV sec. d. Cr.", U. Bianchi-M. J. Vermaseren (eds.), *La soteriologia dei culti orientali nell'Impero romano*, cit., 109-121; Ead., "La scomparsa di Cibele", *ibid.*, 123-125).

[26] *CIL* VI, 510 = Duthoy 18 n° 23. The inscription is dated 13 August 376.

[27] Art. cit., 363.

[28] *Geschichte*, vol. II², 653. A Christian influence has been suggested by H. Rahner, "Das christliche Mysterium und die heidnischen Mysterien", *EJ* XI (1944), 396f.

unlimited efficacy to the rite, perhaps after it had been repeated, but as the expression of an individual devotion of a particularly lively and enthusiastic kind. Apart from the theme of duration, whether limited or indefinite, of the beneficial effects of the taurobolium, it emphasizes a particular aspect of these effects—that of the "regeneration" which the rite will obtain for man.

We may now ask what the sense of the "rebirth" is which the devotee thinks he has experienced as a result of celebrating the taurobolium.

As against the views of Loisy,[29] Lagrange has demonstrated that there is no evidence for connecting the taurobolium with Attis, whose experience of death and subsequent "resurrection" the *tauroboliatus* repeats by descending into the pit to receive the blood of the animal.[30]

It is superfluous to recall that the lateness of the document in question limits its value for determining the primary or the acquired character of the concept of "rebirth" in connection with the rite, making the second possibility more likely.

We should keep in mind, however, that some inscriptions, two of which are dated at the end of the 2nd century A.D.[31] mention, in connection with the taurobolium or the criobolium, a *(dies) natalis* or *natalicium*, on the meaning of which scholars differ. Some have seen the *natalicium* as the day of the celebration of the rite, understood as the moment marking the devotee's

---

[29] *Op. cit.*, 111ff. The author thinks that the taurobolium and the criobolium can be fitted into the context of the Phrygian mysteries—indeed, that they constituted the climax of those mysteries, relating to the "consecration" of the worshipper. As for the mysteries, they would coincide with the March festivals.

A close connection between the "mysteries" and the taurobolium had already been posited by Hepding (*op. cit.*, 197-201; cf. also U. Fracassini, *op. cit.*, 130-144), while Graillot believed that in those "mysteries" which took place on 28 March "the catechumens at least received the criobolium baptism" (*op. cit.*, 178).

It is worth noting, however, that, of the taurobolium inscriptions which are dated, only one falls on 24 March (*CIL* XIII, 510 = *ILS* 4127). It concerns a taurobolium celebrated at *Lactora* by a woman (*Valeria Gemina*) of whom it is said that *vires escepit (sic) Euthychetis*. It has been assumed that the Euthyches here mentioned is a Gallus and that the inscription thus refers to the rite of mutilation performed on the *dies sanguinis*. This would confirm the substitutive character of the consecration of the *vires tauri* in the course of the taurobolium. Of the other taurobolium altars one is dated 12 March (*CIL* VI, 511 = Duthoy 19 n° 24), and another 25 March (*CIL* II, 5521 = Duthoy 36 n° 74).

The sacrifice of a bull which, according to Joannes Lydus, took place in the context of the public ceremonies of March, was aimed at the prosperity of the fields "on the mountains" (*de mens.* IV, 49 see above ch. V, n. 1).

A symbology of death and resurrection connected with the taurobolium has been argued by Graillot (*op. cit.*, 157f.) and by other authors (cf. R. Reitzenstein, *op. cit.*, 45f.). Against: M. P. Nilsson, *Geschichte*, vol. II², 653f.; A.-J. Festugière, "La religion grecque à l'époque romaine", *REG* LXIV (1931), 489f.; K. Prümm, *Der christliche Glaube und die altheidnische Welt*, vol. II, Leipzig 1935, 310-313.

[30] "Attis et le christianisme", 456-459.

[31] *CIL* II, 5260 = Duthoy 37 n° 79: dedication of *Valeria Avita* from *Emerita Augusta*; *CIL* XIII, 11352 = Duthoy 52f. n° 132: taurobolium altar with mutilated inscription from *Divodurum*, dated 199 A.D.

spiritual "birth";[32] others, instead, think it is an anniversary of physical birth, selected for the celebration of the taurobolium.[33]

In the case of Valeria Avita, who dedicates to the Mother of the Gods the altar *taurobolii sui natalici redditi*[34] and of an unknown individual who records having restored *ara(m) t(aurobolicam) ob natalicium [ex] iussu*[35] we can probably choose between one or other of the interpretations suggested. We cannot exclude the possibility that the worshippers in question had chosen their own birthday to perform the rite. This possibility, however, appears less likely in the case of the two *Irinaei*, father and son, who call themselves *criobolati natali suo* in *Pax Iulia*,[36] for we would then have to presume the exceptional circumstance that the birthdays of father and son fell on the same date.

Moreover, the choice of one's own *dies natalis* for the performance of the taurobolium and the criobolium—if the documents cited can indeed be interpreted in this sense—would be equally significant and justify the hypothesis that this coincidence assumed in the eyes of the worshipper a precise religious value. In other words, we would have as a counterpart to physical birth that "renewal" of vital and spiritual energies produced by the purifying effect of the taurobolium or criobolium "bath" conceived as a new birth.

At all events nobody can doubt that, at least in the case of the Roman inscription discussed above, the idea of a spiritual rebirth is connected with the taurobolium. Consequently, in the last days of paganism, and particularly in those circles of the Roman aristocracy which contributed with sincere fervour to its renewal, the taurobolium was also regarded as a ritual act capable of procuring for the participant the certainty of being *renatus*.

Indeed, this notion displays a certain continuity with the cathartic effect which the taurobolium, in its form of a "bath" of blood, seems to present in its basic and essential connotation, if the "purification" obtained by the rite is felt as the beginning of a new life, the sign of a renewal of present existence and a guarantee for the future one.

That the cathartic effect of the taurobolium was not of a purely ritual order, at least in those pagan circles of the 4th century where it was particularly popular, but assumed important ethical aspects, is shown by the language of certain dedicatory epigraphs of the taurobolium altars. Thus, for

---

[32] Cf. H. Hepding, *op. cit.*, 198; H. Graillot, *op. cit.*, 172; C. H. Moore, art. cit., 363.

[33] M.-J. Lagrange, "Attis et le christianisme", 466ff.; J. Dey, *op. cit.*, 77-79; R. Duthoy, *op. cit.*, 106f.

[34] Cf. above n. 31.

[35] Inscr. from *Divodurum* cit. in n. 31. We should also keep in mind the dedication *Natalici virib(us)* from *Burdigala* (*CIL* XIII, 573 = Duthoy 49 n° 124).

[36] Duthoy 37 n° 78: *M(atri) D(eum) s(acrum)/ duo Irinaei, pater et/ fil(ius) criobolati/ natali suo, sacer(dotibus)/ Lucio Antist(io) Avito/ G(aio) Antisti(o) Felicissimo.*

example, the already cited Lateran altar[37] claims to bring as a "sacrificial offering" (τὸ θῦμα) "the works, thought, behaviour, superior life, all that is good in the soul" of the worshipper.[38] In the inscription placed in remembrance of the rite, Clodius Hermogenianus defines Cybele and Attis, with whom Hermes is also associated, as *dii animae suae mentisque custodes*[39] and Ceionius Rufius Volusianus calls them "great gods and his protectors",[40] stressing the intimate and personal bond which ties him to the Phrygian deities.

The connection of the Great Mother with the sphere of ethical values, moreover, already present in the metrical inscription of the sanctuary of Phaestos,[41] must have fairly ancient Anatolian origins if we consider that the observance of numerous precepts of both a ritual and a moral order imposed on the religious community of Philadelphia is guaranteed by the "custodian of the (sacred) dwelling", Agdistis, who makes sure that men and women have ἀγαθὰς διανοίας and piously observe their religious duties.[42]

Finally we should consider whether the taurobolium, having turned, in the 3rd century, from a sacrificial and expiatory rite into an essentially cathartic and individual one, also has initiatory aspects and can thus be placed amongst the "mystic" cults.

There are no valid elements for establishing a relationship between the taurobolium and the mysteries of Cybele and Attis, despite the "reconstructions" attempted by various authors who wish to make room for this rite in the mystery *iter*.[43] Its history, moreover, makes a direct and original connection between the two contexts more improbable than ever.

Nor is there a link between the March festival and the taurobolia, performed in the most varied periods of the year without there being any apparent coincidence with the festival cycle, except in a few rare cases.[44] We know that the indication *initium Caiani* in the Philocalian Calendar for 28

---

[37] See above n. 24.

[38] "ἔργα νόον πρῆξιν βίον ἔξοχον ἐσθλὰ πρόπαντα". Cf. the translation by P. Fabre, art. cit., 13f. and that by Lagrange, "Attis ressuscité?", 566. Rose believes that this line reproduces a "liturgical formula of Persian origin" (art. cit., *JHS* XLV, 1925, 181).

[39] *CIL* VI, 499 = Duthoy 14 n° 13: a. 374.

[40] *CIL* VI, 512 = Duthoy 19f. n° 25.

[41] Cf. above ch. V, n. 7.

[42] In O. Weinrich, *art. cit.*, 5, lines 50-54. It is probably to her qualities as a goddess safeguarding the norms of ethics and justice as well as to those as a dispenser of well-being and fertility, that, together with Lambrechts, we can attribute the presence of Cybele on a figurative stele of the 2nd-3rd century A.D. with a dedication to the Anatolian god *Hosios* and *Dikaios*, frequently invoked in Phrygia and in Lydia as the protector of flocks and fields ("Documents inédits de Cybèle au Musée d'Eskişehir", cit., 215-218, figs. 6-9). Cf. above p. 87, n. 9.

[43] Cf. above n. 29.

[44] Cf. above n. 29.

March, formerly interpreted as referring to the celebration of the taurobolia after the close of that cycle,[45] in fact has nothing to do with it.[46]

Nevertheless the rite would assume a very individual initiatory character if, as some authors claim,[47] the special treatment of the *vires* which takes place even in its earliest manifestations were a substitute for mutilation as practised by the Galli. It would then be a "consecration" of the man to the goddess, performed by way of the animal. Yet it is hard to accept this interpretation in those cases, so frequent, and actually prevalent in the earliest "phase" of the taurobolium, when the rite was performed at the expense and under the supervision of women, or, in the case of the "public" taurobolia, *pro salute Imperatoris*. At all events, if the "initiatory" character of the rite corresponded to that very particular type of "initiation" practised by the Galli, it would have a different significance to that of the initiation of a mystery cult.

In certain taurobolium inscriptions of the 4th century, however, we have a language with clearly mystery connotations used to define the rite, and there is also a tendency to associate it with obviously mystic practices and cults. Thus the dedicator of the taurobolium altar of Athens, who, in the figurative representation associates Cybele with Eleusinian Demeter,[48] records having participated in the mystic rites of Lerna and says he is a daduchus of Kore. He speaks of the taurobolium as of a τελετή of which the συνθημάτα κρυπτά are evoked.[49]

A similar language appears in the second altar of Athens, itself defined σύνθημα τῆς τελετῆς,[50] and in the Greek inscriptions on certain taurobolium altars in Rome.[51] The taurobolium of Rufius Ceionius who, amongst his

---

[45] Thus, for example, H. Graillot, *op. cit.*, 174.

[46] A. D. Nock, *JRS* XXXVIII (1948), 156-158.

[47] Thus, for example, M.-J. Lagrange, *Attis et le christianisme*, cit., 467-470; J. B. Rutter, art. cit., 235-238.

[48] *IG* III, 172; J. N. Svoronos, *Das Athener Nationalmuseum*, vol. I, 474-484; vol. II, Taf. LXXX; M. P. Nilsson, *Geschichte*, vol. II², 651, Taf. 12; M. J. Vermaseren, *The Legend of Attis*, 26 Pl. XV, 1-3; Id., *CCCA* II, 116f. n° 389, Pls. CXVII-CXIX; Duthoy, *op. cit.*, 9ff. n° 5.

[49] *Ibid.*, line 3: "...τελετῆς τ[ῆ]ς Ταυροβόλου"; line 10ff.: "...βωμὸν ἔθηκε Ῥέη/'Αρχέλειως, τελετῆς συνθήματα κρυπτὰ χαράξας/Ταυροβόλου πρῶτον δεῦρο τελειομένης".

[50] *IG* III, 173 = Duthoy 11ff. n° 6: "...ἐτελέσθη/ταυροβόλιον ἐν 'Αθήναις, ὅ/περ, παραλαβὼν Μουσώνιος/ὁ λαμ(πρότατος) τῆς τελετῆς τὸ σύνθημα τὸν βωμὸν ἀναί/θηκα" (27 May 387). Cf. Vermaseren, *CCCA* II, 117f. n° 390, Pls. CXX-CXXII.
The mystery connotation of this languages emerges, amongst other things, from the use of the term σύνθημα which denotes, as we know, the sacred formula pronounced by the initiate in the course of his ritual *iter* to show that he has performed the acts prescribed by the cult.

[51] *CIL* VI, 509 = *IG* XIV, 1018 = Duthoy 17f. n° 22, v. 4f.: "χριοβόλου τελετῆς ἢ [δ'ἔτι τ]αυροβόλου/Μυστιπόλος τελετῶν [ἱερῶν ἀ]νεθήκατο βωμόν" (a. 370); *CIL* VI, 30.780 = *IG* XIV, 120 = Duthoy 21f. n° 30, v. 5ff.: "''Οργια συνρέξαντε θεαῖ παμμήτορι 'Ρείηι/χριοβόλου τελετῆς καὶ ταυροβόλοιο φερίστης/αἵμασι μυστιπόλοις βωμῶν ὑπερτίθεσαν"; cf. L. Moretti, *Inscriptiones Graecae Urbis Romae*, Fasc. 1, nn. 1-263, Roma 1968, n° 126; J. Bousquet, "Epigrammes romaines", *Klio* LII (1970) [Mélanges G. Klaffenbach], 38f. who read ἐργάμασι μυστιπόλοις (of the 4th century); *CIL* VI, 30.966 = *IG* XIV, 1019 = Duthoy 22 n° 31: Sabina who says she has consecrated the altar "to Attis and to Rhea" as σύμβολον εὐαγέων τελετῶν, and has also participated in the mystic rites of Deo and the "terrible nights of Hecate".

religious functions, numbers that of hierophant of Hecate and *pater sacrorum* of Mithras, is called a "mystic rite".[52]

In the celebrated inscription recording the many political and sacred functions performed by Vettius Agorius Praetextatus, his wife Fabia Aconia Paulina who, following in her husband's footsteps, participated in the most important Greek and Oriental mystery cults,[53] sees in her husband the mystagogue who introduced her to the "bull's initiations" (*teletis taureis*).[54]

In the spiritual climate of an age of profound social and religious changes, those who remained true to the traditional religions found a basis for their own religiosity and their own world picture above all in the mystery cults through complex "Sophic" interpretations of the myths and the rites contained in these cults. This feature would account for the obviously initiatory and mystic connotation assumed by the taurobolium. The rite, which drew its cathartic efficacy from shedding the blood of an animal, fitted into a religious context which on the one hand presented itself as the cult of a "national" deity, intimately connected with the destinies of Rome and the Empire,[55] and on the other was animated by a mystic religiosity both markedly individualistic and deeply felt, expressed in great public festivals, but also in esoteric and secluded rites.

The taurobolium displays this duplicity of aspects throughout the course of its history. It was a public and official rite performed "for the health" of the Emperor and probably itself instituted within the cult of Cybele by an act of imperial religious policy, and it was a "private" rite, for the benefit of the individual.

This second dimension, which was gradually to prevail, made it an "initiatory" rite in circles of the Roman aristocracy in the last part of the 4th century. Such a qualification, moreover, can be applied to the taurobolium in an extremely broad and analogical sense, since it lacks that esoteric character and that relationship with a divine vicissitude celebrated cultically which characterises the initiations of the mysteries. We could say that the taurobolium assumes a "mystic" connotation through having been adapted

---

[52] *CIL* VI, 511 = Duthoy 19 n° 24: "*tauroboli(que) simul magni dux mistici sacri.*" It should also be observed that *simbola tauroboli* are mentioned in the context of the inscription.

[53] *CIL* VI, 1780 = Duthoy 21 n° 29: "*Sacratae apud Eleusinam Deo Iaccho Cereri et Corae/ sacratae apud Laernam Deo Libero et Cereri et Corae/ sacratae apud Aeginam Deabus, tauroboliatae, Isiacae/ hierophantriae Deae Hecatae Graeco sacraneae Deae Cereris*".

[54] *CIL* VI, 1779 = Duthoy 21 n° 28, vv. 25-27: "*Te teste cunctis imbuor mysteriis/ tu Dindymenes Atteosqu[e] antistitem/ teletis honoras taureis consors pius*".

[55] Cf. S. Aurigemma, "La protezione speciale della Gran Madre Idea per la nobiltà romana e le leggende dell'origine troiana di Roma", *BCAR* 1909, 31-65; A. Bartoli, "Il culto della Mater Deum Magna Idaea e di Venere genitrice sul Palatino", *MemPontAcc* VI (1942), 229-239; P. Lambrechts, "Cybèle, divinité étrangère ou nationale?", 44-60; P. Boyancé, "Cybèle aux Mégalésies", *Latomus* XIII (1954), 337-342 (repr. in *Études sur la religion romaine*, 195-200).

by the worshipper himself to the other initiations in which he had participated, thereby acquiring a religiously defined status.

The title of the *tauroboliatus* was thus situated, in the mind of the devotee and in the concrete efficacy of his religious experience, in a homogeneous series of religious attributes with an initiatory and esoteric basis—initiate of Dionysus, of the Eleusinian goddesses, of Mithras, etc. Let this be said, however, without diminishing the objective differences between the celebration of the taurobolium and the mystery rites in question.

Religious historical research will undoubtedly stress these differences with the object of obtaining a clear definition of the specific significance and of the morphology of the various contexts. But it must not lose sight of the process by which the rite of Cybele, starting with a sacrificial character, accentuated the individual and cathartic element to gather round itself a mass of religious and ethical values which made it appear, in certain circles in late Antiquity, a cultic act capable of conferring an initiatory qualification and of procuring a sense of inner renovation.

This latter sense is based on that element of individual purification inherent in the taurobolium and fundamental to the initiatory practice of the most varied mystery cults, κάθαρσις being one of its premises and also one of its specific objectives. We can therefore understand how, in this vast and flexible historical process, we can come across the statement—isolated though it is in our documentation and very probably a sign of a personal religiosity rather than of a specific doctrinal element but none the less relevant in its particular religious significance—that the *tauroboliatus* of the Mother of the Gods is *in aeternum renatus*. Because of this we can detect, in the objective structures of a rite with a complex history and with a crudely naturalistic procedure, an elevated soteriological value, no longer limited to a cycle of earthly existence (the "twenty years" of the cathartic efficacy commonly attributed to the taurobolium), but projected into an eschatological dimension.[56]

---

[56] On this topic cf. also G. Sfameni Gasparro, "Significato e ruolo del sangue nel culto di Cibele e Attis", *Atti della Settimana di Studi "Sangue e antropologia biblica nella letteratura cristiana"*, cit., vol. I, 199-232.

CONCLUSION

I shall end this analysis of documents by adding a few words about those considerations to which the various sources I have examined have given rise and by summing up the general state of the problem.

In view of the specific sense in which I have used the terms "mystic" and "mystery"—a sense which I defined at the beginning of this study—the reader is entitled to some conclusion about their applicability to the cult of the Great Mother and Attis, however different the various forms it adopted in time and space. We have indeed been able to observe that, despite the persistence of certain basic characteristics of the goddess and her ritual, the cult of Cybele does not present a uniform physiognomy. I refer, of course, above all to the orgiastic aspect of the ritual, with its attendant and typical manifestations of possession and *mania* which persist throughout its history, from the Hellenized forms of the prevalently female groups of the Classical age to the "Phrygian" ones of the mythical-cultic cycle of Attis and the Galli. The cult appears, rather, as a flexible network of elements which do indeed have connections with one another, but which frequently develop along partly independent lines, at least in certain circles and historical situations.

On the one hand, then, we have the religious complex gravitating round the Great Mother of the Gods as a divinity in whom we can still perceive specific Oriental antecedents but who appears to have been fully integrated in the Greek religious sphere. In her cult, so widespread in Greece and the Hellenized world, we can detect, in the enthusiastic-orgiastic moment, that mystic component to which I referred earlier, while in some places there are attestations, as from the Hellenistic period, of institutions of a mystery type including a specific initiatory practice.

We have no way of knowing whether there was a continuous line of development from the former to the latter or whether the latter can be fitted into that characteristic process which led, in the Hellenistic period, to the constitution of mystery structures in religious phenomena previously defined in a mystic sense, like the Dionysiac cult of the thiasoi, so similar in many ways to the religion of Cybele, or like various Demetrian and Cabirian cults. Some influence or pressure of the Eleusinian model on the religious milieu of the Great Mother with the object of forming within it mystery institutions seems most likely.

At all events, in the passage of the cult of the Great Mother from the mystic form, expressed in the moment of divine possession which is so typical of it, to the mystery form, attested in certain parts of the Greek world, we see the persistence of those strongly Hellenized traits of the goddess' personality and ritual which characterise this aspect of her religion.

After the 4th century B.C., however, we find significant traces on Greek soil of the Phrygian elements of the cult and the myth, particularly when a male paredros, Attis, appears beside the goddess and we hear of the ritual practices of the Galli.

It is hard to reach any conclusion about the connections between these two components of the cult of the Great Mother Cybele. It would be going too far to lay such emphasis on the differences between them as to create a clear borderline between a completely Graecised Mother of the Gods and a Cybele who has retained all her original Phrygian connotations, expressed in the mythical-ritual complex gravitating round Attis.

Neither of these images would truly correspond to the historical reality which knew peculiarly "exotic" traits in the solemn Mother of the gods. A "mountain" goddess, sovereign of an uncultivated world inhabited by beasts, the mistress of lions, venerated to the sound of sacred instruments producing a violent and orgiastic music—this is how she appears in the Homeric Hymn *To the Mother of the gods*.

On the other hand, even the Phrygian forms of the cult of Cybele appear to have undergone a process of Hellenisation on a mythical and ritual level. This is hard to assess in view of the impossibility of a comparison with Oriental sources relating to the original manifestations of that cult, but it was certainly active in the constitution of those same forms as they were handed down by the Greek world.

Towards the end of the 3rd century B.C., at all events, a new element intervenes in the complex history of the cult of Cybele, when the Roman aristocracy turns to Pergamum with a precise religious policy in mind, in order to receive from it the aniconic idol of the Great Mother of Pessinus. We then witness a process partially analogous to that which had taken place on Greek soil. If a series of spontaneous and autonomous cultural contacts between individuals and communities (probably represented at first by the Greek settlers in Asia) led to the introduction of the figure of the Phrygian goddess in the religious panorama of the Greek world, and to a more or less profound process of Hellenisation of her character and her cult, the official accession of the *Mater Magna Idaea* in Republican Rome entailed a rigorous selection of the elements composing the goddess' personality and ritual.

We thus come to the constitution of a deity perfectly integrated in the Roman *pantheon*, considered the protectress of the city in so far as she was tied to the city's Trojan origins and had saved it when its very existence was threatened by foreigners. She consequently had her shrine on the Palatine, the heart of Romulean Rome, and was honoured with annual patrician festivals, the *Megalensia*, celebrated according to the *mos maiorum*, but without any of the mystic-orgiastic aspects of the Oriental cult.

Nevertheless, a staff of Phrygian priests accompanied the goddess to Rome to celebrate her rites in the traditional manner within her sanctuary. Even Attis, as far as we can see from the excavations performed by Romanelli in the area of the shrine of Cybele on the Palatine, came to the city in the train of the Great Mother. According to Cicero (*De leg.* II, 9, 22; cf. II, 16, 40), the Phrygian priests were allowed to practise sacred begging on a particular date and Dionysius of Halicarnassus describes a Phrygian couple, with sacred images on their breasts, wandering through the city μητραγυρτοῦντες to the sound of tympana and flutes (*Ant. rom.* II, 3-5).

Despite the precautions of the civic authorities, then, the people learned to know the Phrygian form of the cult of the Great Mother. There is no doubt that, at the end of the Republican period and the beginning of the Empire, the general interest in Oriental religions was accompanied by an increasing popularity of that cult for, from the reign of Claudius onwards, those same authorities thought it necessary to effect a series of reforms, introducing at successive moments into the public ritual the entire March festival cycle centred on Attis.

The mythical-ritual complex referring to Attis, both in the forms known in Greece and, still more, in those of the Roman festivals of the Imperial period, clearly displays the features peculiar to a mystic cult in its quality as a ceremony re-evoking the significant moments of a divine vicissitude, characterised by deep *pathos* but also orientated towards a positive outcome. Aside from Frazer's outdated scheme of the "dying and rising god", Attis appears, in so far as he is the object of such a rite, as a figure subject to vicissitude, a divinity connected with the sphere of chthonic fertility, and most especially with arborescent and florescent vegetation.

I believe that all the evidence examined hitherto, whether it refers to the myth or to the cult, points to this assessment of the religious historical consistency of this superhuman figure.

In the roman Imperial period (the earliest source in which Attis appears in an explicitly mystery context is constituted by the inscriptions of the *Attabokaoi* from Pergamum), the cult, as we have seen, also included the esoteric-initiatory form of the mysteries. These, though definitely referring to the Great Mother Cybele (who sometimes still appears, even in this period, as their sole object) must have retained a privileged position for the young paredros, if the adept, at the end of his ritual *iter*, acknowledged himself a "*mystes* of Attis".

The historical and typological relationship between the two aspects of the cult cannot be clearly defined in its specific details owing to the difficulty of deciding whether those esoteric forms only attested in a late Hellenistic period already existed in an Anatolian environment before any contact with the Greek world. Nevertheless the mass of evidence examined leads one to suspect that the formation of mysteries in the Phrygian cult was not an original element but a later addition, the result of an encounter with Greek religious structures familiar with the phenomenon in various forms.

The basic cause of the formation of an esoteric-initiatory ritual within that cult appears to have been its typical quality as a "mystic" cult in the sense which I explained earlier. The profound "participation" in the interaction between the divine, cosmic and human levels, as it takes place in the public rites of March, and the re-evocation of a divine vicissitude which constitutes its essential structure, are elements morphologically analogous to the components of a mystery context of the Eleusinian type. We can therefore assume that owing to the pressure of the Greek religious model at a time when there was a prevalence of individualistic tendencies and an interest in cults with a private and secluded character, the mystic elements of the Phrygian cult were adapted to an esoteric-initiatory ritual practice in which the personal aspect of the participation of the adept in the divine vicissitude took absolute precedence.

Still more difficult is the problem of the "soteriological" content of the cult in view of the diversity of its expressions in time and space.

Here we return to the question, put at the beginning of the present study, about the religious historical definition of the concept of salvation. Without claiming to arrive at such a definition, for which it would be necessary to appeal to the widest possible range of religious phenomena, I have preferred to take as my starting point a fairly broad meaning of the notion in question, and to leave it up to the analysis of the cult of Cybele to reveal a formulation capable of characterising the complex of advantages and guarantees which the adept could expect in that sphere.

This task was not easy owing to the quality of the documentation available. There are no sources that can be directly ascribed to the original Anatolian context. Even the sacred writings of a later period, the works of Western authors interested in the religion of Cybele (like the *Thronismoi metrooi* of Orphic origin recorded in Suidas' Lexicon or the treatise of Proclus which Marinus reports in Proclus' biography) have, with a very few exceptions (Julian, Sallustius, Macrobius), been lost. Our evidence, then, is mainly reduced to brief allusions, often polemical or satirical, to authors of different periods and backgrounds, or to the testimony—sadly unexpressive from our point of view—of the figurative monuments or dedicatory epigraphs from whose stereotyped formulas it is frequently impossible to reach any definite conclusions.

Even if the description of the ritual data can be considered sufficiently objective for the periods to which the various authors refer, the mythical traditions have reached us in such a state of elaboration that it is extremely difficult to appreciate their true religious significance behind the multiple accretions to which the most varied interpretations ("physical", euhemeristic, "mysterio-sophic") have led.

However that may be, a first result of our research into the available sources has been to investigate the reliability of a formula which establishes an exclusive and necessary relationship between the "form" of the mysteries and the existence of positive eschatological prospects for the individual. Limited though the expressiveness of the documents may be, it has been possible to conclude that, while no source attributes a specific guarantee of immortal bliss to the initiate, those prospects are not completely absent from the cult of Cybele.

Perceptible only at a fairly late period, however, they cover more or less indiscriminately the entire range of its religious manifestations, from the public form of the March ritual (the celebration of the *Hilaria* as the "salvation from Hades") to the sacred eunuchs and, at least in Roman aristocratic circles of the 4th century, to the practice of the taurobolium which can be viewed, albeit in a single case known to us, as a means of "rebirth" for all eternity.

The guarantees of a positive destiny in the hereafter entitle us to speak of soteriology, unknown though it is to us in its specific details. As far as we can judge from our documentation, however, these guarantees do not seem to constitute a central and absolutely characteristic element of the religious sphere in question, but they may have matured in the course of time owing to the assimilation of widespread contemporary aspirations and tendencies. It is in this sense that—in the context of the accentuation of the cosmic aspects of the deities in question, in the forms illustrated by the patera of Parabiago and the Attis of Ostia—we can account for the presence of the idea of the celestial immortality of the soul in documents which can be related, even if only conjecturally, to the context of Cybele.

A series of converging data reveal, moreover, a special concern with the infraterrestrial situation of man, in the broader sphere of cosmic life, especially on a chthonic and animal level. It is to this that the qualities and specific attributes of the Great Mother who dominates nature both in its uncultivated aspect (the mountain, beasts) and in its vital and fertile energies refer.

The goddess' medical and cathartic faculties, particularly concentrated on children and flocks, complete this perspective and account for the attribute of *soteira* which so frequently accompanies her. Her capacity to infuse *mania* turns into a beneficial possession which takes hold of the man who practises her cult, putting him into a state of bliss and in an immediate relationship with the deity—a condition which reveals a particular aspect of the mystic consistency of the cult.

But it is above all the mythical-ritual complex relating to Attis which expresses a religious vision based on the notion of the deity as a guarantor of cosmic existence. Indeed, however variously composed and elaborated the forms in which it has reached us, we are entitled to consult the Phrygian myth about the main significance of the religious context in question. That it is at least partially reliable is proved by its fundamental connections with the ritual practice which more faithfully retained the authentic and original religious values of that same context.

The theme which runs through the so-called Phrygian version of the myth of Attis is really that of the divine origin of the vegetal elements making up the natural setting in which the characters move. The almond tree or the pomegranate is born from the earth fertilised by the blood of Agdistis and its fruit gives birth to Attis. Nana is fed by the Mother of the Gods with the fruits of this tree, or with acorns and figs. Attis' blood produces the violets surrounding the pine-tree under which his mutilation took place. This mutilation, the cause of his death, is produced by a deity, Agdistis, just as the gods populating the initial scene of the episode had decided to mutilate the hermaphrodite Agdistis in order to regulate her violent and disorderly vital energies.

At the same time the pine-tree which, in the mythical narrative, is the background of the tragic end of the vicissitude, is in actual fact an alternative expression and a privileged manifestation of the Phrygian god, as emerges from its cultic rôle and the rich iconography in which Attis and the tree appear in intimate symbiosis.

The idea is thus established that life and vegetal fertility spring from the death of a deity and, more precisely, from parts of his body (the *vires*, blood). This notion is expressed, too, in connection with the girl, the bride of Attis, who also meets a violent death as the result of mutilation and gives birth, with her blood, to the purple violets. According to Arnobius' version of the myth it is from her tomb that the almond tree grows. We should observe, moreover, the association between marriage and dying which, aside from the banal motif of Agdistis' jealousy, is an essential component of the myth—the association of the sexual act and the ensuing procreation with death.

These various elements, each of which could seem, at first sight and out of the general context, the fruit of mythological elaborations based on the "physical" theories of late theologians, concur in their reciprocal interaction to form a unitary ideological structure, with an internal coherence and organicity, in which the notions of life, procreation and death are intimately connected and examplified in the vicissitude of a deity subject to crisis and disappearance.

This vicissitude is clearly reflected in the cultic practice. Indeed, the peculiarity of the Phrygian ritual cycle is its character of re-evocation of the various moments of Attis' *pathos*, as it is described in the corresponding mythical versions.

The vicissitudes of Attis, as we have seen, end once and for all in death. Unlike a Persephone or (at least in part) an Adonis, Attis does not "return" periodically; he does not have an annual "epiphany" which, mythically conceived in the form of an alternating presence in the Underworld and on earth (or amongst the Olympic gods), finds its ritual sanction in the cult, whether it be esoteric or public.

Attis appears rather as "surviving in death". The pine-tree of the March festivals does not express the idea of a periodic manifestation of the deity, but rather, in its quality as an evergreen, it reveals him as *praesens numen* even in the concealment and fixity of death. Death, moreover, has been intrinsically productive on a vegetal level, of whose cyclic rhythm Attis is now the guarantor and divine supporter.

If we wonder what prospects, aside from the late elaborations which took place under different ideological influences, were open to the adept through the celebration of the March ritual, we must keep in mind the particular content of that ritual, clearly characterised by the re-evocation of a divine vicissitude with multiple and deep connections with nature.

Various meanings have been attributed to these connections in the long course of the history of the Phrygian cult, and the original ideology expressed in it underwent inevitable transformations. Yet the persistence of the cult itself up to a late period, in the form and with the mythical roots I have described, would seem to testify to a relative stability of the fundamental notion essential to it.

The annual re-evocation of Attis' doleful destiny, with its joyful conclusion in the certainty of his survival (even in disappearing and death, which nevertheless produces spring buds and the evergreen presence of the pine-tree) and of his privileged position beside the Great Goddess, could appear to the devotee as a renewal of his own existential essence in an ordered cosmos whose natural rhythms are guaranteed and supported by divine entities. It could thus appear as a specific chance of "salvation".

SELECT BIBLIOGRAPHY

Abel, A. et alii, *Religions de salut* (Annales du Centre d'Étude des religions, 2), Bruxelles 1962.

Akurgal, E., *Phrygische Kunst*, Ankara 1955.

Albizzati, C., "La lanx di Parabiago e i testi orfici", *Athenaeum* XV (1937), 187-205.

Albright, W. F., "The Anatolian Goddess Kubaba", *AOF* V (1928-1929), 229-231.

Alfieri, N.-Arias, P. E., *Spina. Guida al museo archeologico in Ferrara*, Firenze 1960.

Alföldi, A., *Die Kontorniaten. Ein verkanntes Propagandmittel der Stadtrömischen heidnischen Aristokratie in ihrem Kampfe gegen das christliche Kaisertum*, Budapest-Leipzig 1943.

Allo, E. B., "Les dieux sauveurs du paganisme gréco-romain", *RSPh* XV (1926), 5-34.

Altheim, F., *Römische Religionsgeschichte*, II. *Von der Gründung des kapitolinischen Tempels bis zum Aufkommen der Alleinherrschaft*, Berlin-Leipzig 1932.

Archi, A., "Trono regale e trono divinizzato nell'Anatolia ittita", *Studi micenei ed egeo-anatolici* I (Incunabula graeca XI), Roma 1966, 76-120.

Atallah, W., *Adonis dans la littérature et l'art grecs*, Paris 1966.

Aurigemma, S., "La protezione speciale della Gran Madre Idea per la nobiltà romana e le leggende dell'origine troiana di Roma", *BCAR* 1909, 31-65.

Barnett, R. D., "The Phrygian Rock Façades and the Hittite Monuments. Plates VIII-X", *BiOr* X (1953), 78-82.

———, "Ancient Oriental Influences on Archaic Greece", S. S. Weinberg (ed.), *The Aegean and the Near East*, Studies presented to Hetty Goldman, New York 1956, 212-238.

———, "Some Contacts between Greek and Oriental Religions", *Éléments orientaux dans la religion grecque ancienne*, Colloque de Strasbourg 22-24 mai 1958, Paris 1960, 143-153.

Bartoli, A., "Il culto della Mater deum magna Idaea e di Venere genitrice sul Palatino", *MemPontAcc* VI (1942), 229-239.

———, "Tracce di culti orientali sul Palatino imperiale", *RendPontAcc* XXVIII (1954-1955) (1956), 13-49.

Beaujeu, J., *La religion romaine à l'apogée de l'Empire*, I. *La politique religieuse des Antonins (96-192)*, Paris 1955.

———, "La religion de la classe sénatoriale à l'époque des Antonins", M. Renard-R. Schilling (eds.), *Hommages à Jean Bayet* (Coll. Latomus LXX), Bruxelles 1964, 54-75.

Benoit, A., "Les mystères païens et le christianisme", F. Dunand et alii, *Mystères et syncrétismes*, Paris 1975, 73-91.

Bianchi, U., "Initiation, mystères, gnose (Pour l'histoire de la mystique dans le paganisme gréco-oriental)", C. J. Bleeker (ed.), *Initiation*, Leiden 1965, 154-171.

———, *The Greek Mysteries* (Iconography of Religions XVII, 3), Leiden 1976.

———, *Prometeo, Orfeo, Adamo. Tematiche religiose sul destino, il male, la salvezza*, Roma 1976.

———, "Prolegomena. The Religious-Historical Question of the Mysteries of Mithra", U. Bianchi (ed.), *Mysteria Mithrae*. Atti del Seminario internazionale su "La specificità storico-religiosa dei misteri di Mithra con particolare riferimento alle fonti documentarie di Roma e Ostia", Roma e Ostia 28-31 Marzo 1978 (EPRO 80), Roma-Leiden 1979, 3-60.

Bieber, M., "The Images of Cybele in Roman Coins and Sculpture", J. Bibauw (ed.), *Hommages à Marcel Renard* (Coll. Latomus CIII), vol. III, Bruxelles 1969, 29-40.

Bittel, K., "Untersuchungen auf Büyükkale. b. Das Phrygische Burgtor", *MDOI* XCI (1958), 61-72.

Bloch, H., "A New Document of the Last Pagan Revival in the West", *HThR* XXXVIII (1945), 199-244.

———, "The Pagan Revival in the West at the End of the Fourth Century, A. Momigliano (ed.), *The Conflict between Paganism and Christianity in the Fourth Century*, Oxford 1963, 193-218.

Bömer, F., *P. Ovidius Naso. Die Fasten*, Vols. I-II, Heidelberg 1957-1958.

———, "Kybele in Röm. Die Geschichte ihres Kultes als politisches Phänomen", *RM* LXXI (1964), 130-151.

Bolkestein, H., *Theophrastos' Charakter der Deisidaimonia als religionsgeschichtliche Urkunde* (RGVV 21, 2), Giessen 1929.

Bouyer, L., "Le salut dans les religions à mystères", *RSR* XXVII (1953), 1-16.

Boyancé, P., *Le culte des Muses chez les philosophes grecs. Études d'histoire et de psychologie religieuses*, Paris 1936.

——, *Études sur la religion romaine*, Rome 1972.

Brelich, A., "Politeismo e soteriologia", S. G. F. Brandon (ed.), *The Saviour God. Comparative Studies in the Concept of Salvation presented to Edwin Oliver James*, Manchester 1963, 37-50.

——, "Offerte e interdizioni alimentari nel culto della Magna Mater a Roma", *SMSR* XXXVI (1965), 27-42.

Bremmer, J., "The Legend of Cybele's Arrival in Rome", M. J. Vermaseren (ed.), *Studies in Hellenistic Religions* (EPRO 78), Leiden 1979, 9-22.

Briem, E., *Zur Frage nach dem Ursprung der hellenistischen Mysterien*, Lund-Leipzig 1928.

Cadoux, C. J., *Ancient Smyrna. A History of the City from the Earliest Times to 324 A.D.*, Oxford 1938.

Calza, G., "Il santuario della Magna Mater a Ostia", *MemPontAcc* VI (1942), 183-205.

Calza, R., "Sculture rinvenute nel Santuario", *MemPontAcc* VI (1942), 207-227.

Carcopino, J., "Note sur une inscription métroaque récemment découverte", *RendPontAcc* IV (1925-1926), 231-246.

——, *Aspects mystiques de la Rome païenne*, Paris 1942⁶.

——, *La basilique pythagoricienne de la Porte Majeure*, Paris 1944⁸.

Chapouthier, F., *Les Dioscures au service d'une déesse. Étude d'iconographie religieuse*, Paris 1935.

——, "Cybèle et le tympanon étoilé", *Mélanges syriens offerts à M. Dussaud*, Vol. II, Paris 1939, 723-728.

Colpe, C., "Zur mythologischen Struktur der Adonis-, Attis- und Osiris-Überlieferungen", W. Röllig (ed.), *lišān mitḫurti. Festschrift W. F. v. Soden*, Neukirchen-Vluyn 1969, 23-44.

Conze, A., "Hermes-Kadmilos (Taf. 1-4)", *AZ* XXXVIII (1880), 1-10.

Cosi, D. M., "Salvatore e salvezza nei misteri di Attis", *Aevum* L (1976), 42-71.

——, "La simbologia della porta nel Vicino Oriente. Per una interpretazione dei monumenti rupestri frigi", *AFLPad* I (1976), 113-152.

——, "Firmico Materno e i misteri di Attis", *AFLPad* II (1977), 55-81.

——, "Attis e Mithra", U. Bianchi (ed.), *Mysteria Mithrae*, cit., 625-638.

——, "Aspetti mistici e misterici del culto di Attis", U. Bianchi-M. J. Vermaseren (eds.), *La soteriologia dei culti orientali nell'impero Romano*, Atti del Colloquio Internazionale su "La soteriologia dei culti orientali nell'Impero Romano", Roma 24-28 settembre 1979 (EPRO 92), Leiden 1982, 485-502.

Christou, C., *Potnia theron. Eine Untersuchung über Ursprung, Erscheinungsformen, und Wandlungen der Gestalt einer Gottheit*, Thessaloniki 1968.

Cumont, F., "Le taurobole et le culte de Anahita", *RA* XII (1888), 132-136.

——, "Le taurobole et le culte de Bellone", *RHLR* VI (1901), 97-110.

——, "A propos de Cybèle", *RA* VI (1917), 418-425.

——, *Les religions orientales dans le paganisme romain*, Paris 1929⁴.

——, *Recherches sur le symbolisme funéraire des Romains*, Paris 1942.

——, *Lux Perpetua*, Paris 1949.

De Labriolle, P., *La réaction païenne. Étude sur la polémique antichrétienne du Iᵉʳ au VIᵉ siècle*, Paris 1948⁹.

Delcourt, M., *Hermaphrodite. Mythes et rites de la Bisexualité dans l'Antiquité classique*, Paris 1958.

Detienne, M., *Les jardins d'Adonis*, Paris 1972.

Dey, J., ΠΑΛΙΓΓΕΝΕΣΙΑ, Münster 1937.

Di Capua, F., "Un'epigrafe stabiese e il culto della 'Deum Mater' presso le sorgenti di acque minerali", *RAAN* XXI (1941), 75-83.

Dieterich, A., "Die Göttin Mise", *Philologus* LII (1893), 1-12.

——, *Mutter Erde. Ein Versuch über Volksreligion*, Leipzig 1925³.

Dodds, E. R., *The Greeks and the Irrational*, Berkeley-Los Angeles 1951.
——, *Euripides, Bacchae*, Oxford 1960.
Dölger, F. J., ΙΧΘΥΣ. *Das Fischsymbol in frühchristlicher Zeit*, I. *Religionsgeschichtliche und epigraphische Untersuchungen*, Roma 1910.
——, "Die religiöse Brandmarkung in den Kybele-Attis-Mysterien nach einem Texte des christlichen Dichters Prudentius", *Antike und Christentum. Kultur- und religionsgeschichtliche Studien*, Bd. I, Münster i. Westfalen 1929, 66-72.
Doren, M. van, "L'évolution des mystères phrygiens à Rome", *AC* XXII (1953), 79-88.
——, "Peregrina sacra. Offizielle Kultübertragungen im alten Rom", *Historia* III (1955), 488-497.
Dupont-Sommer, A.-Robert, L., *La déesse de Hiérapolis-Castabala (Cilicie)*, Paris 1964.
Duthoy, R., "La Minerva Berecyntia des inscriptions tauroboliques de Bénévent (CIL IX. 1538-1542)", *AC* XXXV (1966), 548-561.
——, *The Taurobolium. Its Evolution and Terminology* (EPRO 10), Leiden 1969.
Egger, R., "Sanctissima Mater", *Studi in onore di Aristide Calderini e Roberto Paribeni*, Milano 1956, 239-250.
Eliade, M., "La Mandragore et les mythes de la "naissance miraculeuse" ", *Zalmoxis* III (1940-1942), 3-48.
Espérandieu, É., *Recueil général des bas-reliefs de la Gaule romaine*, T. I, Paris 1907.
——, *Recueil général des bas-reliefs, statues et bustes de la Germaine romaine*, Paris-Bruxelles 1931.
Fabre, P., "Un autel du culte phrygien au Musée du Latran", *MEFR* XL (1923), 3-18.
Farnell, L. R., *The Cults of the Greek States*, vol. III, Oxford 1907.
Fasce, S., *Attis e il culto metroaco a Roma*, Genova 1978.
Fauth, W., "Adamma Kubaba", *Glotta* XLV (1967), 129-148.
Ferguson, W. S., "Attic Orgeones", *HThR* XXXVII (1944), 61-140.
Ferron, J.-Saumagne, Ch., "Adon-Baal, Esculape, Cybèle à Carthage", *Africa* II (1967-1968), 75-110.
Festugière, A.-J., *Études de religion grecque et hellénistique*, Paris 1972.
Fishwick, D., "The Cannophori and the March Festival of Magna Mater", *TAPhA* XCVII (1966), 193-202.
——, "Hastiferi", *JRS* LVII (1967), 142-160.
Floriani Squarciapino, M., *I culti orientali ad Ostia* (EPRO 3), Leiden 1962.
Foucart, P., *Des associations religieuses chez les Grecs. Thiases, Eranes, Orgéons*, Paris 1873.
——, *Les mystères d'Éleusis*, Paris 1914.
Fracassini, U., *Il misticismo greco e il cristianesimo*, Città di Castello 1922.
Frankfort, H., *Kingship and the Gods. A Study of Ancient Near Eastern Religion as the Integration of Society and Nature*, Chicago-London 1948 (1969⁶).
——, "The Dying God". Inaugural Lecture as Director of the Warburg Institute and Professor of the History of Pre-classical Antiquity in the University of London, 10 November 1949, *JWI* XXI (1958), 141-151.
Frazer, J. G., *The Golden Bough. A Study in Magic and Religion*, Part IV, I *Adonis-Attis-Osiris*, London 1936³.
——, (ed.), *Publii Ovidii Nasonis Fastorum Libri sex. The Fasti of Ovid*, vol. III, London 1929.
Freijero, A. B., "Documentos metroacos de Hispania", *AEspA* XLI (1968), 91-100.
Friedländer, P., *Documents of Dying Paganism. Textiles of Late Antiquity in Washington, New York and Leningrad*, Berkeley-Los Angeles 1945.
Fritze, H. von, "Der Attiskult in Kyzikos. Taf. III", *Nomisma* IV (1909), 33-42.
García y Bellido, A., *Les religions orientales dans l'Espagne romaine* (EPRO 5), Leiden 1967.
Gatti, C., "Per la storia del culto della 'Magna Mater' in Roma", *RILomb* LXXXII (1949), 253-262.
Gérard, J., "Légende et politique autour de la Mère des Dieux", *REL* 58 (1980), 153-175.
Goetze, A., *Kulturgeschichte des Alten Orients*, III, 1. *Kleinasien* (Handbuch der Altertumswissenschaft, III Abt., I Teil, Bd. III, III, I), München 1957².
Goossens, W., *Les origines de l'Eucharistie. Sacrament et sacrifice*, Paris 1931.
Graillot, H., *Le culte de Cybèle Mère des Dieux à Rome et dans l'Empire romaine*, Paris 1912.

——, "Mater Deum salutaris. Cybèle protectrice des eaux thermales", *Mélanges Capart*, Paris 1912, 213-228.

Grandmaison, L. de, "Dieux morts et ressuscités", *RechSR* XVII (1927), 97-126.

Gressmann, H., *Die orientalischen Religionen im hellenistisch-römischen Zeitalter. Eine Vortragsreihe*, Berlin-Leipzig 1930.

Guarducci, M., *Cristo e San Pietro in un documento precostantiniano della necropoli vaticana*, Roma 1953.

——, "Cibele in un'epigrafe arcaica di Locri Epizefirî", *Klio* LII (1970), 133-138.

——, "Il culto di Cibele a Locri", *AlmC* 1972-73, 25-29.

——, "L'interruzione dei culti nel *Phrygianum* del Vaticano durante il IV secolo d.Cr.", U. Bianchi-M. J. Vermaseren (eds.), *La soteriologia dei culti orientali*, cit., 109-121.

——, "La scomparsa di Cibele", U. Bianchi-M. J. Vermaseren (eds.), *La soteriologia dei culti orientali*, cit., 123-125.

Gurney, O. R., "Tammuz reconsidered: some recent developments", *JSS* VII (1962), 147-160.

Gusmani, R., "ΑΓΔΙΣΤΙΣ", *PP* XIV (1959), 202-211.

Guthrie, W. K. C., *Orpheus and Greek Religion*, London 1952².

Hadzisteliou Price, Th., *Kourotrophos. Cults and Representations of the Greek Nursing Deities*, Leiden 1978.

Hanfmann, G. M., *The Season Sarcophagus in Dumbarton Oaks*, vols. I-II, Cambridge 1951.

Hanson, J. A., *Roman Theater-Temples*, Princeton 1959.

Harris, E.-J. R., *The Oriental Cults in Roman Britain* (EPRO 6), Leiden 1965.

Harrison, J. E., "The Meaning of the Word ΤΕΛΕΤΗ", *CR* XXVIII (1914), 36-38.

Helck, W., *Betrachtungen zur grossen Göttin und den ihr verbundenen Gottheiten*, München-Wien 1971.

Hemberg, B., *Die Kabiren*, Uppsala 1950.

Henrichs, A., "Despoina Kybele: ein Beitrag zur religiösen Namenkunde", *HSPh* 80 (1976), 253-286.

Hepding, H., *Attis, seine Mythen und sein Kult* (RGVV 1), Giessen 1903.

Herrmann, L., "Catulle et les cultes exotiques", *NC* VI (1954) [Mélanges Roger Goossens], 236-246.

Jacobsen, T., *Toward the Image of Tammuz and other Essays on Mesopotamian History and Culture*, Cambridge (Mass.) 1970.

Jeanmaire, J., *Dionysos. Histoire du culte de Bacchus*, Paris 1951.

Karwiese, St., *Attis in der antiken Kunst*, Diss. Wien 1967.

——, "Der gefesselte Attis", *Festschrift für Fritz Eichler zum achtzigsten Geburtstag dargebracht vom Österreichischen Archäologischen Institut*, Wien 1967, 82-95.

——, "Der tote Attis", *JÖAI* L (1968-71), 50-62.

Keil, J., "Denkmäler des Meter-Kultes", *JÖAI* XVIII (1915), 66-78.

Keil, J.-Premerstein, A. von, *Bericht über eine zweite Reise in Lydien* (Denkschriften der kais. Akad. d. Wiss. in Wien, Phil.-hist. Kl., Bd. LIV, II), Wien 1911.

——, *Bericht über eine dritte Reise in Lydien und den angrenzenden Gebieten Joniens ausgeführt 1911 im Auftrage der kaiserlichen Akademie der Wissenschaften* (Denkschriften der kais. Akad. d. Wiss. in Wien, Phil.-hist. Kl., Bd. LVII), Wien 1914.

Kobylina, M. M., *Divinités orientales sur le litoral nord de la Mer Noire* (EPRO 52), Leiden 1976.

Kötting, B., *Christentum und heidnische Opposition in Rom am Ende des 4.Jahrhunderts*, Münster 1961.

Köves, Th., "Zum Empfang der Magna Mater in Rom", *Historia* XII (1963), 321-347.

Lagrange, M.-J., "Mélanges I. Attis et le christianisme", *RBi*, n.s. XVI (= XXVIII) (1919), 419-480.

——, "Mélanges II. Attis ressuscité?", *RBi*, n.s. XXIV (= XXXVI) (1927), 561-566.

——, *Introduction à l'étude du Nouveau Testament. Quatrième Partie, Critique historique. I Les mystères: l'orphisme*, Paris 1937.

Lambrechts, P., "Cybèle, divinité étrangère ou nationale?", *BSBAP* LXII (1951), 44-60.

——, "Attis à Rome", *Mélanges G. Smets*, Brussel 1952, 461-471.

——, "Les fêtes 'phrygiennes' de Cybèle et d'Attis", *BIBR* XXVII (1952), 141-170.

——, "La 'résurrection' d'Adonis", AIPhO XIII (1955) [*Mélanges Isidore Levy*], 1-34.

——, "*Attis: van Herdersknaap tot God* (Avec un résumé français par G. Sanders), Brussel 1962.

——, "Documents inédits de Cybèle au Musée d'Eskişehir", *Hommages à Marie Delcourt* (Coll. Latomus CXIV), Bruxelles 1970, 211-218.

Lane, E., *Corpus Monumentorum Religionis Dei Menis* (CMRDM), vols. I-III (EPRO 19), Leiden 1971-1976.

Laroche, E., "Koubaba, déesse anatolienne, et le problème des origines de Cybèle", *Éléments orientaux dans la religion grecque ancienne*, Colloque de Strasbourg 22-24 mai 1958, Paris 1960, 113-128.

Le Bonniec, H., "«Tradition de la culture classique». Arnobe témoin et juge des cultes païens", *BAGB* 4, 2 (1974), 201-222.

Leipoldt, J., *Sterbende und auferstehende Götter. Ein Beitrag zum Streite um Arthur Drews' Christusmythe*, Leipzig-Erlangen 1923.

——, *Die Religionen in der Umwelt des Urchristentums* (Bilderatlas zur Religionsgeschichte, ed. H. Haas, 9-11 Lieferung), Leipzig-Erlangen 1926.

Levi, A., *La patera d'argento di Parabiago*, Roma 1935 (R. Ist. d'Arch. e Storia dell'arte. Opere d'arte, fasc. 5).

Linforth, I. M., "The Corybantic Rites in Plato", *UCPCPh* XIII, 5 (1946), 121-162.

——, "Telestic Madness in Plato, Phaedrus 244 DE", *UCPCPh* XIII, 6 (1946), 163-172.

Loisy, A., *Les mystères païens et le mystère chrétien*, Paris 1914.

Manganaro, G., "La reazione pagana a Roma nel 408-409 d.C. e il poemetto anonimo 'Contra paganos' ", *GIF* XIII (1960), pp. 210-224.

——, "Il poemetto anonimo Contra Paganos" in *ND* XI (1961), pp. 23-45.

Matthews, J. F., "The Historical Setting of the 'Carmen contra Paganos' (Cod. Par. Lat. 8084)", *Historia* XIX (1970), 464-479.

Mau, G., *Die Religionsphilosophie Kaiser Julians in seinen Reden auf König Helios und die Göttermutter. Mit einer Uebersetzung der beiden Reden* (Studia Historica 88), Leipzig 1908.

Mellink, M. J., "Early Cult-Images of Cybele in Asia Minor", *AJA* LXIV (1960), 188.

Meslin, M., "Réalités psychiques et valeurs religieuses dans les cultes orientaux (Ier-IVe siècles)", *RH* DXII (1974), 289-314.

——, "Agdistis ou l'androgynie malséante", M. B. de Boer-T. A. Edridge (eds.), *Hommages à Maarten J. Vermaseren* (EPRO 68), Leiden 1978, vol. II, 765-776.

Metzger, B. M., "Considerations of Methodology in the Study of the Mystery Religions and Early Christianity", *HThR* XLVIII (1955), 1-20.

Momigliano, A., *The Conflict between Paganism and Christianity in the Fourth Century*, Oxford 1963.

Moore, C. H., "On the Origin of the Taurobolium", *HSPh* XVII (1906), 43-48.

——, "The Duration of the Efficacy of the Taurobolium", *CPh* XIX (1924), 363-365.

Mylonas, G. E., *Eleusis and the Eleusinian Mysteries*, Princeton 1961.

Neuman, G., "Die Begleiter der phrygische Muttergöttin von Boğäzköy", *NAWG* VI (1959), 101-105.

Nilsson, M. P., *Geschichte der Griechischen Religion*, vols. I-II, München 1955-1961².

——, *The Dionysiac Mysteries of the Hellenistic and Roman Age*, Lund 1957.

Nock, A. D., *Sallustius Concerning the Gods and the Universe*, Cambridge 1926.

——, *Conversion. The Old and the New in Religion from Alexander the Great to Augustine of Hippo*, Oxford 1933.

——, *Essays on Religion and the Ancient World*, vols. I-II, Oxford 1972.

Ohlemutz, E., *Die Kulte und Heiligtümer der Götter in Pergamon*, Würzburg-Auhmühle 1940.

Otten, H., *Die Religionen des alten Kleinasien* (Handbuch der Orientalistik, I Abt., Bd. VIII, I, I), Leiden 1964.

Pelletier, A., *Le sanctuaire métroaque de Vienne (France)* (EPRO 83), Leiden 1980.

Pensabene, P., "Nuove indagini nell'area del tempio di Cibele sul Palatino", U. Bianchi-M. J. Vermaseren (eds.), *La soteriologia dei culti orientali*, cit., 68-108, tavv. I-X.

Pépin, J., "Réactions du christianisme latin à la sotériologie métroaque. Firmicus Maternus, Ambrosiaster, Saint Augustin", U. Bianchi-M. J. Vermaseren (eds.), *La soteriologia dei culti orientali*, cit., 256-272.

Pettazzoni, R., *I misteri. Saggio di una teoria storico-religiosa*, Bologna 1924.
——, *La confessione dei peccati*, vol. III, Bologna 1936.
——, "Les mystères grecs et les religions à mystères de l'antiquité. Recherches récentes et problèmes nouveaux", *CHM* II (1954), 303-312; 661-667.
Picard, Ch., *Éphèse et Claros. Recherches sur les sanctuaires et les cultes de l'Ionie du Nord*, Paris 1922.
——, "ΠΟΤΝΙΑ «ΑΝΔΡΩΝ ΤΕ ΘΕΩΝ ΤΕ». Note sur le type de la Déesse-Mère entre deux assesseurs anthropomorphes (Pl. I-III)", *RHR* XCVIII (1928), 60-77.
——, "Le phrygien Hector était-il Galle de Cybèle?", *RA* XLIII (1954), 80-82.
——, "Dionysos Pais et Attis enfant", *AEph* I (1953-54) (1955) [Eis mnemen G. M. Oikonomou], 1-8.
——, "Le théâtre des mystères de Cybèle-Attis à Vienne (Isère), et les théâtres pour représentations sacrées à travers le monde méditerranéen", *CRAI* 1955, 229-247.
——, "Sur quelques documents nouveaux concernant les cultes de Cybèle et d'Attis: des Balkans à la Gaule", *Numen* IV (1957), 1-23.
——, "La rencontre sur le mont Dindymon et la passion d'Attis: d'après un cratère de bronze hellénistique", *RA* (1960), II, 63-72.
——, "Le rôle religieux des théâtres antiques", *JS* (1961), 49-78.
——, "Sabazios, dieu thraco-phrygien: expansion et aspects nouveaux de son culte", *RA* (1961), II, 129-176.
——, "Le dieu thraco-phrygien Sabazios-Sabazius a Vichy", *RACentre* I (1962), 10-30.
——, *Manuel d'archéologie grecque. La sculpture. IV. Période classique IVe siècle (Deuxième Partie)*, Paris 1963.
——, "Le trône vide d'Alexandre dans la cérémonie de Cyinda et le culte du trône vide à travers le monde gréco-romain", *CArch* VII (1964), 1-17 Pl. I-V.
——, "Rhéa-Cybèle et le culte des portes sacrées", L. Freeman Sandler (ed.), *Essays in Memory of Karl Lehmann* (Marsyas. Studies in the History of Art, Suppl. I: A special Volume), New York 1964, 259-266.
Poerner, J., *De Curetis et Corybantibus* (Diss. Phil. Halens. XXII, 2), Halis Saxonum 1913.
Pouilloux, J., *La forteresse de Rhamnonte (Étude de topographie et d'histoire)*, Paris 1954.
Prümm, K., "Die Endgestalt des orientalischen Vegetationsheros in der hellenistisch-römischen Zeit", *ZKTh* LVIII (1934), 463-502.
——, *Religionsgeschichtliches Handbuch für den Raum der altchristlichen Umwelt. Hellenistisch-römische Geistesströmungen und Kulte mit Beachtung des Eigenlebens der Provinzen*, Rom 1954².
——, s.v. *Mystères*, L. Pirot-A. Robert-H. Cazelles (eds.), *Dictionnaire de la Bible, Supplément* XXX, Paris 1957, 10-173.
——, "I cosiddetti 'dei morti e risorti' nell'Ellenismo", *Gregorianum* XXXIX (1958), 411-439.
Quasten, G., *Musik und Gesang in den Kulten der heidnischen Antike und christlichen Frühzeit* (Liturgiegeschich. Quellen und Forsch. 25), Münster i W. 1930.
Ramsay, W. M., "Studies in Asia Minor", *JHS* III (1882), 1-68.
——, "Some Phrygian Monuments [Pl. XXVI-XXIX]", *JHS* III (1882), 256-263.
——, "Sepulchral Customs in Ancient Phrygia", *JHS* V (1884), 241-262.
——, "Sketches in the Religious Antiquities of Asia Minor (Plates I-IV)", *ABSA* XVII (1910-1911), 37-79.
——, s.v. *Phrygians*, Hastings, *ERE* IX (1917), 900-911.
——, "Pisidian wolf-Priests, phrygian goat-Priests and the old-Iranian Tribes", *JHS* XL (1920), 197-202.
Reitzenstein, R., *Die hellenistischen Mysterienreligionen*, Leipzig 1927³.
Renard, M., "Attis funéraires de Toulouse", *Latomus* XI (1952), 59-62.
Ribichini, S., "Metamorfosi vegetali del sangue nel mondo antico", *Atti della Settimana di Studi "Sangue e antropologia biblica nella letteratura cristiana"*, Roma, 29 novembre-4 dicembre 1982, cur. F. Vattioni, Roma 1983, vol. I, 233-247.
Richard, J., "Juvénal et les galles de Cybèle", *RHR* CLXIX (1966), 51-67.
——, "Remarques sur le sacrifice taurobolique", *Latomus* XXVIII (1969), 661-668.
Ring, G. C., "Christ's Resurrection and the Dying and Rising Gods", *CBQ* VI (1944), 216-229.

Robert, L., "Sur deux inscriptions grecques", *AIPhO* II (1934) [Mélanges J. Bidez], Bruxelles 1934, 793-812.
——, "Une nouvelle inscription grecque de Sardes: Règlement de l'autorité perse relatif à un culte de Zeus", *CRAI* (1975), 306-330.
Robinson, D. N., "An Analysis of the Pagan Revival of the Late Fourth Century, with Especial Reference to Symmachus", *TAPhA* XLVI (1915), 87-101.
Rochefort, G., "Le ΠΕΡΙ ΘΕΩΝ ΚΑΙ ΚΟΣΜΟΥ de Saloustios et l'influence de l'Empereur Julien", *REG* LXIX (1956), 50-66.
Romanelli, P., "Lo scavo al tempio della Magna Mater sul Palatino e nelle sue adiacenze", *MonAL* XLVI (1963), 201-330.
——, "Magna Mater e Attis sul Palatino", M. Renard-R. Schilling (eds.), *Hommages à Jean Bayet"* (Coll. Latomus LXX), Bruxelles-Berchem 1964, 619-626.
Rutter, J. B., "The three phases of the Taurobolium", *Phoenix* XXII (1968), 226-249.
Sabbatucci, D., *Saggio sul misticismo greco*, Roma 1965 (1979²).
Salis, A. von, "Die Göttermutter des Agorakritos", *JDI* XXVIII (1913), 1-26.
Sanders, G., s.v. Gallos, *RAC* VIII, n° 63 (1972), 984-1034.
——, "Les Galles et le Gallat devant l'opinion chrétienne", M. B. de Boer-T. A. Edridge (eds.), *Hommages à Maarten J. Vermaseren* (EPRO 68), Leiden 1978, vol. III, 1062-1091.
——, "Kybele und Attis", M. J. Vermaseren (ed.), *Die orientalischen Religionen im Römerreich (OrRR)* (EPRO 93), Leiden 1981, 264-297, Taf. I-VI.
Showerman, G., "Was Attis at Rome under the Republic?", *TAPhA* XXXI (1900), 46-59.
Schwertheim, E., *Die Denkmäler orientalischer Gottheiten im Römischen Deutschland* (EPRO 40), Leiden 1974.
——, "Denkmäler zur Meterverehrung in Bithynien und Mysien (Taf. CLXXXVI-CXCVIII, Abb. 1-41)", S. Şahin-E. Schwertheim-J. Wagner (eds.), *Studien zur Religion und Kultur Kleinasiens*, Festschrift für Friedrich Karl Dörner zum 65.Geburtstag am 28 Februar 1976 (EPRO 66), Leiden 1978, vol. II, 791-837.
Schwertheim, E.-Şahin, S., "Neue Inschriften aus Nikomedeia und Umgebung", *ZPE* XXIV (1977), 259-264.
Seyrig, H., "Le rameau mystique", *AJA* XLVIII (1944), 20-25.
Sfameni Gasparro, G., *I culti orientali in Sicilia* (EPRO 31), Leiden 1973.
——, "Connotazioni metroache di Demetra nel Coro dell'"Elena" (vv. 1301-1365)", M. B. de Boer-T. A. Edridge (eds.), *Hommages à Maarten J. Vermaseren*, cit., vol. III, 1148-1187.
——, "Interpretazioni gnostiche e misteriosofiche del mito di Attis", R. van den Broek-M. J. Vermaseren (eds.), *Studies in Gnosticism and Hellenistic Religions presented to Gilles Quispel on the Occasion of his 65th Birthday* (EPRO 91), Leiden 1981, 376-411.
——, "Il mitraismo nell'ambito della fenomenologia misterica", U. Bianchi (ed.), *Mysteria Mithrae*, cit., 299-337.
——, "Riflessioni ulteriori su Mithra 'dio mistico' " *ibid.*, 397-408.
——, "Sotériologie et aspects mystiques dans le culte de Cybèle et d'Attis", U. Bianchi-M. J. Vermaseren (eds.), *La soteriologia dei culti orientali*, cit., 472-479.
——, "Significato e ruolo del sangue nel culto di Cibele e Attis", *Atti della Settimana di Studi "Sangue e antropologia biblica"*, cit., vol. I, 199-232.
Sharpe, E. J.-Hinnels, J. R. (eds.), *Man and his Salvation*, Manchester 1973.
Sokolowski, F., "A propos du mot ΤΕΛΕΤΗ", *Charisteria G. Przychocki a discipulis oblata*, Warsaw 1934, 272-276.
Spinazzola, V., *Pompei alla luce degli scavi nuovi di Via dell'Abbondanza (Anni 1910-1923)*, Roma 1953.
Svoronos, J. N., *Das Athener Nationalmuseum*, vols. I-III, Athen 1908-1937.
Toutain, J., "La légende de la déesse phrygienne Cybèle. Ses transformations", *RHR* LXI (1909), 299-308.
Tran Tram Tinh, V., *Le culte des divinités orientales en Campanie en dehors de Pompéi, de Stabies et d'Herculanum* (EPRO 27), Leiden 1972.
——, "Les problèmes du culte de Cybèle et d'Attis à Pompei", B. Andreae-H. Kyrieleis (eds.), *Neue Forschungen in Pompeji und den anderen vom Vesuvausbruch 79 n.Chr. verschütteten Städten*, Recklinghausen 1975, 279-283.

Turcan, R., *Les sarcophages romains à représentations dionysiaques. Essai de chronologie et d'histoire religieuse*, Paris 1966.
——, *Sénèque et les religions orientales* (Coll. Latomus vol. XCI), Bruxelles 1967.
——, *Les religions de l'Asie dans la vallée du Rhône* (EPRO 30), Leiden 1972.
——, "Masques corniers d'orientaux: Attis Ganymèdes ou Arimaspes", *Mélanges de Philosophie, de Littérature et d'Histoire ancienne offerts à Pierre Boyancé* (Coll. École française de Rome 22), Rome 1974, 721-747.
——, "L'aigle du pileus", M. B. de Boer-T. A. Edridge (eds.), *Hommages à Maarten J. Vermaseren* (EPRO 68), Leiden 1978, vol. III, 1281-1292.
Vanden-Berghe, L., "Réflexions critiques sur la nature de Dumuzi-Tammuz", *NC* VI (1954) [Mélanges Roger Goossens], 298-321.
Vermaseren, M. J., *The Legend of Attis in Greek and Roman Art* (EPRO 9), Leiden 1966.
——, "Iconografia e iconologia di Attis in Italia", *Studi romagnoli* 27 (1976), 46-62.
——, *Cybele and Attis. The Myth and the Cult*, London 1977.
——, "Kybele und Merkur", S. Şahin-E. Schwertheim-J. Wagner (eds.), *Studien zur Religion und Kultur Kleinasiens*. Festschrift für Friedrich Karl Dörner zum 65 Geburtstag am 28 Februar 1976 (EPRO 66), Leiden 1978, vol. II, 956-966.
——, *Der Kult der Kybele und des Attis im römischen Germanien*, Stuttgart 1979.
——, "L'iconographie d'Attis mourant", R. van den Broek-M. J. Vermaseren (eds.), *Studies in Gnosticism*, cit., 419-431, Pls. I-III.
Wagner, G., *Das religionsgeschichtliche Problem von Römer 6, 1-11*, Zürich 1962 [tr. ingl. *Pauline Baptism and the Pagan Mysteries*, Edinburgh 1967].
Walter, O., "ΚΟΥΡΗΤΙΚΗ ΤΡΙΑΣ", *JÖAI* XXXI (1939), 53-80.
Weinreich, O., "Stiftung und Kultsatzungen eines Privatheiligtums in Philadelpheia in Lydien", *SBHAW* XVI (1919), 1-68.
——, "Catullus Attisgedicht", *AIPhO* IV (1936) [Mélanges Franz Cumont I], 463-500.
Wendland, P., ΣΩΤΗΡ, *ZNTW* V (1904), 335-353.
Wilamowitz-Moellendorff, U. von, *Der Glaube der Hellenen*, vols. I-II Berlin 1931-1932.
Will, E., *Le relief cultuel gréco-romain. Contribution à l'histoire de l'art de l'Empire romain*, Paris 1955.
——, "Aspects du culte et de la légende de la Grande Mère dans le monde grec", *Éléments orientaux dans la religion grecque ancienne*, Colloque de Strasbourg 22-24 mai 1958, Paris 1960, 95-111.
Willoughby, H. R., *Pagan Regeneration. A Study of Mystery Initiations in the Graeco-Roman World*, Chicago 1930.
Wissowa, G., *Religion und Kultus der Römer*, München 1902.
Wolbergs, Th., *Griechische religiöse Gedichte der ersten nachchristlichen Jahrhunderte*, Bd. I, *Psalmen und Hymnen der Gnosis und des frühen Christentums* (Beitrage zur klassischen Philologie, Heft 40), Meisenheim am Glan 1971.
Wyss, K., *Die Milch im Kultus der Griechen und Römer* [RGVV 15, 2], Giessen 1914.
Wytzes, J., *Der letzte Kampf des Heidentums in Rom* (EPRO 56), Leiden 1977.
Zielinski, Th., *La Sibylle. Trois essais sur la religion antique et le christianisme*, Paris 1924.
Zijderveld, C., ΤΕΛΕΤΗ (Diss. Utrecht), Purmerend 1934.

ADDENDUM

p. XIII n.1   Cf. now B. M. Metzger, "A Classified Bibliography of the Graeco-Roman Mystery Religions 1924-1973 with a Supplement 1974-1977", H. Temporini-W. Haase (eds.), *Aufstieg und Niedergang der Römischen Welt*, II *Principat*, Bd. 17,3 *Religion* (*Heidentum: römische Götterkulte, orientalische Kulte in der römischen Welt* [Forts.]), Berlin-New York 1984, 1259-1423.

p. 2 n.7   Cf. R. Gusmani, "Der lydische Name der Kybele", *Kadmos* VIII (1969), 158-161.

p. 3 n.12   For Mida Monument cf. C. H. E. Haspels, *The Highlands of Phrygia. Sites and Monuments*, vols. I-II, Princeton 1972. Also E. Akurgal, *Die Kunst Anatoliens von Homer bis Alexander*, Berlin 1961, 86-121.

p. 4 n.13   Cf. also E. Akurgal, *op. cit.*, 95-100 Abb. 55-59; K. Bittel, *Hattuscha, Hauptstadt der Hethiter*, Köln 1983, 201ff. I. M. Diakonoff, "On Cybele and Attis in Phrygia and Lydia", *Acta Antiqua Academiae Scientiarum Hungaricae* XXV (1977), 333-340 is of the opinion that the statue does not represent the goddess Cybele at all, but an eunuch. The sculpture now seems to be restored not rightly as the figure of a woman whereas it is a male person (Attis) (*ibid.*, 337-340).

p. 4 n.14   On the iconography of the goddess cf. also C. H. E. Haspels, "Lions", *Mnemosyne* S. IV, IV (1951), 230-234; F. Naumann, *Die Ikonographie der Kybele in der phrygischen und der griechischen Kunst* (Istanbuler Mitteilungen, Beiheft 28), Tübingen 1983.

p. 4 n.19   Cf. E. Akurgal, *op. cit.*, 240-243 Abb. 209.

p. 13 n.30   Cf. P. Lévêque, "Ὄλβιος et la felicité des initiés", L. Hadermann-Misguich-G. Raepsaet-G. Cambier (eds.), *Rayonnement grec. Hommages à Charles Delvoye*, Bruxelles 1982, 113-126. For *olbios* and other connections of Cybele and Dionysos in Orphism cf. also M. L. West, *The Orphic Poems*, Oxford 1983.

p. 14 n.32   For Olympiodorus' Commentary cf. now L. G. Westerink, *The Greek Commentaries on Plato's Phaedo*, vol. I, *Olympiodorus*, Amsterdam-Oxford-New York 1976.

p. 24 n.19   For Samotrace see now S. Guettel Cole, *Theoi Megaloi: The Cult of the Great Gods at Samothrace* (EPRO 96), Leiden 1984.

p. 35 and nn. 33-36   On *Meter Zizimene* see the complete material in M. J. Vermaseren CCCA I (in preparation).

p. 46 ff.   See also L. Lacroix, "Texte et réalités. À propos du témoignage de Lucrèce sur la Magna Mater", JS (1982), 11-43.

     For Firmicus Maternus cf. R. Turcan (ed.), *L'erreur des religions païennes*, Paris 1982.

p. 48   M. J. Vermaseren, "A new bronze Attis-figurine and Donatello", *Actus. Studies in Honour of H. L. W. Nelson*, Utrecht 1982, 441-451; Id., "Attis Karpophoros" to be published in *Hommages W. Blawatsky*, Moscou.

p. 74 n.59   Cf. M. Tacheva-Hitova, *Eastern Cults in Moesia Inferior and Thracia (5th Century BC-4th Century AD)* (EPRO 95), Leiden 1983, 116-118, n° 101.

p. 34 n.31	Cf. L. Robert, *A travers l'Asie Mineure. Poètes et prosateurs, monnaies grecques, voyageurs et géographie*, Paris 1980, 221-240 (Cap. IX. Stace, les carrières et les monnaies de Dokimeion, Attis et Agdistis).
p. 36 n.44	For the cult of Cybele in Alexandria see also P. M. Fraser, *Ptolemaic Alexandria*, Oxford 1972, vol. I, 277-279. The Agdistis' inscription *ibid.* 277; vol. II, 433 n. 722.
p. 36 n.45	Cf. C. H. E. Haspels, *op. cit.*, vol. I, 295-302, nos. 1-17; Th. Drew-Bear, "Local Cults in Graeco-Roman Phrygia", GRBS XVII (1976), 259f., Pl. 9 fig. 2; L. Robert, *A travers l'Asie Mineure*, cit., 293-299.
p. 37 n.51	Cf. now F. Sokolowski, "TA ΕΝΠΥΡΑ: on the mysteries in the Lydian and Phrygian Cults", *ZPE* 34 (1979), 65-69.
p. 55 n.121	*Contra*: V. F. Lenzen, *The Triumph of Dionysos on Textiles of Late Antique Egypt* (Univ. of California Publ. in Class. Arch. 5,1), Berkeley and Los Angeles 1960.
p. 56 n.122	See also D. Sabbatucci, "L'edilità romana: magistratura e sacerdozio", *MemAccLinc* S. VIII, vol. 6/3 (1955), 275-279; C. Gallini, "Politica religiosa di Clodio", *SMSR* XXXIII (1962), 257-272; G. Thomas, "Magna Mater and Attis", H. Temporini-W. Haase (eds.), *op. cit.*, Bd. 17, 3, 1500-1535.
p. 56 n.124	Another text of Statius (*Silv.* I, 5, 36-41) also stress the doleful nature of the phrygians' rites for Attis. Cf. L. Robert, "Maesta Synnas, Stace, Attis et les monnaies", *JS* IV (1962), 43-55.
p. 65 n.4	Cf. also E. Lane, *Corpus Monumentorum Religionis Dei Menis (CMRDM)* IV, *Supplementary Men-Inscriptions from Pisidia* (EPRO 19), Leiden 1978.
p. 67 n.16	Cf. now M. Tacheva-Hitova, *op. cit.*, 163f. n° 4: "[Θεᾶς] Ἰδείας μεγάλης/[καὶ τ]οῦ Διὶ Ἡλίῳ μεγί/[στ]ῳ Σεβαζίῳ ...". On Sabazios' cult see now M. J. Vermaseren, *Corpus Cultus Iovi Sabazii (CCIS)* I, *The Hands* (EPRO 100), Leiden 1983. Cf. also S. E. Johnson, "The present State of Sabazios Research", H. Temporini-W. Haase, *op. cit.*, Bd. 17, 3, 1583-1613.
p. 80 n.90	Cf. M. Guarducci, "L'iscrizione di Abercio e Roma", *Ancient Society* II (1971), 174-203 = *Scritti scelti sulla religione greca e romana e sul cristianesimo* (EPRO 99), Leiden 1983, 310-339; Ead., "L'iscrizione di Abercio e la 'vergine casta' ", *Ancient Society* IV (1973), 271-279 = *Scritti scelti*, 344-352.
p. 84 n.2	Cf. Vermaseren, *CCCA* III, 150 n° 458.
p. 88 n.12	Cf. M. Tacheva-Hitova, *op. cit.*, 90f. n° 42.
p. 90 n.19	All these inscriptions have been published recently by G. Petzl, *Die Inschriften von Smyrna* I, *Grabschriften, postume Ehrungen, Grabepigramme* (Inschriften griechischer Städte aus Kleinasien 23), Bonn 1982. See also Vermaseren, *CCCA* I s.v. Smyrna.
p. 91 n.26	Cf. S. Besques, *Musée National du Louvre. Catalogue raisonné des figurines et reliefs en terre-cuite grecs étrusques et romains* III, *Époques hellénistique et romaine. Grèce et Asie Mineure*, Paris 1972, 43-46, nos. D 251-D 269, Pls. 52-55.
p. 91 n.27	Cf. also S. Mollard-Besques, *Catalogue raisonné des figurines et reliefs en terre-cuite grecs et romains* II, *Myrina, Musée du Louvre et Collections des Universités de France*, Paris 1963, 85 IV, Pls. 103b,f; 104a-c,e-f; 164 IV, Pls. 198g, 199b; 190 XIII, 4 Pl. 225i.
p. 92 n.39	M. Tacheva-Hitova, *op. cit.*, 71f. n° 2 (*CIL* III, 14211⁴); 72 n° 3 Pl. XIX.

136   ADDENDUM

p. 99 n.80   See now L. Musso, *Manifattura suntuaria e committenza pagana
                nella Roma del IV secolo: indagine sulla Lanx di Parabiago* (Studi
                e materiali del Museo della civiltà romana N. 10), Roma 1983.
p. 102 n.106   *CIL* III, 763 = M. Tacheva-Hitova, *op. cit.*, 92f. n° 47, Pl. XXXI.
p. 116f. nn.51-54 The taurobolium inscriptions from Rome in Vermaseren, *CCCA*
                III, 49-61 nos. 226-245.

INDEX

DATE DUE

MAR 16 '91			